THE WORLD WE WANT

Virtue, Vice, and the Good Citizen

Mark Kingwell

VIKING

VIKING

Published by the Penguin Group

Penguin Books Canada Ltd, 1 0 Alcorn Avenue, Toronto, Ontario, Canada M4V 3B2

Penguin Books Ltd, 2 7 Wrights Lane, London w8 5TZ, England

Penguin Putnam Inc., 3 7 5 Hudson Street, New York, New York 1 0 0 1 4, USA

Penguin Books Australia Ltd, Ringwood, Victoria, Australia

Penguin Books (NZ) Ltd, cnr Rosedale and Airborne Roads, Albany, Auckland 1 3 1 0, New Zealand

Penguin Books Ltd, Registered Offices: Harmondsworth, Middlesex, England

First Published 2 0 0 0

1 0   9   8   7   6   5   4   3   2   1

Author representation: Westwood Creative Artists

94 Harbord Street, Toronto, Ontario M 5 S 1 G 6

Printed and bound in Canada on acid free paper ∞

CANADIAN CATALOGUING IN PUBLICATION DATA

Kingwell, Mark Gerald

    The world we want: virtue, vice, and the good citizen

ISBN 0-670-88924-5

1. World citizenship.   2. Citizenship.   I. Title.

JZ1320.4.K56 2000   323.6   C00-931038-X

Visit Penguin Canada's web site at **www.penguin.ca**

CONTENTS

PREFACE

This is a small book about a big topic: what it means to be a citizen in a rapidly changing world. In the venerable philosophical tradition, it asks more questions than it answers. But it flows from the conviction that critical reflection on the possibilities of political life is one of the highest duties of humanity – that, indeed, such reflection is a form of political action as important as any demonstration or protest. Democratic politics is a parliament, a parley of voices, and not just in the states that explicitly say so. Within that continuous, sometimes raucous conversation, there are times when we must step back from the fray to get our bearings. Sometimes we need to rethink what we are up to – for that too is part of our ongoing discussion. The only thing more dangerous than a total lack of political argument is political argument without awareness of its own pre-commitments.

It was my friend Charlie Foran who first remarked, some four years ago, that it might be a good idea to write a more accessible version of the arguments about justice and civility I had made in my first, academic book, *A Civil Tongue*. (Or rather I think he simply said it was an idea – I supplied the adjective.) But I was occupied for some time with other things and it wasn't until Cynthia Good at

Penguin Canada suggested something similar that I started to think seriously about doing it.

The present book is not simply a restatement of those earlier arguments, however, and it goes well beyond the issue of civility. I hold to the idea that civility, understood as the willingness to engage in public discourse, is the first virtue of citizens. Understood properly, civility gives us a way to navigate our political differences without needing to eliminate them. But a new approach to the subject of citizenship seemed necessary.

We have changed a great deal, both as people and as citizens, during the last fifteen years. The world we confront no longer has the shape it had even two decades ago, when I began my study of political philosophy. It sometimes seems to lack any shape at all, to be swirling into ethereal (or hyperreal) patterns and nodes, senseless volumes of electronic traffic, flurries of conversation that appear and disappear as quickly as a dropped cellphone call. In many places national boundaries mean less, but linguistic and ethnic differences mean more. War is smaller in scale than in recent memory, but it is far more ambiguous, intractable, and nasty. Money flows more quickly than ever, but it still somehow manages to gather and puddle in certain places, for certain people rather than others. There is a huge volume of exciting cultural possibilities to confront, yet little sense of ease in finding one's true identity or understanding one's place within the grand, bland cultural marketplace.

All of this means that our task as humans has lately become more difficult. Concerned about our own need to belong and to feel worthy – concerned to create a better world from the sometimes chaotic materials of everyday life – we now have to work harder than ever to make our voices heard, to make our desires real, to bend events to our ends. We also have to work harder to understand what it means to be politically responsible, to know what we owe to others as well as to ourselves. I remain convinced that a new form of global citizenship will prove available to us, and that this intricately interdependent social order of ours will eventually tend towards justice. But to ensure that those things are true, we first need to buck the received wisdom and routine imperatives of the day. We need to slow down, take time, and reflect on our possibilities. That is what this book is for.

———

One never starts from scratch when it comes to working out a public position on a public matter. Portions of this book have appeared before, usually in other forms or to different purposes.

Part of Chapter 2 was delivered as the 1998 Harold Innis Memorial Lecture at the University of Toronto's Innis College, with the title "The Banality of Evil, the Evil of Banality" (November 1998). Versions of the same lecture were later given at the Queen's University philosophy colloquium (November 1998), and at a conference on media and democracy at the University of Colorado, Boulder (March 1999). A revised version was then published in the *Queen's Quarterly* (Fall 1999); also in *Deliberation, Democracy, and the Media,* edited by Simone Chambers and Anne Costain (Rowman and Littlefield, 2000).

I discussed some themes of Chapter 3 at a meeting of the Cambridge University Moral Sciences Club (November 1999) under the title "The Virtues of Political Liberalism"; also, in much earlier incarnations and with various titles, at the Universities of Toronto, Calgary, and British Columbia; and at the American Philosophical Association, Central Division, in Chicago (1996–97). In a first stab at using philosophers as characters in a conversation about political virtues, I published parts of the same chapter in *Philosophical Forum* (Spring 1996) with the title "Defending Political Virtue."

Sections of Chapter 4 first appeared as articles in the magazines *Azure* ("The Dream House," July/August 1999), *Harper's* ("Arcadian Adventures," March 2000), and *Adbusters* ("Long Live the New

Flesh," June/July 2000). Other sections of that chapter were included in a lecture called "Building Dwelling Acting," which I delivered at the Tulane University School of Architecture as part of a symposium on architecture, ethics, and globalism (March 2000). An expanded version of the lecture was published in the *Queen's Quarterly* (Summer 2000), and later in *Tulane Papers on Ethics and Architecture*, edited by Graham Owen (Tulane University Press, forthcoming).

Chapter 5 adapts some material that first appeared as short opinion articles in the *National Post* (February and March 1999) and *This Magazine* (November/December 1999). A condensed version of that chapter was delivered as a plenary address to the Conference on Reimagining Politics and Society at the Millenium, organized by the Center for Ethics and Meaning, New York (May 2000), with the title "The Good Life."

Finally, I gave a compressed statement of the book's whole argument as the George Grant Memorial Lecture, University of King's College, Halifax, with the title "Citizens: Political Commitment for a New Era" (January 2000). The lecture was then published in pamphlet form by King's. A still more condensed version was used in a paper I wrote for the Canadian Department of Justice as part of a Deputy Minister's conference on access to justice (March 2000); and later discussed at the Center for the Study of Law and Society, University of California, Berkeley (April 2000).

I thank the convenors and participants of all these colloquia, and the editors of the publications, for their inspiration, interest, and criticism. I hope they will feel well served by the results. My particular thanks to Steven Bittle, John Brown, Boris Castel, Natasha Hassan, Roger Hodge, Walter Kemp, Lewis Lapham, Mark LeVine, Gordon McOuat, John O'Sullivan, Gerald Owen, Nelda Rodger, Sarmishta Subramanian, and Mel Watkins.

"Do not write the conclusion of a work in your familiar study," Walter Benjamin counselled aspiring writers. "You would not find the necessary courage there." I have tried to follow this excellent advice.

Time for the writing of this book was made possible by a research leave from the University of Toronto, which I spent as a Visiting Fellow at Clare Hall, Cambridge, during the fall of 1999; and as a Visiting Scholar at the Berkeley Law and Society Center, during the spring of 2000. I think it is a welcome coincidence that my thoughts about citizenship should be pursued in this post-national way, and in the same countries that first provided my higher education – though to say that is perhaps to do an injustice to Scottish nationalism, since Cambridge is far from Edinburgh, not only in miles.

My friends and colleagues Alex Oliver (in Cambridge) and Chris Kutz (in Berkeley) were mainly responsible for the great pleasure and productivity of those two visits. I thank as well the President and Fellows of Clare Hall, the Cambridge University Faculty of Philosophy, and the Program in Jurisprudence and Social Policy at Berkeley. Douglas Bell, Sara Borins, Lavinia Greenlaw, Gerry Kingwell, and Joan Steigerwald all contributed to this project in different but essential ways. My Toronto friends proved no less supportive at long distance, and I offer special thanks here to Alison Gordon, Allison Grace, Allan Hepburn, Naomi Klein, Ceri Marsh, and Suzanne Stein. My agent, Jennifer Barclay, and my editor, Jackie Kaiser, were unfailingly enthusiastic as I struggled from thought to page. Jennifer Heyns provided helpful and exacting permissions assistance. And Meg Taylor copy-edited the manuscript with extraordinary skill.

I have a few more general debts. Students in my University of Toronto graduate seminars on citizenship, politics and culture, multiculturalism, and theories of justice (1995–98) challenged and focussed my thoughts on politics considerably. My undergraduate students over the same period have been insistent in their demands for clarity and topicality. Without all these people there would be, for me, no world worth wanting. As usual, none of them is responsible for any errors, miscues, or sweeping generalizations that remain — including that one.

Finally, this book is dedicated to my nieces, Natalie Kingwell and Aidan Olivia Louise Kingwell: future citizens of the world.

Chapter 1

THE WORLD WE HAVE

It is a common experience in this, the age of casual multiculturalism. There I was, on a crowded 767, heading to London from Toronto, when I realized that nobody around me was speaking English – nobody at all, except the Québécoise flight attendant, who looked as if she might have preferred not to. The two Germans next to me were reading Ken Follett novels in translation. The man across the aisle was talking to his little boy in a mixture of Spanish and French, for reasons that escaped me. The two women farther up were, as far as I could make out, arguing in Italian.

Tourists on their way to the next destination? Maybe. International shoppers off to Harrod's and Jermyn Street? Possibly – a man in the departure lounge had let it be known that he was just zipping over to Amsterdam for the weekend to pick up a few things he need-ed. (Diamonds? Drugs? Sex toys?) Or were they just a group of all-sorts Canadians on their way to England? In the arrival area later there was a flurry of passports, a shuffle of multiple identities. The passengers conjured their variable selves without hesitation. Some of them, armed with logo-embossed briefcases and branded golf shirts, were clearly servants of a higher, corporate power: citizens of the world as it now lies, carved up into markets and territories, catchment areas and satellite PCS coverage zones. These new global citizens, whatever their mother tongue and regardless of their sometimes halting command of English, the lingua franca of the New Internationalism, all speak fluently the language of the customs declaration and the luggage carousel. They know the grammar of taxis and hotel shuttles and courtesy cars. *Which passport? Whichever gets me through the barrier faster.*

It is time for us to rethink the idea of citizenship, to reconceive the structures of political commitment and membership against the background of our shape-shifting world. These sky-people, harbingers of the world we are fast creating, are the first clues as to why. They tell us that old ideas of civic membership no longer compel our attention or answer our needs. Their presence is a reminder that the political structures to which those old ideas were wedded are not yet dead, but they are suffering – and are as nothing compared to the real powers of our world, the real centres of loyalty for most people (however undeserved that loyalty may often be). And if we are the sky-people ourselves, the ones who have found a reasonably comfortable place amid all these changes, who have the frequent-flyer programs and the higher degrees and the international connections, then the challenge is that much more proximate.

We begin with what is not news. Corporations and firms have not simply taken over the mechanisms of production and consumption. They have equally usurped our private selves and our public spaces. They have created bonds of belonging far stronger than any fractured, tentative nation could now hope to offer, providing structures of identity, ways of making sense of one's place in a complex world. They are also far more powerful, and richer, than many nations: the annual budget of France was only three-quarters of the combined value of America OnLine and Time Warner when those two media giants merged in January 2000, and Kmart's 1998 U.S. sales were equal to the estimated budget of the entire Russian military. But corporations are not democratic, and they do not possess the political legitimacy that is necessary to justify that kind of power. We have global markets, however unjust and skewed; and we have a global culture, however banal and enervating. What we don't have, but desperately need, is a global politics to balance and give meaning to these troubling universal realities.

This book is an attempt to begin a discussion about the nature of citizenship in a world where national identities and institutions may no longer serve – a post-national, even post-cultural, world. I say "begin" to acknowledge the limits of what is sayable here. We ask questions and hope they take root, lead to more questions (and maybe a few answers); we cannot expect to lay the issue of citizenship to rest in some final way. The questions I want to ask are implicitly open-ended, even endless. How can we get back the sense of public commitment and public good associated with citizenship when our identities are a grab bag of traditional norms and free-floating possibilities? How can we go beyond the stalled intramural disputes of so much current politics and find a new sense of belonging for the shared global spaces – including nonmaterial spaces such as the Internet – which we now so blithely inhabit? What does it mean to be a citizen in a world of fractured identities, global monoculture, and crumbling civic nationalism? How do we make sense of a situation where the uniform spread of cola, television, and market rationalism is accompanied, anomalously, by resurgent ethnic hatreds, cultural tribalism, and wars of insane bloodline vehemence?

We tend to think of the problems of globalization and cultural identity as peculiar to our times. In fact they are rooted in ancient problems of civic belonging. And the crisis we now face is at least as old as the century that has just ended, indeed much older. It is, in its way, a crisis of the modern world's attempt to make itself ever anew, the high-velocity novelty that dominates our lives. We cannot begin to understand that world without tracing the idea of citizenship from its roots in ancient Greece through to the contemporary world of consumerism and cultural banality. The key to unlocking the confusions and conflicts of the present day, in other words, is to be

found in our own history, how we came to be here. We need to rum-
mage a little in the attic of our world to find the old photograph or
broken toy that will make insight possible. This may seem an odd
claim to make in our fast world, where a mass of newspapers, full of
breathless wisdom, is pulped every single day. *History? Don't have
time for it.* We think we already know the story, think we've already
heard what there is to hear about political commitment. We assume
that voices from the past have nothing to say to us, that they cannot
really understand the things that vex us. Or we simply believe,
finally, that attending to them is too much work, too much of a burden when there is so much that we have to do.

All these forms of resistance must be overcome. My first aim in
this book, therefore, is to provoke reflection on the idea of citizenship at a time when such reflection is in painfully short supply,
whether from pressures of time or from assumptions of certainty –
whether from *busyness* or from *knowingness*, the twin distracting
deities of our day. As I will suggest in the pages that follow, these
linked preoccupations are an attempt to sidestep the anxiety we
actually feel about ourselves and our world. Disruptive and incon-
clusive though it will certainly be, we have to force an entry to the
depths of that anxiety if we are to make any progress whatsoever.

But I am also making a polemical argument in favour of an inclusive and participatory model of citizenship. For, while it is true that
current models of citizenship sometimes appear irrelevant or even
dangerous, based as they so often are on the nationalism and jingo-
ism of imperial expansion, it is too early to give up on citizenship
altogether. We cannot be confident that the vision of a post-national,
postmodern consumer future – a vision that fires the imaginations
of the mainly white, male, and affluent media and money elites of
North America and Europe – will actually foster justice. Arguments
that corporations will end up serving the public good far more
efficiently than governments must be assessed in terms of accountability, inclusiveness, and equity. Assertions of general and growing

happiness, claims that "we are closer to capitalist utopia than ever before" (as one financial services worker I know recently put it), must be challenged and probed. Is that likely? Is it the sort of utopia we should be satisfied with?

The notion of citizenship itself is not obsolete, as if it were no more than a 14.4 modem or an old version of Netscape. Citizenship is a way of meeting one of our deepest needs, the need to belong; it gives voice and structure to the yearning to be part of something larger than ourselves. By the same token, citizenship is a way of making concrete the ethical commitments of care and respect, of realizing in action an obligation to aid fellow travellers – in short, of fostering justice between persons. At its best, a best we have yet to realize, citizenship functions as a complex structure for realizing our deeply social nature, even as it acknowledges and copes with the terrible vulnerability of humans, the myriad fragilities and risks of our existence on the mortal plane.

Citizenship is, in short, one of the profound categories that make us who we are, one of the crucial ways humans go about creating a life for themselves. Without it we are cut adrift from each other – and from ourselves.

There are four kinds of motivation at work whenever we think about citizenship, descending in order from the large scale to the small. I have mentioned the international situation already, and it is indeed the primary scene for any current argument about citizenship.

But alongside this, and partly as a result of it, we observe the dismal state of sovereignty in our own particular nations. Countries that were formed in the eighteenth- and nineteenth-century rounds of unification, or emerged in strength after the upheavals of world war in the twentieth, no longer appear viable. In many cases, including Canada, the nation of yesterday is increasingly reduced to the

economic colony of today, beholden to market forces. A member of
the G7 (or G8 if that other crumbling nation-state, Russia, is invited; or even more lately, G20), Canada nevertheless lacks power in
arranging its own affairs. Some of this is de facto, as when our cultural experience is overrun by wave upon wave of American consumer products. But some of it comes from sheer lack of will, as
when, during the Vancouver meeting of the Asia-Pacific Economic
Cooperation Summit in 1997, Canadian leaders were cowed and
even embarrassed by the demands of a visiting foreign dictator who
did not wish to confront a few student protesters.

The example resonates well beyond these borders. National sovereignty, always tenuous in its hold on life, seems to be a patient on
life-support in an era of underfunding, American economic dominance, and free-form electronic marketing. Determined nationalists
may fight rearguard actions in the face of these changes, but their
cause looks more and more doomed – and liable to issue in an
untenable isolationism or vicious right-wing retrenchment. (There
is nothing that arouses racist sentiments more quickly than a dispute
over contaminated beef, or a liberal refugee policy plus a few well-
publicized cases of boat people.) But this may be an opportunity in
the form of a crisis. For it is precisely the looseness of current
notions of national identity in countries such as Canada, Australia,
and the Netherlands that will, in the end, provide the more open-
ended models of citizenship we need for a more complicated and
interrelated world.

Fine. Yet, our day-to-day lives are rarely lived at the level of
nations, and for most of us the fabric of existence is determined far
more by municipal than by national character. Hence a third kind of
motivation in our thinking about what it means to be a citizen:
cities. Cities are now, like it or not, the gathering places of global
culture and diversity. They are powerful bases of wealth and culture,
often more powerful than the countries of which they are a part.
They are also magnets for artistic talent, intelligence, entrepreneurial

drive, and lust for life. Head offices and independent theatre companies alike find them congenial and necessary. At their best, they are
free-ranging, energized conversations, restless and inventive con-
fabs set amid the tough beauty of concrete slabs and glass-and-iron
towers. The successful world cities, the truly great places to live on
this planet, are those able to embrace the world's complexity, make
it their own. In this regard, places like Sydney or San Francisco or
Amsterdam – or the city where I live, Toronto – may have something to teach us about civic belonging at another level of political
and economic order.

How? There is not yet anything like a "Toronto model" of citizenship, but there may be enough successful coexistence here, under
conditions of extreme and growing cultural diversity, to indicate a
possible way forward. Paeans to Toronto are not hard to find – outside Canada anyway. Here's the rosy picture: The United Nations has
called Toronto the most ethnically diverse city in the world, with 41
percent of its population born outside the country. Ray Bradbury
called it "the most perfect city in the western hemisphere." *Fortune*
magazine has ranked it first overall as a place to work and live, the
functional capital of the country the U.N. ranks likewise. *The New
York Times* wrote not long ago that "[t]his is a city of immigrants without slums, without graffiti, and without gridlock, dynamic but sel-
dom frenetic, a metropolis with clean and healthy downtown
neighborhoods. In short, a city that works."

The *Times* reporters should have taken a closer look, however: at
the homeless people panhandling on the street, the rising pollution
levels, the gang-related violence in Chinatown and Scarborough,
and the brutal day-long traffic jams on the 401 and the Don Valley
Parkway. They might also have spent some time listening to people
from the rest of Canada, who continue to regard Toronto as a place
just as arrogant as New York without the excuse of good shopping
or theatre. Still, it is my city and a place where I believe multinational citizenship is a reality. In search of viable models, we rightly

look to what works, even if it doesn't work perfectly. That is the other side of genuine political theory: abstraction must meet reality at some point.

The fourth kind of motivation is more personal still, and it involves the circumstances each of us brings to the practice of political activity. In 1995 I published a scholarly book about justice and citizenship that argued for the centrality of civility as a virtue of citizens. I claimed that the key to resolving and managing the deep conflicts of pluralistic politics was a willingness on the part of citizens to tolerate imperfect solutions. In order to make a social order of diverse goals tend towards justice, it was necessary for each citizen to internalize the virtues of dialogue, in which the claims of others are considered and one's own claims are phrased in terms intelligible to others. Ideally, this specifically political form of civility – which began with the character of the individual citizen – would radiate outward to encompass a thriving debate about the basic conditions of social life. It would represent what the Italian liberal socialist Carlo Rosselli in the 1920s called *a pact of civility* among free citizens. This is not a social contract so much as it is a form of civic friendship in which we give without necessarily expecting to receive in return. In practice, we might hope to find this kind of civility operating in everything from the conventions of legal debate, which formalize disputes in the interest of justice, to routine exchanges between neighbours, who often find that a few kind words do as much to make good relations as Robert Frost's celebrated fences.

This was political theory in a very hopeful mood, of course. There is plenty of evidence that citizens are anything but civil as the differences, and hence the friction, between them grow. (Rosselli himself was gunned down by Fascist thugs in 1937 after becoming involved in a plot to assassinate Mussolini.) But that is only more reason, I thought, to try to identify the qualities necessary to deal with those differences, to minimize that friction. Civility in the political sense is on a continuum with the more mundane social virtues of politeness and consideration. We can start by examining and advocating those qualities in order to build up a more robust, and less variable, form of relation between citizens. But civility is much more than mere politeness, and politics has to cope with a good deal of fierce disagreement, some of it unresolvable. As a basic sense that we are participating in a social project, a project with goals that at some level we all share, civility is the enabling condition of a larger debate about the world we want. Without it, there can be no political organization that goes beyond the self-interested bargaining and culture of complaint that currently dominates our sense of politics. And hence there can be no real justice.

Soon after this, for various reasons good and bad, civility became a kind of rallying cry for political commentators in the United States, most often on the ideological Right. Missing the point about the distinction between politeness and civility, they used the word as an all-purpose counter to everything from breakdowns in workaday manners, through the increase of profanity in literature, to the excesses of daytime television. They decried the decline in moral values that these blights supposedly represented, and called for more vigorous personal etiquette – and more stringent codes of conduct in schools, universities, and other public spaces. In short, calls for more civility quickly revealed themselves as exercises in self-serving moralizing and cynical insistence on a nonthreatening form of public debate, one that left everything as it is.

These developments were part of a larger annexation of the radical potential that many, myself included, still believe resides in the idea of political virtues, and civility in particular. Not surprisingly, because civility is a virtue of daily life, the idea of the virtues more generally became a fashionable topic at about the same time. In the hands of scholars, this move away from rigid rules and towards more contextualized ethical reflection was welcome. But it was the writers of popular works on the virtues who rose to prominence, with William Bennett's books of homespun reactionary wisdom only the most successful example of the pieties conservative writers love to peddle. Lamentations about the decline of civility led, with troubling inevitability, to calls for a revival of puritanical bourgeois virtues like godliness, thrift, and celibacy.

Both trends – the rehabilitation of civility and the emphasis on virtues – suffered the usual fate of ideas that spring up too quickly in this overheated cultural economy. Soon there was a backlash of journalistic disdain and mockery. The Yale law professor Stephen Carter, who wrote two thoughtful books on civility and integrity, respectively, was chided in *Time* magazine for being obvious and preachy. Smarter-than-thou columnists gave him and the other advocates of civility a thorough going-over, and the very idea of civility, always one that requires careful nurture to survive the chill winds of parody, was effectively ridiculed. The notion that civility might be the first virtue of citizens, a basic willingness to see oneself as part of a larger shared undertaking, was killed off just as it gained the field. An important connection between civility and justice – a sense that without the orientation to a common discourse, there can be no arguments about what is or is not just – slipped through our fingers.

———

The idea of citizenship was born in vicious exclusion, and many – too many – of its nationalistic expressions are brutally exclusive still. It was an elite class of male landowners who first laid claim to the reasoning faculties that alone, in their view, made them competent to influence policy. The history of citizenship has been a hard-won, incremental expansion of that focus to include ever more categories of people, from foreign-born men to low-born men to men without property or of different skin colours to even, eventually, women. In the eighteenth century the ideal of citizenship is given perhaps its most inclusive articulation with the Kantian notion of universal reason. With this bold theory in place, all persons are eligible to claim a political status because their very capacity to judge, their ability to reason itself, makes them legislators.

But moral and political theory outstripped political practice, and universal reason is no proof against prejudice if one can simply set off certain groups of people as inherently irrational. In any event, citizenship has been effectively restricted in numerous ways down to our own day, most obviously by birthplace and bloodline, enforced by isolationism and xenophobias of varying intensities. The cosmopolitan ideal has gone largely unrealized and, except in certain idealistic quarters, mostly unmourned. Theorists and policymakers alike have been content to discuss citizenship in national terms, fixing immigration and refugee policies from a usually unquestioned base of prior commitment to the nation-state. That is, the criteria and privileges of citizenship are assumed to be tied to such states, which are in turn tied to geographical territories that can, in theory anyway, be defended at the border.

With the rise of the global market and transnational communications, we now face a stiff (and obvious) challenge. For the notion of the nation-state cannot, in its current form, survive the changes that have already fundamentally altered the geography and conceptual configurations of the world. Inverting the earlier trend, political theory has not kept pace with these changes, for reasons that are clear enough in outline: fear of the homogenizing effects of a cosmopolitan order, deep and irreconcilable differences in culture and ideology, an inability to imagine workable forms of transnational governance. There is, further, the dead weight of inevitability to contend with. On the Left, the globalization of markets and its various attendant pathologies are greeted more in sorrow than anger, and cries of woe rise up without, it seems, much hope of changing anything. On the Right, globalization is viewed as equally unstoppable and, if not exactly positive in the sum of its effects, certainly useless to resist.

Citizenship can be defended, then, but it can no longer be conceived the way it was a thousand, hundred, or even fifty years ago. The oldest models of civic belonging are forms of virtual racism, tribal fear given a political formulation. Later they were based on adherence to a body of civic and, usually, religious nostrums: they were fluently ideological, but no less exclusive. More lately still, democratic states have adopted a model of citizenship based on neither blood nor conviction but on procedural exercise and access to a body of rights – a constitutional notion of belonging, in other words, that matched the open-ended and liberal ideals of the emerging capitalist West. None of these three historical models – the models based in blood, belief, or law – has been complete in its attempted domination of the political realm. None of them realized the perfection their advocates frequently claimed. By the same token, none of them can really serve us fully now. What we need is a new model of citizenship based on *the act of participation itself*, not on some quality or thought or right enjoyed by its possessor. This participatory citizenship doesn't simply demand action from existing citizens; it makes action at once the condition and the task of citizenship.

Such an understanding of citizenship bears an affinity with recent calls in public debate for a reinvigoration of "civil society," something that is thought to be a function of "social capital" accumulated and spent in the form of voluntary associations and civic-minded groups. I have sympathy with this notion, and with the ground-level actions it is invoked to guide; but the enthusiasm of reception offered to the idea of civil society in diverse quarters should also give us pause. Without institutions of democratic legitimacy and without the norm of justice that alone makes citizen participation valid, social capital is at best politically ambidextrous and at worst morally vapid. The Harvard sociologist Robert Putnam spearheaded the analysis of civil society with his image of Americans "bowling alone": cultivating purely private ends instead of the associational ones of a previous era. But, as critics have noticed, social capital can reside as much in Ku Klux Klan meetings and fascist rallies as in community-service volunteering – a point captured vividly by the Princeton graduate students who coined the satirical counter-phrase, "bowling with Hitler."

The liberal individualism that gave rise to the conditions we see now is not an opaque or monolithic tradition, though, and its subjects, the individuals of the early modern imagination, are not simply bundles of appetite that can be controlled or manipulated. We, and our desires, are more complex than either liberal economics or socialist perfectionism would like to think. Inclusiveness does not imply, as intemperate conservative critics sometimes claim, an elite moral dogmatism that is bent on making the world virtuous and dull, taking everyone's toys away in pursuit of a bloodless lack of conflict. Inclusiveness is not boring, and virtue is more consistent with fun than these cranky complainers, with their own forms of elitism much in evidence, can recognize. Moreover, the aim of politics is not, in my view, the final elimination of any and all conflict. Conflict can be productive and it can be exciting; it can also be vicious and destructive. The first task of citizenship is to recognize the difference.

"Citizen" is of course just one role among others in a full and well-ordered life. We are also mothers and fathers, students and professionals, moviegoers and householders, and many other things besides. Even a cursory survey of the range of human life would have to conclude that we inhabit, with varying degrees of enthusiasm, at least six roles that are not distinctly political. Let's consider them for a moment.

We are (1) *inquirers*, seeking the truth about our lives and the universe in which we live. We are (2) *moral agents*, seeking to discern, do, and defend what we consider is the right thing. We are (3) *householders and consumers*, involved in a daily round of dwelling, eating, and entertaining. We are, necessarily, (4) *workers or economic agents*, engaging in the labour that makes dwelling possible. We are (5) *cultural beings*, who enjoy the fruits of human creativity in everything from staged performances and recorded music to the pictures we hang on our walls or the television we watch and books we read. And we are (6) *intimates*, creators of love and emotional connection in our relationships with our friends and families.

Now, I say none of these roles is distinctly political because each can, and often is, pursued without any explicit awareness of the things that are usually considered matters of politics, like voting or influencing policy. For many people, assuming these six roles is more than enough to fill a happy and productive life. For many people, furthermore, politics appears negligible next to the demands of these six roles and, if heeded at all, is often seen as merely instrumental to something "higher" or maybe just of more immediate concern. That is, politics is tolerated as the enabling condition for the things that really matter, and however we rank roles (1) through (6), whatever relative weights we give them, politics is left out of central consideration.

But this is a mistake. Among these many roles of modern life, citizen — what we might call "Role Seven" — is instead the primary one, and one that, in widely different local conditions, shares some essential commonalities. Moreover, everything pursued in roles (1) through (6) is, in fact, political — more deeply so than many of us would readily accept. Politics pervades human life, from relations of exchange in the workplace to every transaction or encounter with another person on the street. Even our closest relationships arguably have a political dimension in the implicit assumptions and expectations of gender and personal identity. Accepting this, it might seem obvious to argue that citizenship could ground our other commitments, could orient us as people. And yet, this is far from being so, not least because our ideas of political commitment are these days so often truncated or distorted, and hence considered dispensable. Citizenship is a role now in danger of losing its privileged position in human life, through various forms of withdrawal from the political realm: into consumerist fetishism, into cultural separatism, into self-regarding isolation. These withdrawals, which hollow out the sphere of civic life and public good, are gratifying only in the short term. Abdicating our duties as citizens, we surrender the field to the ambitious and the credulous.

It is no exaggeration to say that the value of individual autonomy, which we have over centuries carved out of the hierarchies and tyrannies of earlier ages, is on the verge of self-defeat as we enter this new century. Without a background of commonality, without some form of civic responsibility, autonomy degenerates into mere special pleading. Without a strong notion of commitment to other people and our shared undertakings, without a sense that we are together creating a just world, a world not ruled by cheap acceptance of inevitability or the easy superiority of wealth, our hard-won individualism loses its deeper significance. It becomes a victory without genuine spoils, personal comfort not only restricted in number to the very luckiest few but also cramped in scope, bereft of meaning. This is luxury with no objective beyond itself, freedom minus any sense of direction.

———

Three extraordinary encounters lie at the centre of this extended discussion of citizenship in a globalized world. They are signal confrontations between friends, all drawn from the history of Western philosophy. In their way, they are also milestones in an unusually productive and extended conversation about how to live as a citizen. As human encounters about the political, they open up in their vividness new spaces for reflection and argument concerning what we are doing now, what we have become – and what we might create in future.

There is, first, Socrates in argument with his well-meaning friend Crito, explaining why he will choose death over political exile. Explaining, that is, the depth of gratitude he owes even to the state that has condemned him to die; and why his commitment to an independent moral standard demands the highest expression of citizenship: dying for the state – even at its own decree. Socrates willingly drinks the hemlock his fellow citizens have decided is his reward for a life of searching social criticism. This commitment contrasts strongly with the situation in which most of us find ourselves, and with the individualism that, for three centuries, has lain at the heart of our political thinking. Why is Socrates' act so alien to us? Because individualism, once universalized as a value, revealed its inherent instability. To recover from the one-sidedness of our current prejudices, we don't all need to be Socrates, but we do need to be Socratic – and we need to listen again to his imagined voice within us.

Then there is Montaigne's compressed, intense engagement with his friend Étienne de la Boétie, in which he explores the conflicted worldliness of the late sixteenth century – where one can simultaneously confront an exhilarating global viewpoint and a wealth of depressing local hatreds. Montaigne is arguably the first modern philosopher, himself a politician – he was mayor of Bordeaux for two terms – and his writings display the intellectual as a man of the world, struggling to make sense of his newly expanded awareness. As well as arguing explicitly with his friend, he implicitly grapples with the dominant mind of a generation before his, Machiavelli. Along the way he articulates a clear sense of the virtues of citizenship in a troubled and diverse world, a sense at once worldly and idealistic, tempered by experience but tending towards justice. This account of the political virtues, so relevant still, adds to the indispensable faculty of imagination a more concrete *disposition to act*.

And finally, there is the critic Walter Benjamin in correspondence with his close friend, the social theorist Theodor Adorno. Adorno, a brilliant musicologist and philosopher, survives the Second World War to become one of the century's great pessimists, a man who fingered the evils of a mass-produced culture's disturbing conformity and cheap consumerism long before such complaints became staples of media criticism. Benjamin, an unparalleled connoisseur of everyday life, is more optimistic in the years before the war, but he too notes the deep difficulties of forging political awareness when the times are gripped by capitalist triumphalism. Through their letters and other writings, they pursue a struggle with the very ideas of modernity, identity, and emancipation – and along the way give us perhaps modernity's highest expression, the critical conversation. They remind us that in a world dominated by capital, there is no easy path to the exercise of citizenship but that the idea of utopia still has its expression, sometimes in the least likely places.

Plato needs no defence as a philosophical genius. And his dialogue *Crito*, while early and sometimes considered minor, is a defining moment in the working through of the civic ideal of democratic commitment and belonging that dominates the ancient world – even as that ideal is modified and distorted, sometimes fatally, by later republican experiments in Rome and elsewhere. But the other figures who appear in the following pages may be less familiar, or anyway less certain of enjoying *prima facie* approval. They deserve that and more. Both Montaigne and Benjamin are attractive, worldly figures who write outside the bounds of standard scholarly procedure. Working three and a half centuries apart, they adopt a similar style of montage and dialectical commentary to examine the rich materials of everyday life.

Montaigne in his *Essays* and Benjamin in *The Arcades Project* work by means of amassed detail and quotation, by way of the probing comment and broken-off remark rather than the extended argument. Their works are kaleidoscopic, labyrinthine, personal, and endlessly digressive. Quite apart from the many profound insights that stud their pages, their attraction lies in this fractured honesty.

The *Essays* and *The Arcades Project* were both left unfinished at the time of each author's death, in each case a death untimely and intimately linked to political circumstance: Benjamin falling ill while on the run from the Nazis, a man deprived of citizenship or home, and finally taking his own life with an injection of morphine in an obscure mountain village near the French border; Montaigne succumbing to the pressures of loneliness, the pain of chronic illness, and the anxieties of his disorderly times. In this, they are perhaps the appropriate heirs of Socrates, himself a victim of hasty political judgment by his fellow citizens.

Though each of these three discussions can be read separately, they also constitute an overall argument that proceeds dialectically. We move from a conflict between moral objectivity and the need to universalize rights; through a burgeoning conception of political virtue based on skepticism and tolerance; to an awareness of the limits of individualism, and the possibilities of hope, under conditions of cultural diversity and global consumer capitalism.

Though you will find here some of the familiar materials of history and philosophy, listening in on these conversations is no academic exercise. It is, instead, a reflection – in both the thoughtful and the mirroring sense – on our current predicament. I mean our situation as inhabitants of a fast, overwhelming, and often unjust global context. But I also mean, more basically, our situation as time-bound creatures. Life, as Kierkegaard said, has the unfortunate characteristic that it must be lived in a forward direction but can only be understood backwards. We are forever stuck in that literally preposterous position, and seeking more confident futurism and prognostication is no solution to it. Novelty and its paradoxical twin, nostalgia, are our current fetishes; but piling up more of them will not help us much. Only more reflection will help.

That is why this book is not a policy paper, and why you won't find here yet another glib analysis, pro or con, of globalization and corporatism. In what follows I will fashion, I hope, no smooth additions to the fund of what the sociologist Pierre Bourdieu calls *the already-thought*: that stock of nicely turned phrases and easily digestible notions that, slipping neatly into the comfortable categories of a shared complacency, too often passes for critical thinking these days. (Compare David Foster Wallace on a larger but related point: "Popular culture is the symbolic representation of what people already believe.") These slick formulations are merely more knowingness, knowingness in particularly virulent form, even (or especially) when dressed up in the rhetorical guise of sharp contrarian opinion. Defences of globalism or cultural evolutionism slide quickly into determinism, and determinism, as always, facilitates passivity. We begin to think we can do nothing to make this a world we want because the "inexorable" flow of capital, or technology, or memes, is larger than any of us. Larger than any of us they may be; larger than all of us, no. Citizenship, if it means anything, means *making our desire for justice active*. It is not something we can do alone.

If you are so minded, you can certainly read many thousands of pages "explaining" the new global world, and then telling you what you can't do about it. I myself believe life is too short for that; also that it ultimately just reinforces what is already so. Theodor Adorno, writing in the blistering denunciatory spirit of his later years, saw such fluent predigested pages as the active enemies of thought. "Only what they do not need first to understand, they consider understandable," he wrote in his elliptical little book *Minima Moralia*; "only the word coined by commerce, and really alienated, touches them as familiar." (To be sure, Adorno ultimately saw communicability itself as the enemy of thought, which for some of us constitutes going too far.) Here, as elsewhere, writing is a tightrope walk, a delicate matter of placing one foot in front of the other to reach the goal of clear thinking without falling into the abyss of superficiality or familiarity. This book, which is nevertheless written in plain English, is not an explanation of any kind but rather an invitation to greater critical reflection.

I realize that to make even that sort of argument for a notion of inclusive transnational citizenship is, in the present circumstances, bold if not foolhardy. But I hope I have tempered that boldness, and its underlying condition of political optimism, with an acknowledgement of the difficulties we face. Ever since Plato tried to work out his gloom at Socrates' execution by writing the *Republic*, political theory has revealed itself as an undertaking that, done properly, works only by simultaneously acknowledging its pessimism and yet not falling into despair. In that spirit, I do not argue that there is one, and only one, form of citizenship that is valid. I do not suggest that individuality, in its late-modern multiplicity, its urban variety and complex role-playing, will or should reduce to a single determinate character.

Nor do I argue, naively, for a world government that is unlikely to come anytime soon, and unlikely, were it present, to meet the challenge to everyone's satisfaction anyway. When I argue for transnational citizenship I do not imply that the nation-state should be abolished forthwith – certainly not in the present circumstances. Significantly, recent protests against the World Trade Organization have turned on arguments for the continuing necessity of accountable national government. Global trade organizations, like global markets, often operate in invisible and unrepresentative ways that impose policy without regard for local interests, thereby merely perpetuating processes of wealth concentration that already favour the fortunate and powerful few.

What the protesters called for, in what were perhaps the first major acts of organized transnational citizenship, was less of the roughshod transgression of national sovereignty that has marked the WTO and, before it, the GATT. Those on the inside of the convention centre in Seattle, and their supporters in various equally unaccountable institutions like newspapers, delighted in depicting the people outside as idealistic throwbacks, loony eco-warriors, and ignorant opponents of the irreversible. They were gravely mistaken. The people outside were as globally minded as anyone on the planet, and as savvy. The difference is that they were acting as citizens, not merely as brokers of interest. Like them, I argue that a global world is a fact of life, but a fact that we can bend to our desires and needs. Sometimes national government will be the appropriate place to demand accountability. Sometimes it will be municipal government. Often we will have to find wholly new forums and strategies to influence the existing structures of world governance (which are not yet structures of world government).

I believe reflection on the idea of citizenship reveals some important shared features of life with other persons, whatever our variations in local conditions: that we are all vulnerable and fragile; that we all feel pain; that we all need to belong; that we all possess an imaginative capacity to feel concern, even love, for others. These shared features can be abstracted from the sea of variation and articulated with some limited success – for example, in the United Nations Universal Declaration of Human Rights. They can also, with a full awareness of the cultural and moral pluralism alive in a complex world, be teased out and made the scene for further thought and discussion.

You may nevertheless want to ask, Who is this "we" that I speak of so cheerfully, as if I knew already where a global community were to be found and who was part of it. That is a good question; in fact, so good a question that it's sometimes thought to be an argument-stopper in political theory, one of those challenges that expose the futility of any attempt to speak across the vast differences that separate humans even within relatively homogeneous nations. But that position gives the game away too quickly and, under cover of cleverness, surrenders politics to the forces of inevitability. The best answer to the "Who, we?" question is really this: let's find out. We should not fall prey to the self-contradictory argument that we can only speak of community if we already have a community we can point to. Human communities are not best imagined as exercises in picking out pre-existing essences or identifying clusters of in-groupers. Instead they are discursive achievements, processes of seeking and finding conversational partners and forging with them, painfully and by increments, the shared public institutions that will work for us. We are what we make of ourselves.

The idea of citizenship is not the only way we can pursue our commonalities and needs, not the only way to entertain our long-ings and dreams. But it is a crucial one; and, when linked to the deep insight that we owe a duty of justice to our fellow citizens, the con-cept of citizenship sheds its dark origins in the project of *keeping people out* and, reversing the field, becomes a matter of *bringing people in* – not loving them or liking them or even agreeing with them, much of the time, but making room for them to be at home too.

Books, like lives, are always unfinished even when they end, for to write is to struggle with contingency, to impose a certain false order upon the endless, and endlessly frustrating, nature of thought. When it is genuine, thinking is essentially and eternally disruptive. It never leaves anything as it is – even itself. A central virtue of the encounters that lie at the heart of this discussion is that they give an engaging particularity – a messiness, a conversational urgency – to what might otherwise be rather tidy and abstract arguments. They also illustrate the very contingency that these thinkers all, in their different ways, try to acknowledge in argument. Together they paint a vivid, backwards-looking self-portrait of the modern age, a chal-lenging, provocative – and infinite – reflection of our desires and confusions, our wishes and dreams. Listening to these voices from the past, we begin to hear ourselves, our own voices articulating the characteristic worries and hopes of the age – which are also the timeless worries and hopes of humans in community.

As with all such reflection, we begin with a simple question: What is it to be a citizen? We end, again typically, with a sense that the simple question is a lot more complicated than it looks. It spawns numerous other questions, maybe even ones that tend to undercut our original certainty about where the questioning was supposed to begin, where it was supposed to go. Questions like these: Where do I belong? To what am I loyal? What is the point, if any, of this life I struggle to lead? Cultural and political isolation are no longer options for any of us, regardless of nationality or passport. Whether we are discussing countries or the individuals who inhabit them, whether we are talking about markets or communications technology, we must accept that global interdependence is now a reality for us. Any argument about political commitment begins here. It begins now.

Chapter 2

RIGHTS AND DUTIES

Excellent friend. You are an Athenian. Your city is the most important, and renowned for its wisdom and power. Are you not ashamed that, while you take care to acquire as much wealth as possible, with honour and glory as well, yet you take no care or thought for understanding or truth, or for the best possible state of your soul?
— Socrates, in Plato's *Apology*

The Perfect Citizen

The year, by a certain sort of reckoning, was 399 B.C. It was, by any sort of reckoning, spring in the south of Greece. The season of cultivation and rebirth. And the old man, a cobbler of widely acknowledged physical ugliness, sat alone in the cell, thinking about what he had done.

It was very early, the long dawn of springtime. The light was feeble and so was his mood, normally one of jaunty self-confidence. What had possessed him? He should have known better, at a grizzled seventy, than to respond so sharply. It was that young idiot Meletus standing up to denounce him that did it. To think that a scant-beard like that should be accusing *him* of impiety and corruption, as if the pursuit of his own ignorance in those marketplace discussions had really been some calculated device to undermine conformity among the young.

Well . . . what if it had? Would that be so unforgivable?

No, no, that wasn't right. He shouldn't give in to their ignorance. He was not condoning impiety, even if those fools in the galleries were no more able to think clearly about it than that dim-witted bigot Euthyphro, so enthusiastic about indicting his own father for murder. Didn't they see the simple problem? You could not define piety as the quality of being loved by the gods, if you also claimed their reason for approving an action in the first place was that it was pious. The gods love what the gods love! That's not news! Just think about it for a moment: is an action pious because the gods love it, or do they love it because it is pious? There's your problem, Euthyphro, off to condemn your closest kin, the man who gave you life, with such certainty. So certain you know what's right. You don't even know that you don't know!

Simple, really, but amazing how many of them missed it. All this talk of the gods loving things, and where has piety itself gone in the meantime? True piety might be, in a way, refusing to claim one knew what piety was *and seeking it all the same*. But they never quite grasped that. God knows the idea was foreign to them, the great and the wise, the beautiful citizens of Athens. They just couldn't see how much deeper their ignorance was than his, so divinely foretold at Delphi. The old man knew he was ignorant, but to *not* know that you did not know, and to claim knowledge when you did not have it – what better description of damnation!

And now to be accused of something he hadn't even done, to be accused at all when what he did was for Athens alone, for the good of them all, with all of them standing there like that, arrogant and haughty and uncomprehending as usual. Democrats! Ever since the wars, ever since the Thirty, they'd been growing in boldness. He knew the trumpery charges were not the real issue, that they were really after him for the deeper challenge he posed to their cheap religious authority and shoddy claims to knowledge, the way the young men trailed after him and watched him embarrass their pompous elders. But it was irritating anyway.

More than irritating. His friends, young and old, scattered throughout the crowd, had registered their dismay when he rose to speak. Young Plato taking notes, as usual; you could almost see him sifting it all in his head, making it into something else. Plato – he probably thinks of the old man as some kind of *martyr*, when really he was mostly just annoyed. Crito, the old man's kinsman, was there too. Older than the others, he looked concerned. Crito knew the frame of mind the old man was in. They could all sense what was coming. They could feel the passion bubbling under the light tone, the practised ironic pose.

It really was no more than the truth. The established citizens were afraid. It wasn't atheism and corruption they feared, but inquiry. *The gods themselves are not higher than the moral truth* – that was hard for them to swallow. Custom and convention, obedience and ritual, are all very well for children, but it is time for glorious Athens to take on the estate of adulthood. It is time for Athenians to think for themselves, and to find the truth that lurks beneath their observances and laws. All this talk of material wealth and worldly success, instead of asking how they ought to live, what was worth doing.

It wasn't just the elders, though. He saw how completely most of the younger men accepted the thoughtless ideas of success – and how upset they became when they got an inkling of another way of thinking about life. All of them, young and old, should welcome what he was doing. He hadn't been kidding about his suggestion for another sentence, though perhaps it was better they had thought so. Not pay him, for that would make him no better than a sophist; but give him the same dining rights enjoyed by the athletes at the Prytaneum. Why not? Some of those boneheads couldn't even carry on a conversation. And there they sat, day after day, feeding at the public trough.

Well, fine; they had brought their own kind of glory to the city. His contribution was no less than theirs, though, if the old citizens could only see it. Worshipping false gods! Did they really think he cared for anything more than Athens, that he would ever do something unfaithful to her best interests? It was unthinkable. He had been angry, of course, and once he started he really couldn't stop. It happened that way sometimes. Somebody said something stupid and, bad manners or not, you had to set them straight. That whelp Meletus made too easy a target, really. He hadn't been briefed well enough – a couple of quick logical moves and his position was a shambles.

He had to make that point about genuine impiety and the fear of death, too. They would not manipulate him into accepting exile as an alternative to execution. Anytus even wanted him to go voluntarily – as if he could simply walk away from Athens, the mother of all he was. That's what they really wanted, of course, his going meekly away. Even they could see he was right when he said a dead Socrates would be a much bigger annoyance than a live one. Well, they were not going to get it. Yes, he would continue his thinking and questioning even at the risk of death. To fail in that – to surrender the quest he was on, for fear of bad opinion or punishment – would be the only true impiety, a real failure of duty. Then he actually *would* be guilty of the charges they had brought against him! Ironic, really, when you thought about it. The prescribed cure was in fact the cause of the disease. They didn't seem to find that funny, but he did.

But hemlock? That was clever, he had to admit it. They knew he'd been going around saying that real wisdom was all about learning how to die. That the philosopher was always practising for death. Yes. Hadn't he said himself just that afternoon that death was not to be feared, because to fear something unknown is to pretend foolishly to a knowledge we do not possess? Of course, that was an argument that always sounded better when he said it to someone else than when he put it to himself alone.

Still, it was basically right. It was part of acknowledging ignorance as the first step to true knowledge. And of course fear, like everything else, should finally be guided by reason – that was why he hadn't tried to sway the jury with an emotional appeal. We haven't been given this gift of thought only to disregard it in favour of sentiment or superstition. Where thought would lead was still unclear, but at least a conscious lack of clarity was better than a false, dangerous certainty. That narrow-minded fundamentalist Euthyphro was a fool, but they were all a bit like him, really, despite their mockery. It was certainly true, as he'd said, that wickedness runs faster than death. Even if death catches us all in the end.

And so here he was, and truly he didn't feel very afraid. He was getting on. It was easy to be so reckless when his life was already almost gone, and old age loomed. Plato didn't like his talking this way – it seemed less noble – but it was true. He might have thought differently about all of this when he was thirty. They knew he secretly prided himself on his steadfastness. Eating the raw onions before battle. Going barefoot in winter – and he a cobbler, too. Never complaining.

Now he was going to learn a thing or two about discomfort. But he had to put a good face on it, hadn't he? Thirty days had passed since the ship had sailed, and soon it would return and, those ritual obligations discharged, his sentence would be carried out. Plenty of people had come by in the meantime. He only had to keep it up a little longer. For their sake, if not for his own.

———

Crito came in alone. An honourable man visiting his troubled old friend in prison. The jailer knew him, and made no trouble.

He had been many times before in the past month, as they waited for the ship to return from Delos. It was due the next day, and time was short. This wasn't going to be one of those fan-club meetings, when the young men crowded around Socrates, shoving each other and struggling to get a word in, to be the person he favoured with his intense gaze and frightening questions. Some of them came away shaking their heads, others looking pale and shattered, others still with beaming smiles of apparent idiocy. That was fine for the market-place, and for the children. But not for him. Crito had a proposal to make, and he didn't want a throng of groupies jostling for position and trying to argue with him or with Socrates.

The man was a prize oaf, however brilliant he might be. Didn't he realize that his simple presence in the agora, his desire to ask those questions, was disruptive? He didn't believe he had corrupted the young, but in a way he certainly had. They were not the same any-more. They were argumentative, unhappy – troubled by things their elders had not questioned, had taken for granted. But that wasn't the point now. The point now was to get him away before these other idiots could kill him. There he was, sleeping peacefully with every sign of ease. Meanwhile he, Crito, hadn't had a good night's sleep since that farce of a trial a month ago.

Crito's appeal is straightforward, his urging heartfelt. He has bad news to share with his imperturbable friend, waking from his peace-ful sleep: the ritual ship was about to land, probably by the next morning, and the execution would then be enacted. He and Socra-tes are old friends; they have talked many times on topics both mun-dane and philosophical. He has come with a simple appeal. Socrates should take the opportunity to slip out of the jail. A plan is ready, and a route chosen. All they need is the old man's cooperation. He begins to speak . . .

He first argues that Socrates' death will deprive him, Crito, of a valued friend. Maybe unwisely, he quickly adds that public opinion will judge him and his other friends harshly if Socrates dies, because people will think they did not do enough to rescue the convicted man, even though they had ample opportunity and financial means. On that count, Crito tells Socrates that he has enough money to make the escape good, and that he is confident Socrates will be welcomed in Thessaly. Simmias of Thebes, among others, is prepared to foot the bill. His other friends are all waiting to help. Then, a bit wildly, Crito urges Socrates to think of his three sons – the little boys Sophroniscus and Menexenus, the young man Lamprocles – who will be left in an orphanage if their father does not take the opportunity to make a break for it, submitting to the death sentence instead. (There's also his wife, Xanthippe, to consider, but Crito, a good Athenian of his time, does not actually see fit to mention her.)

These are worldly arguments, and here Crito represents the voice of pragmatism over principle. But Socrates answers him in the voice of conviction, confident of his moral position and assured of the political consequences of that position. A voice few of us are likely to hear today, least of all, perhaps, in our own heads. There is none of the habitual Socratic irony in this conversation, none of the teasing and aggressive interrogation characteristic of his engagements with his younger friends – or with his enemies. Socrates speaks from his heart. He dismisses Crito's concern with popular opinion, and then waves away the rather telling point, made as Crito rallies in the argument, that popular opinion, like it or not, put Socrates in his current position. Popular opinion can do neither good nor ill, it can only speak its biases.

Crito is frustrated. "Frankly," he tells Socrates, "I'm ashamed for you and for us, your friends: it may appear that this whole predicament of yours has been handled with a certain feebleness on our part. What with the bringing of your case to court when that could have been avoided, the actual conduct of the trial, and now, to crown it all, this absurd outcome of the business, it may seem that the problem has eluded us through some fault or weakness on our part – that we failed to save you, and you failed to save yourself, when that was quite possible and feasible."

Socrates is unmoved. He replies with what will emerge as the central statement of his position, the essence of his idea of citizenly duty. "I cannot now reject the very principles that I previously adopted," he says reasonably, "just because this fate has overtaken me; rather, they appear to me much the same as ever, and I respect and honour the same ones that I did before." As always, it is not simply living that is to be valued, but living justly and well. And so for Socrates, to return injustice for injustice would be a clear violation of his sense that a good life is one that inflicts no harm whatsoever. It would contradict at a stroke his entire position, his entire life.

But Crito wants to know: why should evading a *bogus* conviction constitute an injustice? This is the central question of the remaining dialogue between the two, and the crux of this anguished reflection on the rights and duties of citizenship. Here, to make his point, Socrates assumes the voice of the laws of Athens themselves.

"Suppose," he says to Crito, "that while we were preparing to run away from here – or however one should describe it – the laws and constitution of Athens were to come and confront us and ask this question. 'Now, Socrates, what are you proposing to do? Can you deny that by this act which you are contemplating you intend, so far as you have the power, to destroy us, the laws, and the whole state as well? Do you imagine that a city can continue to exist and not be turned upside down, if the legal judgments that are pronounced in it have no force but are nullified and destroyed by private persons?'"

The way this question is phrased is important. It has sometimes been argued that the laws are asking what would happen if *everyone* disobeyed the law, and suggesting thereby that Socrates is bound by the strictures of a social contract like the ones that become familiar in later political philosophy. Here citizenship is understood as a kind of bargain between citizens, an exchange of loyalty for services effected through the mechanism of the state. This impression is strengthened when, later in this imagined conversation with the laws, they demand of Socrates why he has not forsworn the benefits of Athenian citizenship if he had a problem with its constitution. "[A]ny Athenian," they say, "on attaining to manhood and seeing for himself the political organization of the state and us its laws, is permitted, if he is not satisfied with us, to take his property and go away wherever he likes. . . . On the other hand, if any one of you stands his ground when he can see how we administer justice and the rest of our public organization, we hold that by doing so he has in fact undertaken to do anything that we tell him."

In social contract theory, this argument is known as *tacit consent*. Socrates has not been asked the explicit question whether he accepts the laws of Athens, but he has conspicuously accepted the fruits of Athenian society even when he was free to go elsewhere – much more free, in fact, than most citizens are today, since there was no issue of passport control or work visas. Indeed, Socrates is uncommonly accepting of Athens' charms, having never travelled beyond its walls except on military campaign and, once, to attend some games and spectacles on the nearby Isthmus. More than that, he has fathered children in the city, and therefore extended his commitment to the Athenian way of life into the indeterminate future. He has enjoyed the benefits. How can he evade the costs?

Warming to the theme, the laws take on the quietly demanding tones of a bunch of goodfellas: "Now first answer this question. Are we or are we not speaking the truth when we say that you have undertaken, in deed if not in word, to live your life as a citizen in obedience to us? You had seventy years in which you could have left the country, if you were not satisfied with us or felt that the agreements were unfair. You did not choose Sparta or Crete – your favourite models of good government – or any other Greek or foreign state. It is quite obvious that you stand by yourself above all other Athenians in your affection for this city and for us its laws."

Socrates can make no answer, and neither, in his turn, can Crito. But significantly, the argument here is not really a contractarian one – or rather, is not one in the form we usually recognize, where individual citizens bind together to secure their rights and avoid anarchy. Plato is not suggesting with this interplay that Socrates is bound to abide by the law because of an agreement, tacit or otherwise, with his fellow citizens. On the contrary, his obedience is enjoined because of *a relationship with the laws themselves*. It is not his fellow Athenians who speak to him, but the voice of the laws as supernatural realities – the very idea of Law. And though the laws occasionally suggest that Socrates' escape would violate a previous contractual agreement, they also go much further. They view escape as, in essence, a personal attack upon them, a form of patricide.

"Come now, what charge do you bring against us and the state, that you are trying to destroy us?" they ask. "Did we not give you life in the first place? Was it not through us that your father married your mother and begot you? Can you deny, in the first place, that you were our child and servant, both you and your ancestors? And if this is so, do you imagine that what is right for us is equally right for you, and that whatever we try to do to you, you are justified in retaliating?"

This strong hint of authoritarianism has bothered readers of the *Crito* for centuries. How can it be squared with the defence of free expression apparently contained in the *Apology*, a dialogue drawn from a scene just a month earlier, when Socrates argued for his innocence? How can Socrates be at once a champion of free-thinking and rational challenges to social power, and a craven child suffering the wrath of a disapproving father? Crito, remarkably, makes no objection when the laws assume this new tone in Socrates' speech. Why not? Pragmatist that he is, surely the proper rejoinder is to point out that Socrates does not really have to suffer this stern, paternalistic judgment. Unlike a son or a slave, he can simply avoid the punishment threatened by a father or master. These analogies, which the laws use so blithely, are excessively weak. No citizen is so nearly beholden to the laws – especially when their judgment, as in the present case, may be faulty.

Crito says none of this, but, looking back on their conversation, *we* must. And Socrates' answer is there in the discussion, even if it is likely to fall oddly on our ears. Without Athens, Socrates says, he is not merely less than himself, he is *nothing*. It is literally unimaginable to him that he should be anything other than Athenian. This is only partly a matter of not wanting to find himself in some other place – Thessaly or Sparta – where he might not be welcomed, or where his scofflaw tendencies, following an illegal escape, would be constantly noted. It is much more about recognizing the validity of the laws' claim that for him to escape would be to destroy them.

Why? Because for Socrates, the laws are made legitimate not through the acts of his fellow citizens, as in a contractarian or democratic constitution, but instead because they track a higher, universal justice. The laws are valid in themselves, not because they are chosen by a particular group of people. That is why the choice is posed starkly when they speak to him: he must either persuade them *in the name of that same universal justice* that they are wrong, or else submit to their judgments. And, significantly, the fact that these judgments are meted out by imperfect citizens, who might be vindictive or otherwise motivated, does not alter the basic case. "If you cannot persuade your country you must do what it imposes," the laws tell him. "Both in war and in the law courts and everywhere else you must do whatever your city and your country command, or else persuade them in accordance with universal justice."

Even if we would not accept without qualification a category such as "universal justice," in which an essentialist like Plato has so much faith, the point may still hold in this way: to break a given unjust law is one thing, a justifiable or even demanded act of civil disobedience. But to evade the law's punishment as well is to undermine the very idea of law, and instantly to nullify the effect of disobeying an unjust one. The kind of critical engagement Socrates has had with his city, constantly calling it to rational and moral account, is gravely weakened if he is unwilling to suffer the consequences of it. The laws argue that such an evasion of punishment works to destroy them, because it violates the enabling principle of all law, namely, that it will be subject to enforcement. An individual law or judgment may be just or unjust, but without the reality of enforcement, there is no law at all.

The laws say this: "As it is, you will leave this place, when you do, as the victim of a wrong done not by us, the laws, but by your fellow men. But if you leave here in that dishonourable way, returning wrong for wrong, and evil for evil, breaking your agreements and covenants with us, and injuring those whom you least ought to injure – yourself, your friends, your country, and us – then you will have to face our anger in your lifetime, and in that place beyond when the laws of the other world know." Socrates recognizes the power of this argument, and moreover sees clearly that he would destroy himself as well as the laws in the act of dodging punishment. This is not submission to authoritarian will, or even persuasion by the interests of his fellow citizens. It is instead a recognition of the self-contradiction entailed in escaping his own convictions – a recognition that is mixed liberally with more self-serving motives. Among other, higher reasons for his decision, Socrates will not suffer himself to be thought of badly after he is gone. He is going to do the right thing even if it kills him. This self-regard is more considerable than the general tone of Platonic adulation would like, but it comes through the discussion with Crito almost despite itself.

So, having adopted the stance of a moral purist, Socrates nevertheless reminds Crito of the negative consequences that will befall his friends and (especially) his reputation if he flees. He says he cannot go somewhere else because it would violate his commitment to rational inquiry – but equally it would obliterate his good name as a man of principle. "Will you approach these people and have the impudence to converse with them?" the laws demand, almost mocking now. "What arguments will you use, Socrates? The same which you used here, that goodness and integrity, institutions and laws, are the most precious possessions of mankind? Do you not think that Socrates and everything about him will appear in a dis-reputable light?"

This issue of the complicated relationship between personal integrity and reputation is one that weighs heavily on the mind of Plato — it is a main focus of the first parts of the *Republic,* for example — but in this conversation between Socrates and Crito, it is unstable. This flaw in the character of Socrates should be accepted for the benefit that it is. Here we see him as near to death as anyone knowingly is, rationally assessing his position. It would be amazing if no hint of personal pride or *amour-propre* were discernible. More than humanizing an otherwise astringent character, however, the instability provides an important clue to thinking about citizenship. Socrates is proud: he is proud to be an Athenian, proud of himself for the gadfly role he has taken on in Athens, even proud to be sub-mitting to the will of Athenian law in this brave, thoughtful fashion. Thoreau believed civil disobedience was the highest duty of citizen-ship. Horace thought it was sweet and right to die for one's country. Socrates combines both sentiments: what greater act of citizenship can there be than to die at the hands of one's own country, precisely while engaged in its service as a political critic?

We can no longer wonder that Crito, that well-meaning, good-hearted practical man, could not even begin to persuade his friend of the wisdom in escaping. There is literally nowhere for Socrates to escape to. He is home, and he cannot leave home without destroying both it and himself in the process. And so he will die, contented — and more than a little stubborn. As he says himself, effectively ending any further discussion with Crito: "The sound of these arguments is ringing loudly in my head, and makes me unable to hear the others. As far as these present thoughts of mine go, you may be sure that if you object to them, you will plead in vain. Nonetheless, if you think you will do any good, speak up."

Crito, glumly, can think of no argument to offer in response to that. "No, Socrates," he concedes. "I have nothing to say."

Never has citizenship been so profoundly defended. And never since, frankly, have the perfect conditions of its realization been available. We may even wonder if they were truly available in Socrates' time. Socrates can talk this way to his friend Crito, speaking to himself in the voices of the laws, only because he is rock-solid in his belief that the laws are a part of him, and he of them. He sets himself up as a kind of perfect exemplar of political commitment, a pure reflection of ideal and universal justice. There is no troubling distance here between his sense of himself, even his sense of himself *as a citizen*, and the political realm to which he belongs. There is no acknowledgment here that actual laws and the worldly justice they try to serve are always the imperfect creations of fallible people.

These convictions, so foreign to us, are the real source of his decision to suffer execution. What bothers him is not that fleeing Athens would constitute a betrayal of his friends and fellow citizens, but that it would constitute a betrayal of himself. This is crucial. Socrates doesn't make an argument that the decision against him is legitimate because it was arrived at democratically – no surprise there, for neither he nor Plato were enamoured of the new Athenian democracy. Nor, however, does he claim to find the decision valid because he has entered into an agreement with his fellow citizens, in a non-aggression pact on the Hobbesian or Lockean model. No, the decision to suffer the punishment of Athens is made because of a personal relationship Socrates has with the rule of law itself.

The choice is therefore easy for him because the only other option is thoroughly irrational. This, surely, is something that lies a good distance even from vibrant forms of contemporary patriotism, which depend so much on irrational passion. The contemporary philosopher Jonathan Lear remarks that at least in the eyes of their philosophers, the ancient Greeks enjoyed in their political discussions an *ideal speech situation.* Given the small size and exclusiveness of their polity, public discourse was both full in extent and fully participatory. It was able to generate purely rational results because none of the usual pathologies of discourse – exclusions and truncations, distortions and deceptions – could get in the way. They were ruled out by definition.

That, anyway, was the theory. Werner Jaeger, rather more cynically, has noted that early democratic Athens did not destroy its aristocracy so much as it tried to turn its entire citizen body into one. And did so, prominently, at the expense of slaves, guest-workers, and women, who could enjoy neither the benefits nor the responsibilities of citizenship. Thus their political results were indeed as close to a pure reflection of citizens' desires as we can imagine – though the price was that those desires came exclusively from a proportionally very small section of the entire social population. The state is not conceived here as a series of familiar compromises and bargains in the art of the possible. It is not shot through with fundamental, opaque irrationalities and ungovernable passions. Politics is rather the creation of the best possible polity out of the deep inner needs of its citizenry – who are only some of its members.

Socrates is working with these assumptions, indeed is giving them voice for everyone. The laws say to him, thunderingly: "Are you so wise as to have forgotten that compared with your mother and father and all the rest of your ancestors your country is something far more precious, more venerable, more sacred, and held in greater honour both among gods and among reasonable men?" We may hear that demand and think, Forget it. Patriotism that all-consuming is not citizenship, it is fanatical devotion – nationalist fervour. Just the sort of thing that leads to wars and genocide. Socrates is critical of his city's inhabitants, but never of the very idea of the city. He is willing – perhaps all too willing – to die for Athens.

This will not quite do for us. Today we must ask, Can the democratic experiment of Greece, and this confrontation between

Socrates and Crito, really teach us anything about citizenship? Surely the distance in context is so great, the gap in ethical and spiritual background so yawning, that nothing of interest can come from these reflections?

Well, certainly the Greek democracy bears only passing resemblance to what we have forged in our own time. It was an emergent political form that by brilliant steps took a tribal culture and transformed it into a small functional state. This was possible only because a number of conditions were met simultaneously. The heroes of early Greek democracy – Solon, Cleisthenes, Pericles – possessed vision and luck. The local economic conditions were favourable, there was relative peace and stability, and the nascent citizens of Athens were blessed with philosophers of courage and insight. Among other things, they believed, as Aristotle most famously put it, that humans were political animals, *zoon politiken*, that they could not realize their nature in isolation from one another.

The emerging citizens of this polity in turn believed in an equality of competence in judgment (*isonomia*) and in the value of self-sufficiency (*autarkia*). Socrates sets himself up as a moral expert in his conversation with Crito, but it is important for the larger story that his fellow citizens were not often given to expert guidance. That is, they trusted in their own judgment – even as they excluded many people from full possession of that faculty. In the rosy picture, democratic politics in Greece is a smoothly functioning combination of sound practical judgment (*phronesis*) and civic action (*praxis*). Offices were held by lot, cases were decided by the assembled citizen body, and each citizen was, crucially, expected to defend the city with his life in times of conflict.

The last point is particularly significant, since the roles of warrior and citizen have historically been more closely identified than any other. (The role of worker or taxpayer, which today is often linked to citizenship, is of much more recent vintage. Even the connection between ownership of land and citizenship is, relative to the ancient ideal, a late development.) In many civic republican states, only those willing to die for the city could expect to enjoy the benefits of citizenship – a notion updated in popular form in the right-wing corporatism of Robert Heinlein's *Starship Troopers*, say, where non-warriors do not have citizenship and are viewed not unlike drones in a beehive.

Certainly military service, and especially death in combat, is a noble expression of commitment to a body politic. But this connection, so strong and persistent, is also potentially dangerous, if the military virtues associated with the warrior are not separated from the civic virtues of the citizen. A tragic depiction of this danger is Shakespeare's Coriolanus, who finds his skills at soldiering inadequate to the slippery demands of politics. On the other side, a more positive illustration of the problem might be seen in the mutiny of French soldiers in 1917, when the incompetence of their generals moved these warriors to put their citizenly identities first and refuse to be slaughtered. But then, the French have always been effective at realizing that mixture of pragmatism and romance that makes for good citizenship.

In the ancient Greek ideal of the state, there was also a strong commitment to public spaces. The famous agora in which Socrates strolled and argued was twenty-six acres square, and citizens regularly met each other there and at gymnasia, religious celebrations, markets, or festivals of drama. We see these details alluded to in Plato's dialogues as well as elsewhere in the extant sources. The *Republic* opens with Socrates returning from a spectacle of religious observance in the Piraeus, the port of Athens. The *Symposium* celebrates the winner of a drama competition. These public spaces, so crucial to Athenian political life, are the necessary complement to the purely private spaces of everyday life, the spaces of what Marx would label "the realm of necessity."

He meant necessity in the sense of basic needs, the place where animal functions are met in order to pursue higher goals elsewhere.

For the Greeks, this realm was important – one must have some-where to eat and sleep – but not for solace or luxury, as it so often is for us today. "Personal comfort was virtually unknown among the Greeks," Ernest Renan writes in his *Essais de morale et de critique*. "These citizens of small towns, who raised in their midst so many admirable public monuments, resided in houses that were no more than modest, houses in which vases (though masterpieces of ele-gance, to be sure) constituted the only furnishings." It is only when one ventures out of the house, into public, that the dialogue of citi-zenship is made possible, where the realization of our full political selves is accommodated. (An unromantic but necessary caveat here: these Athenian citizens had so much time to talk politics only because their slaves were doing all the routine domestic and commercial work. Functionally, the guarantors of the Greek's ideal speech situa-tion were not the brilliant philosophers but the sweating workers.)

Plato, though he was sensitive to the harm the democratic state had done to Socrates, and though he was forced to flee Athens him-self after the trial depicted in the *Apology*, was not in doubt that a certain kind of democratic principle is still basic in securing legiti-macy. This despite, too, his famous depiction of democrats as crazed libertines in the latter stages of the *Republic*. Plato's principle is democratic in a rather different sense than we are nowadays familiar with, however. It is not that legitimacy is conferred by *the will of the people*, but rather that the people in a just state are individual reflections of the justness of the political order. That is why Plato can make what, on the surface, looks like a straightforwardly bizarre argument, namely, that out of an absurdly narrow particularity, a political body ruled by a mere five hundred males, Socrates and the laws of Athens speak in a conversation about universal justice. Yet, it is this bizarre claim that makes these Greek eccentrics of enduring interest for citizens everywhere.

How so? Well, as Jonathan Lear once more puts it, there is for Plato an *isomorphism*, not merely an *analogy*, between the inside of self and the outside of society, between an individual and his or her culture. One side of this complex relationship always works to form the other in an intricate weave of codependency, a kind of reflective equilibrium between polis and psyche. There is a dynamic tension in any such relationship, one that under favourable conditions is productive, just, and even rational. If the state is legitimate and its citizens just, then the whole social reality functions as an ongoing articulation of the higher truth that rules the entire universe. In a sense, these early Greek citizens saw themselves as the agents of reason's self-realization through the state. They are fulfilling their natures, becoming what they are meant to be. And wily reason (as Hegel liked to call it) is here in the dialogic process of its own self-interpretation, using the desires and aspirations of concrete individuals, struggling to make lives for themselves, as part of its larger internal progress.

That is the ideal case, of course. At the same time — and this is the tragedy of the philosopher-king in Plato's *Republic* as much as of Oedipus in Sophocles' Theban Plays, or indeed of Socrates in the *Crito* — there is a fundamental limit on the prospect of full rational awareness, of complete self-disclosure through dialogue with fellow citizens. Our desires are never wholly transparent, even to ourselves. Our preferences are never perfectly lucid, even when the state is closely related to our inner nature. And reason never accounts for everything that moves us in human life — on the contrary. The prospect of rational social justice is always overshadowed by the presence of the irrational, the unjust, the evil aspects of human affairs.

The awareness of that tragic dimension of democratic politics, so strong in Plato's vision, is often obscured today, both by our sense of the alienness of the Socratic execution and by our blithe assumption that as products of modern liberal thinking, we know perfectly well what our desires and preferences are. The first important lesson of the Socrates/Crito encounter, then, is this reminder that when it comes to the world outside ourselves, the social and political world, we are at least as much formed by as forming. More deeply still, this relationship of what we might call isomorphic codependency is always fraught with hidden wishes and irrational turmoils. It is ever on the verge of becoming dysfunctional if we are not watchful and wise.

The second important lesson is that this is not a passive situation. Because reason is in play in the social world, there is always the possibility of social criticism. That is what Socrates repeatedly insisted on in his encounters with his fellow citizens, after all: that we must examine our beliefs, not merely hold them. Critical reflection comes inevitably in the wake of trying to give reasons for why we do things, and this reflection is, importantly, internal to the social practice in which it appears. Consensual approval of the order of things can, in principle, be granted or withdrawn by citizens, though of course such a process is never perfect or free of pathology. We are often willfully blind to things. Just as often, things are invisible despite our best efforts to see.

Socrates therefore represents a limit case in the matter of citizenship, because he goes to his death maintaining the clear sense of internal belonging that led him to his disruptive behaviour in the first place, even as his fellow citizens in effect have reached the conclusion that he is an alien presence, a barbarian in their midst. This effectively externalizes the criticism he represents, making it (they hope) alien and thus ignorable: a manoeuvre we might agree to label the Barbarian Defence. This kind of deflection is not so distant from our own practices as we might think. In a popular version of the same move, unwelcome criticism is declared not barbarous but irrational – not literally alien as being outside the limits of the city's tolerance but intellectually alien as being, allegedly, beyond the rational pale.

We must always be aware of these charges of irrationality in the ongoing tussles of social criticism, the struggles of citizens to make the social world reflect their desires and needs. The details of Socratic method are once more to the point here. Socrates works by questioning. Why? Because nothing else is so effective in calling out the real commitments of his fellow citizens, their often rigid yet prereflective beliefs. But more than this, it works by a complicated process of generating internal conflict between discrete parts of the entire belief-set. Through his questioning, Socrates is able to bring contradictory parts of a single world view into contact with one another, closing the distances that are usually opened by delusion or laziness or complacency. He is thereby able to produce a positive charge of confusion or discomfort that the interlocutor, on pain of irrationality, must attempt to discharge. That is, the interlocutor, confronted by his own beliefs, must face either cognitive contradiction (where one belief he holds belies another) or performative contradiction (where he says one thing even while doing another).

No wonder so many of Socrates' partners in dialogue suddenly have a strong desire to move off to less unsettling social spaces and encounters. Cephalus laughingly retires to less strenuous talk in the *Republic*, Thrasymachus sulks after being trounced later in the same dialogue, Euthyphro hastily excuses himself in the dialogue bearing his name. The Athenians may have used the ultimate Barbarian Defence in expelling Socrates from their midst, but it was at least in part because, as he himself points out at the trial, they know in their bones that his challenges have hit the mark. They were rattled. Socrates has not brought in an external standard of judgment and asked them to live up to it. He has, on the contrary, asked them to do a much harder thing, namely, to live up to the internal logic of their own beliefs. In condemning him, they are only condemning themselves. Their unease in handling him at trial is proof that they sense it.

In this regard, Socrates – or any social critic – is in the precarious position of relating to his fellow citizens somewhat as a therapist relates to a client. That is one reason that Plato must give us Socrates in dialogue form. (The other obvious reason is that it makes the question-based method vividly effective.) Even though Plato is often accused, with ample reason, of being a metaphysical essentialist, he does not choose to deliver his arguments in a traditional discursive manner. Instead, he adopts the complexity and drama of the personal encounter. He wants us to feel in ourselves the unease that Socrates' friends felt when he turned his questions upon them. He wants the dialogues themselves to work like Socratic encounters. Whatever we think of Plato's mature thoughts on politics, and the vexing question of whether he really wanted there to be philosopher-kings, his dialogic approach preserves something of the immediacy of the encounter between critical, engaged citizens.

One of the key moments in the *Republic* concerns the philosopher's responsibility to return to the cave and engage in conversation with his former mates. Socrates acknowledges that the journey down from happy illumination, the place outside the cave where the philosopher can bask in the sun of ultimate truth, will be as hard as the one up to it. The philosopher, returning to his still-chained associates, will be blinded by the darkness to which he returns just as he was blinded by the light of the sun when he first emerged. And his erstwhile fellow prisoners will not welcome him. They will think him mad, and engage full flights of mockery and injury against him. The violence alluded to in the story clearly parallels the violence that was actually done to Socrates when he submitted himself to the judgment of his fellow Athenians. Even knowing this, yet the philosopher must go back down.

Again, why? Because the only duty higher than personal illumination is the duty to engage in conversation with fellow citizens, to try to persuade them what is right. This can be done well or it can be done badly, in arrogance or humility; but it must be done, because reason is not a country of one. Here and there Plato wavers on the point, of course, and the issue of the philosopher's commitment to society is a source of continuing scholarly debate about Plato's meaning. Indeed, there are hints elsewhere in Plato's dialogues that the philosopher can only do himself – and others – grave damage if he enters the realm of worldly political affairs; and the *Republic* is often read as a secret warning against political participation, not an encouragement of it. The philosopher-king remains an ambiguous legacy. Yet Plato finally seems to imply what Socrates himself enacted: that there is some kind of duty on every rational person's part to resolve the internal conflicts of reason. In a sense, reason is the ongoing conversation, the extended self-articulation, of ourselves in community. And whatever we may think about the idea of philosophers also being kings – absurd or terrifying, nonsensical or just good sense – this basic political-therapeutic duty to engage one's fellow citizens cannot be shirked.

The risks, meanwhile, are the same as in the standard therapeutic situation, only writ large. The social critic generates a transference, just as the therapist does, and must anticipate the same flashes of love and hate that come in the wake of any close encounter of this kind. Socrates did not see clearly enough that this would happen; or perhaps he wanted, unconsciously, to smash himself on its rocks. In any case, the larger lesson went mostly unlearned, at least at the time. (As Lear says, Socrates "did nothing to help the Athenian analyze their transference-distortion. Indeed, he seems to have invited and provoked the transference-storm which resulted in his death.") There are, at the same time, significant dangers of counter-transference, when the critic can no longer separate his role as analyst of pathologies from an erotic attachment to the subject of analysis. Thus do critics sometimes become ethnic nationalists, unreasoning patriots, do-or-die xenophobes – or simply happy and comfortable celebrants of the status quo.

The final lesson of the Socrates/Crito encounter, then, is that all of us who possess reason have the capacity, and hence the duty, to be social critics. Here, *can* implies *ought*. Like it or not, our embeddedness in social and cultural formations already means that this duty is demanded of us: we cannot fail to engage in social criticism if we are capable of making judgments at all. This is not a special duty of citizenship but a basic one.

Such a claim may not strike us as obvious, I realize. In a rush of empty individualism, a paroxysm of blind faith in the transparency of our desires, we have lost sight of the complicated dialogue between ourselves and the world of our making. All participation in civic life involves these complicated aspects of our individuality, the ways in which we are more than just ourselves. There are always little models or traces or reflections of the larger world inside our heads: deposits from the world we have, visions of the world we want. And these traces form our identities as citizens as much as any purely internal desires ever could, seemingly (but only seemingly) unrelated to anything besides themselves. Paying too much attention to ourselves, we have done damage to the complex political and social relationship between outside and inside, between us and the world. Our sense of ourselves is nowadays too often on the verge of incoherence or heedlessness. But this damage can be healed, and we need not return to some idealized Greek agora to do it. Such a return in any case would be impossible, for there is no golden age to find there, just a struggle like our own.

Of course our civic engagements, even when they are intended to generate wide commonalities or shared social goals, are likely to begin by being idiosyncratic: we are all here for our own complicated reasons, with our own pressing problems and clusters of demands. Not many people today are as confident as Socrates was that they reflect the nature of justice itself. The problem lately is that we have allowed these internal models of a larger meaning to warp and distort, so that our individuality is no more than a personal brand created in response to a barrage of marketing messages and merchandising imperatives. That is not the creation of a valid social space, a thriving new agora for this new global world. It is six and a half billion people mostly in isolation one from the other, struggling to find their way.

How did we get here?

The Evil of Banality

To pursue that question, let us first ask some slightly more tractable ones. How have we fared in making the world reflect our reason in the sense the Greek philosophers understood? Put another way, what have we achieved in our arguments with the laws, our more recent appeals to universal justice? To answer, we might begin by examining a key document in the rational working-out of our contemporary political commitments – an articulated reflection on the political culture we want, emerging from the one we have.

In 1998, the world marked a half century since the United Nations adopted the Universal Declaration of Human Rights. That document, substantially drafted by a Canadian law professor, John Humphrey of McGill University, offers thirty articles of faith for the shattered global landscape after the Second World War, beginning with the assertion that "all human beings are born free and equal in dignity and rights, endowed with reason and conscience, and should act towards one another in a spirit of brotherhood," and ending with the warning that "nothing in this Declaration may be interpreted as implying any right to act in destruction of the rights and freedoms set forth" within it.

The Declaration is a stirring document, as these sorts of documents go, because it uses without embarrassment the plain language of faith and hope. It is couched in tough-sounding declarative sentences, almost every article beginning with the phrase "Everyone has a right to . . ." or the phrase "No one shall be subjected to . . ." What everyone has a right to includes life, security, freedom, property, work, equal pay for equal work, leisure, due process, free assembly, suffrage, medical care, intellectual property rights, and education. What no one shall be subjected to is, among other evils, slavery, torture, arbitrary imprisonment, slander, seizure of property, and exile. The "will of the people" will be the basis of all legitimate government, according to the Declaration, and that will "shall be expressed in periodic and genuine elections."

Perhaps anticipating objections that would soon be levelled against this so-called rights discourse by various anti-liberal critics, the Declaration also articulates the *responsibilities* and *duties* of humans living in society. In Article 29 – significantly, near the end of the document, almost as a recursive meta-rule – we are told that as a general thing, "Everyone has duties to the community in which alone the free and full development of his personality is possible." Moreover, in the exercise of rights, everyone will be subject to the limitations of law – but only "for the purpose of securing due recognition and respect for the rights and freedoms of others and of meeting the just requirements of morality, public order and the general welfare of democratic society."

The resulting notion of citizenship is stronger than is often defended by liberals, moving towards a more civic republican, or even ancient Greek, view of political activity as part of the set of goods enjoyed by any person in his or her role as citizen. More than this, it extends the range of our understanding of human rights from the prophylactic or protection-based conception – human rights as a shield – towards a host of positive duties and activities.

Now, it is easy to pick over a high-minded statement like this in search of gaffes or missteps; easy too, I suppose, to make the obvious point that despite the language of *everyone having a right to* and *no one shall be subjected to*, people around the world are subjected to and denied rights to all kinds of things on a daily basis. One of the difficulties with the Declaration, from its first acceptance at the United Nations, has been the issue of compliance. Many regimes who are signatories to the document have achieved only partial compliance; moreover, sometimes that compliance is cynical or merely for show. Too often, the presence of human-rights rhetoric on the political podium has deflected attention from the violation of those rights in nearby prisons or detention centres.

That is not as damning an objection as it is often thought to be, however, since documents like the Declaration are – and are intended to be – statements of ideals. In the best case, they function as *regulative* ideals, guiding principles for an imperfect world and not simply as utopian fantasies. That is, they act to edge actual circumstances towards an ideal state rather than asserting that such a state will ever be fully achieved. That a rosy picture does not reflect the nature of the world as it now stands is not, contrary to cynical opinion, a rap against the picture.

In any case, our present engagement with the Declaration should not be of that dismissive kind. It should be, rather, that the sentiments of the Declaration are systematically unstable, and unstable in a way that makes it hard for us to think clearly about our current political context. By "our current political context" I mean one quite different from the world Socrates and Crito enjoyed but where their dispute between pragmatism and principle is still very much alive. I mean a world in which a form of universalism has indeed been achieved in human affairs, but without many of the guarantees that animated the authors and early adopters of the Declaration, and without the sense of moral objectivity that a Socrates could confidently defend more than two millennia before. It is a world that, beneath its slick self-congratulation, has so little political direction or stability that we are not indulging in doom-saying or aimless fear when we say it is in crisis.

———

The story of how this world came to be, of how we crossed the vast distance between Socratic citizenship and our own fractured reality, has many moments of crucial innovation. I am going to focus on one that may seem controversial, but only until we realize its connections to the deep tensions of our own political experience. I start with Immanuel Kant, the Enlightenment thinker responsible for much of our reigning view of the moral and political self and, in turn, for the spirit that animates the Declaration.

There are some echoes of Rousseau in the Declaration – for example, people are born free, the will of the people is supreme. And perhaps the most proximate relation of Enlightenment liberalism to the themes of the *Crito* is via Montesquieu's influential book *The Spirit of the Laws* (*L'Esprit des lois*, 1748), whose rationalist liberalism inspired the Declaration of the Rights of Man and the Constitution of the United States. But in its emphasis on human dignity, and centrality of reason, and the very idea of universalism itself, the U.N. document is clearly driven by Kantian ideals of cosmopolitan order. Indeed, the Kantian legacy cannot be overestimated in the idea of universal human rights, because it is Kant's version of liberalism, building upon the pioneering efforts of the seventeenth-century English philosophers, that takes the ideas of freedom and equality to a higher plane of abstract reality, moving past the fear-driven monarchism of Hobbes or the minimalist religious toleration of Locke to embrace the idea of each and every individual as valuable simply by virtue of being alive.

I will leave aside for the moment any consideration of the dignity and rights of non-human life, and note simply that Kant's triumph is modernity's triumph. Against the old orders of privilege based on social hierarchy, bloodline, and proximity to God, he offers the modern world a vision in which every human, regardless of station or wealth, must be treated as an end in him- or herself, and never merely as a means to an end. Extending the range of that "regardless" clause to take in nationality, race, gender, ethnic origin, sexual preference, and physical ability has been the work of the past two centuries – work that is by no means complete. Whatever we may think of Kant personally – and there was not much to like, if biographical tales can be trusted – he bequeaths to us a twinned vocabulary of individualism and universalism that runs through the modern world like the buzz of conversation at a good party. A human being is worthy of respect simply by virtue of being alive. And that worthiness extends without borders to encompass every individual, ignoring all particularities.

There are difficulties here, however, and many of them. I will mention just two and elaborate only on the second. The first arises as a result of the fact that for Kant and his followers, people were actually worthy of respect not by virtue of being just any kind of entity, but because they were moral agents, and they were moral agents by virtue of being rational. That is, it was a central part of the worthiness of individuals that they could, by the light of reason, perceive the structure of the moral law and their duty to it, and so act as to make the maxim of their action a universal law. That, indeed, is one prominent formulation of Kant's categorical imperative: a test of dutifulness that says that an action is justifiable if and only if it can be universalized for everyone.

The trouble is that the attribute "rational," and its unexamined assumptions, does all the work in this conception of human action. So much so that a negative judgment on a person's actions could lead, without difficulty, to the judgment that they were not fully rational. Or, by the same token, groups of individuals could be ruled out of moral and political play *ex ante* by declaring them incapable of reason. In Kant's usage, they are "minor," much the same way that cops in fifties melodramas might speak of minors – a procedure that will be familiar to women, blacks, the handicapped, children, and many others. (Compare the views of a character in Honoré de Balzac's 1833 novel, *Le Médecin de campagne*: "The proletarians seem to me to be the minors of the nation, and should always remain in a state of tutelage.")

Even if the attribute "rational" is taken to be uncontroversial, there are many heterogeneous elements that tend to creep into Kantian moral decision making, as John Stuart Mill (for one) famously noted a half century after Kant. Calculations of universal extension are notoriously subject to situational limits and various other forms of special pleading. This tends to reduce the allegedly pure dutifulness of the categorical imperative to the decidedly hypothetical instrumentality of calculating consequences for and against a certain action. For instance: lying is wrong, finally, not because it entails a self-contradiction, as Kant insisted, but because it undermines the web of social relations.

Our present concern, though, is the specifically political issues arising from the conjoined discourses of individualism and universalism, in particular the tension that exists between them – a tension noticed and thematized most pressingly in recent years by the political theorist Charles Taylor. That tension comes to the fore in recent political events, but it also nestles in the heart of the Declaration in the unstable relationship between Article 29 and the rest of the document. It is the tension between the avowed focus on the individual, which stresses the uniqueness and worthiness of the individual's life, and the overarching demand for universalism. The latter attempts to transcend the particularities of the individual's life in favour of some commonly held properties of humanness that demand protection and promotion.

The existence of this tension will not come as news to political observers today. We can articulate it in several ways. It's not just that universalism is being challenged in various appalling conflicts that turn on resurgent ethnic nationalisms or tribal blood feuds. We might place those facts, in their very extremity, beyond the political frontier. But even if we chose to do that, we cannot do the same when it comes to the social struggles within Western liberal democracies like our own, the struggles in what has come to be called the politics of identity. The attempts to secure group rights, cultural recognition, or simply a rich acceptance of the reality of each individual, have been written and acted as oppositions to the prevailing liberal norm of those democracies. That norm is perceived to secure individual rights only by robbing individuals of their particularity. In other words, when the idea of individualism is universalized, it has the apparently self-contradictory effect of rendering actual individuals null and void, mere ciphers in a formal array of rights.

This is a familiar story, if also an alarming one, to anyone who has read the newspapers during the past three decades or so. From the civil rights movements of the 1950s and '60s, which sought to work out the implied promise of universalism by securing rights for previously excluded individuals, the 1970s, '80s, and '90s moved into a period in which that kind of victory was rewritten as a defeat. From the point of view of new generations of feminists, race theorists and gay activists, it was not enough to have individual rights. Individual rights were ultimately conceived and made into policy by straight white men who wished, consciously or otherwise, to reduce everyone to a straight white man. Securing those rights was no more than a dangerous deflection from the genuine political task, namely, to secure the particular rights belonging to a specific marginalized group.

Individual rights, once the prize, now become the tool of a new, more subtle form of oppression: they are a particular masquerading as a universal. There is in fact no Kantian standard of universal rationality functioning beneath all our particularities, and so political stability cannot be secured by stripping those particularities away. Subordinating one's particularity to that false universal only means losing one's self, not preserving it. The political imperative, then, is not to secure individual rights under a larger political structure of generalized, and therefore empty, respect, but to demand real respect for *my* particularity in the uniquely valuable project of living my life. Or, if not my particularity *per se*, then that of the exclusive group to which I belong, whatever it may be — especially of course if that group has been, as a group, historically excluded from power and privilege.

I will not rehearse the intricacies of these conflicts here, for they are widely known. Nor will I declare myself on the various conflicts that ensued, except to say that I still believe a language of individualism can be politically useful if, but only if, its limits are constantly acknowledged and any tendency to eliminate otherness or difference is ruthlessly resisted. What must equally be resisted, however, is the celebration of particularity at the expense of larger political goals, the sort of self-regard that closes off all rational challenges by pointing out that the challenger is not a member of the particular group in question. In short, I believe the tension between these two extremes of elimination and separatism can be made productive. (Of course, I'm a straight white man, so you'll have to judge for yourself.)

In thinking about citizenship and rights, the main concern must be the very existence of this conflict between particularity and the prospect of a larger political justice. Human rights are about justice, and the Declaration was an attempt to help secure them – or at least give us some guidelines in working to do that. It was a flawed attempt not because universalizing human rights is the wrong route to take, but only because the very political culture from which it sprang is riven by this deep conflict. It is a powerful and indispensable touchstone in an era where there is much confusion, and even outright cynicism, about human rights. So the fundamental question remains, What can we do about justice when the interests of the individual seem everywhere at odds with the interests of a larger body politic, even one based upon the idea of the individual's interest?

In order to suggest an answer to that question, I am first going to complicate it with another one. It arises from the distance we have travelled from the encounter between Socrates and Crito, and involves tracking some features of our often bizarre political culture. The question is this: What becomes of universalism in a world where the particularity of the individual must always be respected, possibly to the exclusion of other goals?

Well, without too much exaggeration, we can suggest some

proximate tendencies. The prevailing idea of the sovereign individual is, like all prevailing ideas, liable to pathology. If people's identities must be respected absolutely, presumably so must the preferences and desires that proceed from those identities. If an identity cannot be challenged by reference to some larger shared goals, then neither can the preferences and desires that proceed from it. Thus, in a twisted way, we arrive at the toxic forms of narcissism, complaint, and self-justification that pass for individualism today: not just the rock-'em, sock-'em talk shows, in which people act out their pathetic conflicts under Jerry Springer's cynically moralizing eye, but also the high-toned literary memoirs and confessions that are the functional equivalents for people with more money and education.

You may say that I am moving a little too fast here, conflating legitimate claims to identity with these lowest-common-denominator excesses. But, as the Declaration itself teaches us, it's always important to consider the worst case to illuminate a whole field of cases. Not everyone need fear imminent prospects of torture; but everyone should be able to articulate a right not to suffer it. I am highlighting these excesses mainly in order to illustrate a point, namely, that individualism is not the uncomplicated good it may seem to be. While it has brought us much moral and political progress, it has also led to many perversities that have the ultimate effect of undermining justice rather than fostering it.

This becomes even clearer when we take a look at how the discourse of universalism has fared in practice. Again this is a tale of worst cases and excesses, and therefore just part of the full account, but it can be validly argued that the only functional universalism today has little to do with the propagation of justice and almost everything to do with the growing reach and influence of the cash nexus and global economy. This particular story is so depressingly familiar that I will not spend much time making my claim about it.

Capitalism has now decisively entered what the Marxist economist

Ernest Mandel called its third, or late, stage – each stage determined quite precisely by the dominant technology of capital's spread. The first stage, coinciding with the machine production of steam engines since about 1848, was market capitalism. This was eventually encompassed and surpassed by monopoly or imperialist capitalism based on the production of electric and combustion motors since the last decade of the nineteenth century. And that form was in turn subsumed by the post-industrial or multinational capitalism of the 1940s and beyond, based on electronic and nuclear technology.

The stages of capitalism also determine new sets of spatial relations, such that the world of multinational capital is speedily transformed into a weirdly annihilated space in which every point touches every other simultaneously, a rhizome of fibre-optic relations. In a world dominated by multinational capital, not only is everything reducible to exchange value, in the traditional manner, but the exchanges themselves become distorted and metastasized because of a speed and virtuality of exchange that ultimately defies the old logic of supply and demand – not to mention the now archaic idea that markets exist to facilitate the movement of useful products to the people who need them.

Indeed, that rather natural view now has the quaintness of a fairy tale – something captured vividly in the near-failure, in the fall of 1998, of a private transnational derivatives fund. Its sudden plunge into trading free-fall, while its operators were on vacation and the trading program was on automatic, threatened the stability of the entire global economy. If not for the panicked intervention of "various governments and agencies" – a phrase that has for us the same menacing vagueness that the words "certain matters of import to discuss" might have for a character in a Kafka novel – that fund's unforeseen failure would have pitched us all into chaos. That is the reality of the global market today. If you want to call it reality.

———

The first concrete implication of universalism today, therefore, is our universal subjection to these economic forces that appear to function beyond our conscious control. I say "appear" because the belief that they are literally beyond control is one of the most disabling ideas we can surrender to. But if you believe the newspapers, it's far from clear that even those who directly benefit from those forces have a much better idea of how they function than you or I do. The world of late capitalism is more dependent on its material technological base than the earlier stages were, because computer technology is so indispensable to most of what passes for wealth creation in this economy, both as source and as measure, and because that technology so often functions in an opaque, black-box manner.

Sophisticated communications and media technologies also have a tendency to deliver what the critic Fredric Jameson calls a "technological bonus," such that the act of consumption includes not only the first-order product — the film, the shoes, the song, the computer — but also the second-order product of the technology that produced it, in itself. When consumers devour a Hollywood blockbuster, for example, how much of its success comes from their greedy consumption of the money on the screen in the form of special effects? Moreover, there is a peculiar — and highly pleasurable — reduction of this second-order bonus, when, as J.G. Ballard noted of dystopian science-fiction films like *Blade Runner* or *The Terminator*, we observe technology advanced enough to depict the violent decline of advanced technology.

I don't mean to be facetious here, but perhaps the most appropriate tag we could use for the current situation is the name that Homer Simpson, in an episode of the Fox Network's long-running animated television series, gave the Internet provider company he decided to set up in competition with Microsoft's Bill Gates – without benefit of a computer, knowledge of computers, capital, or even a second phone line. But he did have a great name, the sort of name that sends the right message. Homer called his company Compu-Global-Hyper-Mega-Net. And that's as good a description as any of where we now live. (The company, by the way, doesn't hold out against Gates for long: the Microsoft honcho and some thuggish nerds quickly descend on Homer's house to break all his pencils, smash up his desk, and tear out the single phone.)

This situation has numerous political and cultural consequences that we must note. The first is that the de facto universalism of the transnational market has more devastating effects on the idea of the individual's particularity than any liberal attempt to articulate formal rights ever could. It is a function of late capitalism not only that technology and capital go global, but that culture – or anyway a simulacrum of it – goes global too. We now have, all protests and cries of incredulity aside, a genuine global culture. In fact, taking a page from the book of Homer, we could give it a name: Mono-Global-Culture-Corp.

It is not perhaps the culture you or I would consider worth attending to, though I do not presume to speak for anyone on this account. I have myself listened to the music of the Spice Girls without suffering debilitating effects, and watched their surprisingly witty movie, *Spice World*, with keen enjoyment. I have purchased Nike running shoes because, among other things, I wanted to wear the swoosh that Michael Jordan wore. I have never watched *Baywatch* with much pleasure, I'm afraid, mainly because of a scarring childhood experience with the earlier David Hasselhof vehicle *Knight Rider*, but I accept it has its uses as a morality play about the temptations of cosmetic surgery and skimpy bathing suits. I don't drink Coke or Pepsi except at the movies – but then, why not there? Where else does flavoured, sugared, carbonated water cost more than four dollars a cup?

Mono-Global-Culture-Corp is always ripe for parody, but I think it is important not to indulge that tendency, at least for a moment, so that we can note something more significant than the risibility of the product: the net effects of Mono-Global-Culture-Corp on the project of securing individual identity. We hear so much from post-modernist intellectuals about the death of the individual under conditions of global capitalism that it often doesn't sink in that there is a reality to the claim, precisely because of the unparalleled success of a pathological version of that modern aspiration, the universalization of regard for individuals. The net effect is a self-contradiction, but that fact is but rarely noted in the rush to extend the reach of market, technology, and culture to every corner of the world.

It is not crazy to call this three-pronged initiative a global virus, for, like a virus, it free-rides on the otherwise healthy functions of its host, namely, the desires for personal comfort and security that animate individuals, and gradually rewrites those functions to such an extent that the original host is, in a sense, no longer present. In effect, Mono-Global-Culture-Corp, with its enabling technological and market conditions, colonizes individuals around the world one by one until they are assimilated into the smoothly functioning logic of production. And anyone who believes desires cannot be colonized in this way has not been paying attention to their own shopping patterns and connoisseurship of advertising techniques, that third-order consumerism in which we consume our own sophistication along with the ads and the products that feed it.

What becomes of political power under these circumstances? It probably goes without saying that the political influence of individuals, those elements of the will of the people that made for legitimacy according to the Declaration, is attenuated, if not eliminated, in extreme conditions of this kind. Power reduces in many cases to little more than spending power, the vaunted voting-with-our-feet that free marketeers seem to think so much of. But the populism of the market's availability, its wide dissemination of what was formerly thought to be the preserve of an elite few, is often nothing but a false form of democratization. When the contours and offerings of the market are beyond question, when choice is just a game of eenie-meenie between infinitesimally different brands, power of that truncated consumerist sort is little more than a bad joke. The individual disappears even further, reduced to an unconnected series of expressed preferences in market surveys and political opinion polls, whose once-essential differences are no longer discernible even to those who administer them.

Worse than this, though, is the attenuation of legitimate national power and the resulting distortion of its exercise. We see every day more and more obvious manifestations of the bland, bureaucratized, responsibility-deflecting management style of political leaders who have become all too aware of their insignificance on the larger world stage. Bureaucracy, not patriotism, is the last refuge of the scoundrel – especially if the scoundrel cannot avoid constant reminders of his own ultimate powerlessness. Hannah Arendt's vivid depiction of the banality of evil in her 1964 *New Yorker* report, "Eichmann in Jerusalem," gave us an important new way to understand the nature of power, especially when mobilized around technological and economic imperatives of rationalization. In the hands of the functionary, the dutiful servant of larger forces, evil can itself be rationalized as a perverse instance of Kant's categorical imperative: follow the will of the leader without question. Such was Adolf Eichmann's notorious defence of his own role in facilitating the extermination of Polish Jews.

Evil becomes banal, in other words, when it becomes mechanical, routinized, heedless, and thick. Eichmann is no monster out of the Satanic mould; on the contrary, he is a featureless family man with few distinguishing interests and no obsessions. He is simply doing a job. Of course, his ordinariness is precisely what makes him noteworthy, the blunt instrument of a great evil. I won't belabour the point, for this is a familiar story. The connection to the bureaucratized and implacable power of our world is perhaps less familiar.

Drawing comparisons to the Holocaust is always a risky business, and I don't mean to suggest that every attempt to shrug off an instance of police brutality or a policy of complicity with a visiting dictator is equivalent to condoning genocide. But I do mean to suggest that there is a connection, on the continuum of banality, between the exemplar, Eichmann, and many of our more proximate political functionaries, whose indifference to questions of legitimacy and accountability is their most obvious defining feature. Thus does the banality of evil become, under less extreme and even more routine political conditions, the evil of banality — which may nevertheless erupt at any moment into something worse. Indifference can swiftly breed callousness, arrogance, and eventually contempt.

That is one aspect of my inversion of Arendt's famous phrase here. There is of course another. The evil of banality is cultural as well as political, and indeed the two forms are related. What is evil about mass culture is not simply its immense reach and apparently unopposable force, but its relentless downward drag on the rich possibilities of media and performance. It becomes an Augean stable of the mind, in which there is so much volume that though we may fool ourselves momentarily with ever-faster web browsers and more end-of-year best-of lists, no one is sufficiently Herculean to shovel the shit swiftly enough. At the same time, the creation of such lowest-common-denominator product is naturalized by producers and consumers alike by asserting, without argument, that this is simply "what people want."

Depending on where you situate yourself, that claim is either outright cynicism, on the order of there being a sucker born every minute, or a well-heeled elitism that presents itself as democratic geniality: "I don't like television, fast food, and branded clothes, certainly, but you can't argue with the people, and what they want is television, fast food, and branded clothes." This position abdicates responsibility for critical judgment at the same time that it abandons these "people," whoever they are, to a cultural hell allegedly of their own making.

Don't mistake my meaning. I am not taking the elitist, Adorno-esque high road on mass culture, holding myself aloof from commodities and entertainments while disdaining those who don't do the same. The pleasures of popular culture are real; they are certainly inescapable. What is needed is not condemnation of those pleasures, but greater appreciation of them — and their implications. We all act to obscure our complicity in the banalization of the cultural world, and in the social and economic arrangements reinforced by that world. We might even note a new form of reification here: not the translation of social forces into things, as leftist critics used to speak of reification, but rather (to use Jameson's phrase) the "effacement of the traces of production" itself.

What does that mean? Well, consider the unremarkable facts that you can get Nike shoes made in Indonesia in your local Foot Locker store, that the person who made them was paid about sixteen cents an hour to do it, and that you pay your hundred dollars and feel pretty much okay about doing it. Indeed, these facts are so unremarkable that they don't sound like news. What is deeply worrying here is not just the unconscious (or even, sometimes, conscious) acceptance of a brutalizing economic determinism, but also the concomitant modification of attitude — almost always unnoticed when the transaction is successful — by which we lose any connection whatsoever between the objects purchased and the facts of their production. The shoes are just too cool or, more likely, the brand identity just too sharp for me to spend much time obsessing over how these fetish objects made their way to me.

Globalization of the labour market doesn't just allow this disconnection, it demands it. We must *remember always to forget* the conditions of the creation of consumer and cultural goods, because otherwise we might become disgusted with our own needs and desires, and what is necessary to satisfy them. It is in the interest of global markets to keep us from thinking too deeply or too long about the way things are made lest, in alarmed self-disapproval, we begin to withdraw our consumer dollars. The forces of transnational capital want us to remain blithe, happy, and freely spending; all the elaborate and fine-tuned machinery of influence and desire-creation they marshal – advertising, marketing, focus groups, and demographic targeting – is in the service of precisely this. And no nation on earth, certainly no individual, is powerful enough to regulate that kind of influence.

Cultural products no longer come to us signed, as when they were the result of personal artisanship and commitment; they only come branded, with the heavily underscored logos and trademarks of the corporate project. And in that multiple branding, the relentless mechanical reproduction of identical objects whose very goal is to be the same in Tokyo as in Topeka, in Cairo as in Calgary, the objects begin to lose their reality as things created by humans. Style and contour, once identified with artistic genius and individual talent, remain, but they are henceforth emptied of all meaning, retaining only a hollowed-out status of the commercial sheen, the glossy patina that catches the eye – and coaxes the dollar.

More than this, reality itself begins to lose its reality. It disappears, or threatens to at every wavering moment, in a pervasive system of mass reproducibility where there are multiple tokens but no types, many simulacra but no true representations – for there is nothing real left to represent. Cultural products are therefore consumed precisely in a manner that studiously ignores the (usually exploitative) conditions of their mass production and that, further, ignores the implications of that consumption for our sense of ourselves. We are driven towards a form of transcendence – of our limitations, of our cares, of our selves. But what we find when we get there is that the transcendent state we have so avidly sought is ultimately an empty one: a narrative without a subject, a symbol without a referent, a copy without an original.

Banal means trite, as in aesthetically or morally inferior; but it also means, more precisely, commonplace, taken for granted. The banality of evil lies in the commonplace person, the unremarkable functionary, ordering genocide. The evil of banality lies not only in the aesthetic weakness of cultural products today, though there is certainly that; it lies also; and more damagingly, in the self-effacing commonness of it all – a commonness that expunges all traces of a system of production no longer really attuned to the deeper needs and desires of its inhabitants, expunges those needs and desires themselves as meaningful standards of assessment.

The world of mass culture looks as if it is entirely driven by our desires, that nothing else matters to it. And of course there is much to beguile and please us there, even things to cherish and save. But the appearance of responsiveness to human longing is too often a smokescreen for a constantly regenerated disappointment, a planned obsolescence of our cravings. When was the last time you found something there that fulfilled this useful definition of happiness: a satisfaction that goes on being satisfactory?

Hope's Imagination

It would be easy, far too easy, for me to fall into a jeremiad on this topic and leave it at that. I won't indulge that impulse here because the stakes for the future of citizenship are too high. Denunciations of mass culture are ten-a-penny in our world. You could even call them a routine product of mass culture itself, a sort of essential by-product of the grinding machine of television and Hollywood and pop music. First come the cheesy shows and movies and CDs, then the equally indistinguishable laments about them. The trouble is, none of those laments seem to make any lasting political difference whatsoever. They fall by the wayside like so many discarded pop cans. (I know, because I have offered them myself on occasion.) What we really need to examine is not the fact that mass culture is banal — everyone knows that — but what our constant engagement with this banality is doing to us politically.

What I have argued so far is this: in part because of tensions within the twinned discourses of individualism and universalism, and in part because of the success of technological capitalism, individualism has become prey to its own aspirations. Evil has become banal, and banality has become evil. The reasons for this lie tangled in the origin of those aspirations themselves, but they have been aided and abetted by less abstract forces, the forces of technology and money. If you will grant that this picture of our current situation has at least some accuracy, we must now ask what can be done about it.

I have three claims to offer on that score — claims that, taken alone, may seem insubstantial or ambiguous but taken together add up to something powerful. The first is the fact that my earlier scenario of a smooth assimilation of all humans under the rubrics of Mono-Global-Culture-Corp and Compu-Global-Hyper-Mega-Net must be nuanced and limited by an awareness of the rising tide of defiantly hybrid identities and mutating cultures. The world is not in fact surrendering to the global reach of capital with an unbroken sameness, a featureless capitulation to mass culture and market values. Instead, we observe more and more the emergence of wholly new forms of cultural and political identity that incorporate some elements of the dominant story even while preserving many of the distinctive features of the local context: a strange cultural diversity within the larger universalism of human rights. Islamic women take up the language of human rights even while accepting life conditions many Western feminists would consider unacceptable. Japanese workers demand better wages and living conditions without necessarily wanting to challenge, in the style of British or French organized labour, the loyalties and hierarchies of their corporate culture.

Which is another way of saying that these hybrid practices do not necessarily arise in a form that we in the industrialized West would consider emancipatory. They may exist alongside practices that are deeply troubling to cosmopolitan liberals, especially in relation to the discourse on rights: blood feuds, religious fundamentalism, female genital mutilation, bride-burning, and so on. These instances of oppression, which continue to persist in some countries despite both internal resistance and rhetoric of compliance with international human rights, indicate that the exportation of Western values is a more complicated matter than optimistic rationalists would like to believe. At the same time, they also indicate that pathological versions of exported universalism are as unstable as valid ones when grafted onto distinctive local ways of life. Western democracy does not travel abroad without alteration; neither does the so-called free market. (A cautionary note: we in the West should not be smug and ignore our own mixing of the barbaric and the liberal. Consider, for instance, the persistence of the death penalty in otherwise fairly humane American criminal codes.)

The fact of hybrid identities therefore sends a mixed message and offers a challenging point of departure for further debate. Such complicated practices, partly liberal and partly not, chasten the triumphalism of happy-go-lucky global capitalists at the welcome cost of putting the very idea of the universal into question. In a sense, we seem to have returned to the impasse between individual and universal with which I began, only on a larger scale. But the fact of hybrid identities can have another effect, which is to make us rethink the notion of universalism in what might prove to be a productive manner – not despite these troubling examples, still less in easy support of them, but precisely because they are troubling to us in the West. We cannot be sanguine about what remains to be done, neither can we ignore the insistent pull of local context and long-standing traditions when the language of human rights is made politically effective in other parts of the world than our own.

The second claim I want to highlight here, then, is the possibility of rewriting the discourse of universalism to take account of the far-from-smooth extension of that idea throughout the world. Rather than seeking the goal of a pure universalism of rationality, as Kant did, and finding that the only actual universalism is one of money, we might shift the focus to another target. We might seek instead what I am going to call a *universalism of imagination*. Such a shift may have the ultimate effect of reinvigorating documents like the Declaration, and along the way giving us means to rethink our own political commitments as politics becomes, necessarily, more complex and more global.

This suggestion may strike some as misdirected, if only because the notion that we might universalize imagination, that fragile and variable faculty, is so unfamiliar to us. But what I mean is not as odd as it might sound — and is by no means intended as the last word on the subject, only the first. Imagination can be defined as the capacity to see beyond the materials given, in a sense to see what cannot be seen. That means somehow going beyond, and being willing to challenge, one's own personal experience, which is inevitably limited. Only close attention to my experience and its limits, in other words, can teach me the value of what I do not yet know, of what I can only imagine. There is no other way, finally, to make a meaningful connection with someone who is not already like me. The connection is like the third language that is created when we translate from one tongue into another. This third language is neither English nor French, for example, but instead a bridging dialect that proceeds from the good will of two, otherwise separated, native speakers.

Imagination is the faculty of the human mind that responds to story and image, that is most excited by art and has an acknowledged cultural primacy since it is central to aesthetic experience. It has, too, its obvious cultural enemy, namely, the evils of banality I tried to articulate above. But imagination also has a political role, because it is imagination, not pure practical reason, as Kant thought, that responds to the deep pull of justice. The true force of universalism lies not in the act of picking out some dutiful responsibility to an abstract moral law, or in relying on reason to adjudicate the differences that separate us, but in the shared capacity of humans to be pained by the pain of others. The human community is not so much a community of reason as it is, at a basic level, a community of feeling. Reason simply is not equal to the job of politics across differences, because without imagination I do not care about your claims of justice in the first place. Beyond certain minimal demands of logic, such as consistency and non-contradiction, it is very likely true that I care about a claim you make or a reason you offer only if I have some prior commitment to care about you – only if I already grant you status as someone worth listening to. And only an imaginative connection makes that possible.

The value of imagination in politics is something we can validate not by means of a metaphysical theory that trades in essences, but rather by means of describing what the philosopher Richard Rorty has called "a discursive fact" about us. Namely, that we can and do respond to the suffering of others and see ourselves in them. We can all see, without needing any detailed philosophical or anthropological theory, that cruelty is wrong – that, indeed, it might be, as Montaigne says in his *Essays*, the worst thing one human being can do to another. That is why torture is so abhorrent to us, and why declarations of human rights hold their place in our imaginations. But our abhorrence of obvious cruelty begins with much lower-level sorts of insight: that bullying is unacceptable, that insult can have no justification, that humiliation is deeply threatening to anyone's sense of self.

There is a troubling irony here, of course. Imagination, like reason, is no proof against cruelty – sometimes, perversely, it is its ally. This is related to the larger paradox of technology from which so many of our troubles flow: rational progress equals moral regress; ingenuity equals cruelty. In contrast to Eichmann, who represents the moral evil of absence of imagination, Rorty vividly characterizes O'Brien, the quietly menacing torturer in George Orwell's *1984*, as an illustration of what happens to a subtle intellectual when he has nothing good left to believe in. Here is the presence of a thoroughly perverted imagination. O'Brien is reason's servant, to be sure, and reason appears to be his most effective tool – he argues with Winston, doesn't simply inflict pain on him. But O'Brien's imagination is more important even than his ratiocinative abilities. In the end he is not interested in arguing with Winston, and waves away his feeble position-taking and resistance-movement ideology, because he has heard it all before.

What remains then is a brutal, penetrating insight. It is O'Brien's capacity to imagine Winston's terror about rats, to know that this is the thing that will unman his prisoner completely, that makes him such an effective torturer. The crude tools of physical pain are too blunt for O'Brien: not for him the tooth drill of *Marathon Man* or the testicular shocks of the Khmer Rouge. Also too blunt, ultimately, are the instruments of argument and questioning: they do not reach far enough into the soul. The deep cruelty of Room 101 is that it is ruled by fearsome imagination – an imagination so fearsome, in fact, that its effects are psychological disintegration for its own sake, for the pure exercise of power, not for anything as trite as information or confession. When Winston, in his anguish, says, "Do it to Julia," we know that his destruction as a human being is complete, despite the persistence of his physical body – indeed, wickedly, because of it. For he must then endure the memory of that betrayal and the irremediable pain of seeing her again. His final punishment is being made to live with the knowledge that he wished the worst humiliation and pain he could imagine inflicted on the woman he loved. And O'Brien's evil mastery of imagination is made complete when we realize that Julia, in her pain, did the same to Winston.

Imagination is not cruelty-proof, in short – no human capacity is. We must face the possibility that any of us might, under certain circumstances, be a Winston or an Eichmann, or even an O'Brien. But despite all this, we must also accept that without imagination we cannot forge even the provisional commitments that will bind us one to another in a world of difference. If I cannot in some sense see your pain and humiliation as real, then I cannot reliably regard you as worthy of my concern. And if I cannot do that there is very little reason for us to expect that I will respond meaningfully to a claim you wish to make, especially one that might challenge my own comfort or security. This is not to say that *I feel your pain*. Nobody feels anybody else's pain, only their own. But pain has many sources, and the imaginative link of one person to another makes a politically relevant kind of pain – the pain of compassion – possible for us.

Possible, but of course never guaranteed. There is no transcendental account of human imagination that would lock down these claims, no grand theory that would make them foundational in a strong sense. We can rely on our imaginations only provisionally, only contingently. We often fail in imagination: fail to see the effects of an action, fail to see what might be possible that is not yet real, fail to accept the forever incomplete task of creating a perfect human society. But as often – or so, anyway, it seems to me – we succeed. We succeed in responding to the pain of another, succeed in acting for something good even though we know it will not change the world from top to bottom, succeed in believing in the forever valid hope of creating a just human society. Thus is imagination sometimes transformed, whether gradually or in rare explosive moments, from fellow feeling into direct confrontations with power, into the creation of cultural resistance, into more and better-defined arguments about how the world might be.

The third claim I want to mention is that imagination has many sources, some of them unlikely. Popular art and popular culture are not *necessarily* banal. There is much in their production that drives the bulk of words, pictures, and narratives towards banality today, it's true. There is much to be annoyed or depressed by. But there are nevertheless moments, not too few either, when human voices seem to speak through the cumbersome and dangerous machinery of that mass production: when a connection is made between the human being who, somewhere, wrote the pop song or penned the line of dialogue that, right now, takes me or you somewhere we hadn't gone before. At that moment, imagination has snaked through the self-concealing forces of market and money, traced a path through the mechanisms of blandness, and sounded a note of something better. And no amount of mass commodification can, finally, take that away from us.

The link between this kind of experience and political action is not unbroken or obvious. I would be unwise to claim that popular culture, or culture more generally, necessarily leads to political awareness, still less to political action. Most cultural experience does nothing of the kind, and cultural acts directed consciously towards prompting a political response are something else, namely, propaganda. Moreover, cultural signs are often merely symptomatic of larger, material faultlines that cannot be addressed adequately if we remain at the level of cultural analysis. And of course it is possible for our imaginative responsiveness itself to be exploited, the way radio jingles or compelling high-speed miniature narratives of TV ads lodge in our brains, just as much as a good Radiohead riff or a scene from a Hal Hartley film. Or, for that matter, a Beethoven overture or a line from Shakespeare.

And yet the act of consumption, seemingly unavoidable, can itself become unexpectedly liberating, as we rearrange and appropriate the offered materials for our own purposes. We can make of our everyday experience something much more conscious and expressive of our deeper needs than we imagine. We can use routine cultural transactions in a way, perhaps contrary to their makers' intentions, that drives us deeper within ourselves and more searchingly into the world. These tasks are no easier now than they have ever been; they are also no less important. The point, as ever, is that seeing beyond ourselves is the only way to begin realizing the complicated project of emancipation. It is no more than the beginning of that task, not an end to it. Imaginative connections remind us, as nothing else can, that we are, as citizens embedded in cultures, neither entirely free nor entirely imprisoned.

Rather, we are social and cultural creatures through and through. Which is to say, as I argued earlier, that we are both defined by, and defining of, the times in which we live. Plato's isomorphism of inside and outside, of person and culture, continues in our own political situation, even if it no longer arises in the smooth manner whereby Socrates could claim to hear the very voice of the laws themselves in his head and heart. We are not likely to make such a claim, and would perhaps regard anyone who made it as a dangerous ideologue or simply a candidate for institutionalization. We are more mindful, probably, of the cultural structures that seem to stand over against us, alien presences that determine what is on our screens, in our newspapers, creeping into our daily lives. We feel far less confidence, certainly, that the world will respond to what is inside our hearts.

But that is not the point that endures when we begin to think seriously about our commitments and possibilities as citizen-critics. The point that endures, the point Socrates bequeaths to us in his complicated, back-handed way, is that we can never wholly transcend our social contexts, can never fully pass beyond the limits and strictures and distortions of the cultural medium in which we exist. Nor should we try. We are part of the world we find, and we must cast our lot with it. To do anything else is to court self-contradiction, or madness, or merely the arrogance of the culturally superior. We cannot jump over our own shadows. Yet we are never completely dominated by those contexts, never simply cultural robots acting out the plans of distant masters. We are always in the position of becoming more active cultural critics, more committed citizens of a complex global world.

That is a constant challenge, a challenge to accept immersion in banality as inescapable but not necessarily permanent. Action can only start where people live their lives, in the midst of things and relationships and distractions and mindless entertainments – and great art and true love and noble friendship, for they too are part of everyday life. If, instead of all this, and ignoring the ongoing productive duality of self and world, we were to believe in the need for some notional form of cultural excellence – if we were to think that there can be no valid action until we entirely transcend our social and cultural limits, that everything else is falling short, or selling out, or buying in – then we would condemn ourselves, paradoxically, to a never-never land of political nullity.

Pursuing purity, we would capture futility instead. Handcuffed by an aspiration that is no regulative ideal but just a crippling self-loathing, a denigration of our possibilities in which no action is ever good enough because we are not perfect, because we still go to the movies or shop for clothes or eat out now and then, we would end up leaving everything as it is. And, however tempting it might occasionally be, this is certainly not the time to do that.

Chapter 3

VIRTUES AND VICES

I do not go about telling people what they
ought to be doing in this world. There are enough others
to do that — but I say what I do myself.
— Montaigne, *Essays*

A Friendship

They met at a party. It was, he said later, "some inexplicable power of destiny" that brought them together. The year was 1558, and Michel Eyquem, heir to the estates at Montaigne, was twenty-five, a young man of learning, position, and property. He had been educated as a gentleman, which is to say mostly in Latin, with only a smattering of Greek. He had no excessive regard for precision in scholarship.

He liked hunting on the family's wide Dordogne estates as much as he did reading his beloved Catullus, Horace, Seneca, Plutarch, or — more fashionably — Ariosto. He had travelled, though not yet extensively: to the Collège de Guienne, to the universities at Bordeaux and Toulouse, to his first legal post in Périgueux. He had been at the last town for three years and then, just a year ago now, had come back to Bordeaux, where his father, Pierre Eyquem, Seigneur de Montaigne, was mayor. His mother, Antoinette de Louppes, was of an Iberian Jewish family, but of course this dutiful son observed the religion of his father, his station, and his country. He was a good, if not fervent, Catholic.

The feast was a large one in the city of Bordeaux, and their meeting was by chance. Yet they knew of each other, for it was that kind of town. The young Montaigne heir had seen Étienne de la Boétie's little political pamphlet *The Voluntary Servitude*. It was in fact a piece of precocious juvenilia, written by the older man when he was still a teenager, but its energetic argument "in praise of liberty and against tyrants" impressed Montaigne, who, romantic and not yet sufficiently challenged by the world, was young and looking for love.

La Boétie was now a judge in Bordeaux and a devotee of ancient Greek culture. His work "is as fine and perfect as it could be," Montaigne later wrote. "Yet it is far short of the best that he could do; and if in his maturer years, when I knew him, he had conceived a plan, like this of mine, of committing his thoughts to writing, we should now see many rare things which would make our age almost as famous as antiquity. For, in natural gifts particularly, I know of no one who could compare with him." La Boétie knew the younger man too, by reputation. He was, after all, the mayor's talented and ambitious son.

They met, they ate, they talked together long into the night. There was much for them to discuss, since they were both deeply interested in politics and art. They talked of war and crime, of science and discovery. The times were both controversial and violent. Life was rich in incident, varied in texture. It was not uncommon to be killed for what you did, or didn't, believe. A new continent, full of wonders, had lately been discovered, rocking the certainty and superiority of traditional cultures. Empirical investigation of all kinds was flourishing, in optics and mechanics and chemistry, and reason was everywhere challenging the centuries-old stranglehold of faith. Faith, for its part, was fighting back with dogmatism, repression, intolerance and, here and there, some superior philosophizing.

But faith was also violently divided against itself, and the nearby countryside was like a gangland war zone, often littered with the bodies of those who could see no way to reconcile their disagreements about God's plan and their place in it. Homes and possessions were not safe, law was uncertain, intrigues and plots were rife. As so often in the cities of our own day, there were many places you just didn't want to be found after dark. Anyone with sense and means went about armed. They were both lawyers. They were also, of course, trained in the use of weapons. Death and disagreement were not strangers to them. But as scholars, they knew the lessons of antiquity. Though reason was never supreme in human affairs, it sometimes found a way through the thickets of emotion and hatred; and, for the rest of this too-short life, it must be borne with as much fortitude and good humour as one could muster. Ambition is ever tempered by experience. Otherwise, fortune makes fools of us all.

As sometimes happens, there sprang up between them an instant understanding. La Boétie surely saw in the younger man something of himself: a hopefulness, a charm, a winning naiveté. Montaigne had the unusual experience of finding the author of an admired work as admirable in himself as on the page. "We found ourselves so captivated, so familiar, so bound to one another," he wrote of the encounter, "that from that time nothing was closer to either than each was to the other. . . . Having so short a time to live, and having begun so late, for we were both grown men and he some years the elder, we had no time to lose, and none in which to conform to the regular pattern of those mild friendships that require so many precautions in the form of long preliminary discourse."

How short a time to live neither could have known then. La Boétie was to die just four years later, when Montaigne was not yet thirty. The intensity of their communion even in the absence of this knowledge surprised them both, was even a little embarrassing. La Boétie, for his part, diffused some of his passionate feelings by writing a Latin satire on the subject of instant friendship – a sort of literary displacement ritual, performed as much to mitigate or even deprecate his strong emotions as to justify them. But more privately, he composed sonnets in praise of his young friend and delivered them with great love. Theirs was a kind of all-consuming male friendship, full of intellect and emotion, that has, for one reason and another, disappeared almost completely from our cultural experience. Ardent and devoted, it was loving but not physical.

Certainly it was defining for Montaigne. He contrasts it not only with other kinds of friendship, which depend on mere pleasure or utility, but with such closer associations as brotherhood and marriage. (In common with many people both then and today, he did not believe men and women could really be friends.) None of these other bonds compares with his friendship, he tells us; and "even the treatises which antiquity has left us on this subject seem flat to me in comparison with my own feeling. For, in this particular, the reality surpasses even the precepts of philosophy." The two men spoke unabashedly of their passion for one another, a passion that was exclusive, constant, and complete – though not, as Montaigne makes a point of telling us several times, erotic.

He does not shy away from that subject, however, mentioning how more visceral and lustful feelings sometimes bubbled up from la Boétie's poems. He wonders whether what the two of them enjoyed was anything like what the ancient Greeks celebrated as a higher passion between men. But that form of erotic love, he reminds us, was most often between a young boy and an older man, not two adults. (We may be inclined to think he is overestimating his maturity at age twenty-five, but that was nearly middle age in his day.) In the ancient Greek ideal, the boy is ambitious, or anyway eager for tutelage and advancement; and typically the older man is drawn primarily to the boy's physical beauty, not his deeper qualities of character – even assuming there are any. In any case, in its best form this love was, as Plato too had argued in the *Phaedrus*, not sexual but philosophical. "[A]ll that can be said in favour of the Academy's conception," Montaigne concludes, "is that it is a love which terminates in friendship, a definition which does not disagree with that of the Stoics, 'that love is an attempt to gain the friendship of someone whose beauty has attracted us.'"

That definition is from Cicero's *Tusculan Disputations*. It is one of the many learned quotations that are scattered through Montaigne's *Essays*. Or rather, one of the many quotations, misquotations, and transliterations, for Montaigne, relying on his idiosyncratic reading habits and often shaky memory, is nobody's idea of a careful scholar. His famous book is an album of reflections and musings, elliptical in argument, on everything from cannibals to vehicles, from education to cruelty. It is the first book of its kind, one composed entirely of personal trials – *essais* – that, in pursuit of a given topic, actually serve to expose the author in all his wisdom and frailty. Montaigne is conventionally considered the inventor of the personal essay, and for that alone would be justly celebrated, but he is also one of its most accomplished practitioners. His book, first published in 1580 and never out of print since, save for a period in which it was indexed by Roman Catholic authorities, is a literary landmark. Montaigne himself, with no pretensions to the title, is also a contender for the honour of first modern philosopher – a designation usually reserved for a later and vastly more systematic thinker, Descartes.

The reason for Montaigne's claim to the honour is simple. Owing to a felicitous combination of character and circumstance, Montaigne is recognizably an inhabitant of a world like ours. In his intimate, beckoning prose we hear a voice not so different from one of our own: ironic but sincere, learned but not pedantic, worldly yet occasionally naive, above all fully alive and fascinated by himself. His struggles to understand are not scholastic, and his world view is not forbiddingly abstruse, which means he is sometimes a little too casual. As well as wanting to tell us some things about the world, he wants us to get to know him, sometimes at great length. In a manner we can immediately understand as familiar and intimate, he chooses to examine a single person, himself, as a means to finding larger truths about manners, mores, social conventions, knowledge, ignorance, prejudice, wisdom, and a score of other topics.

But always we start with him. We learn in his pages that he does not like fruit, melon excepted, but never met a sauce he didn't fancy. He enjoys scratching his ears, prefers to sleep alone, and has kidney stones that trouble him enormously. He doesn't like naps, between-meal snacks, or breakfast. He rarely goes without gloves and a hat, cannot suffer having his hair cut after dinner, and likes to eat with benefit of a large napkin, since he does not favour that new-fangled invention, the fork. He is moderate, yet tolerant of his appetites: to attack a cough by abstaining from oysters is, he says, to indulge "two evils instead of one." He was, he hints, lusty and successful in youth, less so as time took its toll; though he still prefers, at his advanced age, making love just before bed.

The *Essays* are, in this way, a linked series of autobiographical sketches – linked, that is, not by the subjects they pursue (truth and error, the power of the imagination, the art of conversation, clothing), but by the person of the author who finds the subjects interesting. Montaigne is forever ruled by interest: his is a wandering curiosity, a peripatetic intelligence, always following its nose. Indeed, his nose figures prominently. There is, naturally enough for a rural landowner in an age before refrigeration or regular bathing, an essay on smells, in which we learn that his thick moustache, once touched by glove or handkerchief, holds odours for some time. "It betrays the place where I have been," he tells us. "The close, luscious, greedy, long-drawn kisses of youth would adhere to it in the old days, and would remain for several hours afterwards."

Taking seriously his own lessons on restraint and the dangers of certainty, Montaigne at first offers only annotations and commentary, stringing together quotations from the classical sources with asides and anecdotes. Soon, however, gaining in confidence, he begins to venture more of his own thoughts. He is on the verge of inventing the new literary form. Then, in the early 1570s, the religious civil wars once more intrude on his solitude, and Montaigne must ride out to deal with gangs of robbers and take up arms against the rebels campaigning across his lands. The experience chastens but does not enliven him; his mind, already sensitive, finds the intolerance and persecution of his historical circumstances abhorrent.

In 1576 he has cast his famous personal medal, with the motto *Que sais-je?* (What do I know?) on one side, and an admonition to practise restraint on the other. Montaigne now sees what his unusual life has conspired to teach him, namely, that the power of human reason is not equal to its own devices and desires. We cannot know that which we desire to know. We cannot, moreover, make sense of all that we desire. He becomes stoical and skeptical – if not, as some have argued, a skeptic in the fully modern sense of doubting the very possibility of truth. Like the Stoic philosophers he most admired, his watchwords are self-knowledge and self-discipline.

The first edition of the *Essays* was not the last, and as befits a project that grew ever more autobiographical, it continued unfinished to the time of its author's death. Montaigne travelled extensively from 1580 onward, seeking cures for his kidney stones. As a result, he visited Baden, Augsburg, Munich, Venice, Florence, and Rome – where he had an audience with the Pope and, less happily, had all his books confiscated. In 1582 he was elected mayor of Bordeaux *in absentia* – the news came to him in Lucca, where he was taking the waters – and had to return home to perform his political duty. A second, much expanded edition of the *Essays* was published at this time, in 1583. Montaigne served a second term as mayor, though he was often absent from Bordeaux in Paris or at the Montaigne estates. Soon after the second term ended, he was forced to abandon the estates because of the threat of plague. Yet he spent enough time in his study to bring out another expanded edition of the *Essays* in 1586, and a fourth in 1588. These included the most personal material yet, chiefly about his poor health and recent travels.

When he died, on September 13, 1592, at the age of fifty-nine, Montaigne was at work on yet another round of revisions. The final edition of the *Essays*, prepared by his adopted daughter Mlle de Gournay, was published in 1595 – a book that ended, we may fairly say, only because the author succumbed to the human frailties he so warmly celebrated.

Together, the essays paint a detailed, affectionate, and illuminating portrait of a complex, imaginative, warm-hearted man. They also, after their fashion, defend a profound philosophy of liberal citizenship.

———

It is clear that la Boétie's influence on Montaigne was in all things paramount. The younger man did not write a word that was not within the shadow of his older friend, for Montaigne only began composing the *Essays* in 1571, when he was thirty-eight. By that time he had been at court and seen more of the world and of life, but he had not quite found his mature voice and was still very much shaken by the tragic end to his time with la Boétie.

In 1561, a decade before, Montaigne had been sent to the King on a mission and, in 1562, followed the monarch to Rouen, lately recovered from the Huguenot rebels. He saw there the captured Brazilian natives he was later to describe in his celebrated essay on cannibals – an essay in which he argued, centuries before Rousseau's defence of the noble savage, that the true barbarians were his warring fellow countrymen, not the primitives from the New World.

Soon after he returned to Bordeaux in 1563 he was informed of la Boétie's premature death from a sudden illness. The news plunged him into profound grief. The rest of his life, he wrote later,

compared with the four years of la Boétie's "sweet and companion-
able society," is "but smoke, nothing but dark and tedious night."
Since his death, Montaigne says, "I have dragged out but a languish-
ing existence, and even such pleasures as come to me, far from con-
soling me, redouble my grief for his loss." Without doubting the
extent of Montaigne's sadness, it must be said that he didn't quite
languish, at least outwardly. He married Françoise de la Chassagne
in 1565, receiving her impressive dowry – if not, by his own arguments, her friendship. Three years later he inherited the estates of
Montaigne when his father died, becoming one of the richest and
most influential men of the Bordeaux region.

Montaigne was now a considerable figure of thirty-five years who
had money, land, and power. Yet his ambitions remained uncertain.
He had rejected a high-flying political career after his experiences
with the King, and was to turn down high posts later in life when
Henry of Navarre, working for his own tricky political causes,
attempted to advance the reluctant Montaigne. He practised law
without enthusiasm, and was the first to acknowledge that he had no
penchant for academic work. Yet his library was where he felt happi-
est, surrounded by the old friends of his classical education who,
even if his Latin sometimes deserted him, spoke to him in the voices
of ancient wisdom. It was here, in conversation with his dear
departed friends and heroes, that Montaigne decided his life's work
would be to write about his everyday life. It was not memoir he was
after since, really, he had done nothing to justify that: no grand
ambitions, no elaborate intrigues, no triumphant battles. Nor could
he pretend to himself or anyone else that he possessed the intellectual talent to engage in systematic philosophy. He did have a keen
eye, a taste for irony, and a syncretic, lively mind.

We can hear la Boétie's more proximate wisdom in Montaigne's
decision to begin writing about himself and his experiences – the
pull of friendship as conversation, a conversation now lost and only
imperfectly recovered in the alluring, intimate prose of the essay

form. Friendship is the key to Montaigne's political thought, and his friendship with la Boétie is key to his thoughts about friendship. We must start with the preface to the *Essays* to see exactly what Montaigne is up to. It is a miniature masterpiece. "This, reader, is an honest book," it says – a claim that can only have the effect of immediately arousing a healthy suspicion. What writer, after all, does well by insisting on his own truthfulness? From the start, with this bald insistence on honesty, we must (naturally) suspect dishonesty.

This book, Montaigne says, "warns you at the outset that my sole purpose in writing it has been a private and domestic one. I have had no thought of serving you or of my own fame; such a plan would be beyond my powers. I have intended it solely for the pleasure of my relatives and friends so that, when they have lost me – which they soon must – they may recover some features of my character and disposition, and thus keep the memory they have of me more completely and vividly alive." Not to serve us? We are a little offended. Not for fame? We do not really believe him. And yet the matter is still more complicated. His book, by its own admission, is not intended for us – we cannot already be his literal friends or relatives. So we should read on only if we are prepared to make friends with him right away, if we are willing to grant him friendship before being able to judge him. And if that sounds too demanding, we might remember that underneath everything else, we are relatives in terms of predicament if not direct bloodline.

This odd preface concludes: "So, reader, I am myself the substance of my book, and there is no reason why you should waste your leisure on so frivolous and unrewarding a subject. Farewell then, from Montaigne, this first day of March, 1580." As irony, this is mannered, even a bit clunky. But still, for some reason it works. Beneath Montaigne's studied pose of fighting off the reader's attention with a self-deprecating honesty, shooing us away before we even start reading, there is charm – and real honesty – of a deeper kind. The claimed modesty serves a purpose that is not as simple as mere dissembling. Of course Montaigne wants us to read on, wants us to be interested in him. Yet to say so is, as in any human exchange, especially between people meeting for the first time, to court precisely the danger that we will not. Waving us off so conspicuously, he succeeds in communicating both his desire for our love and his inability to speak of it directly. Naturally, seeing that, we grant it. Flirting with readers is a difficult art; Montaigne is a master.

These tactics and tones suggest a point beyond mere literary curlicues. Friendship requires a leap, not of faith but of *regard*. We must trust to listen to the other whom we do not yet know, must rely on a basic willingness to care about someone who thinks and lives differently from ourselves. Montaigne's instinctive philosophical skepticism made him wary of dogmatism and certainty, vividly aware that human interchanges are subtle and fraught with danger. But he is an expert conversationalist and, as such, knows the peculiar efforts and pleasures to be found in talking with another person. He is a loyal and devoted friend, and yet the times – we can never forget – are not friendly. Making friends is a lot harder, and a lot more important, than it sometimes seems.

For Montaigne, indeed, the lesson of any hard-won skepticism (or, more accurately, non-cognitivism – the inability to know the final truth) should never be anger or prejudice against others who think differently, but instead *toleration of diversity*. The reason is clear. Humans have the limitation that when it comes to knowledge, only the self can really be trusted. And yet the self is restricted in capacity. We must therefore be modest and open-minded, not judgmental and condemnatory: whereof we cannot know, we must not judge. His friendship with la Boétie taught him this valuable lesson about the relation between knowledge and kindness. It is true not because all human relationships could ever hope to be as elevated – Montaigne specifically denies this, singling out their friendship as unique ("Let no one put other, everyday friendships in the same rank as this") – but rather because such an unusual intimacy reminds us at once of our inescapable loneliness and the fragile connections, person to person, that may sometimes transcend it. In Montaigne's eyes, therefore, the highest expression of humanity is friendship, and the highest purpose of human society is therefore to make such friendship possible.

Characteristically, this largely Aristotelian position is further modified by his own circumstances. Montaigne admits that it would be naive, not to mention self-contradictory, for him to suggest that it is possible to be friends with everyone. Much more so than Aristotle, he was aware of the deep differences that can divide people, even when they are of good will and moderate reason. This awareness of the inevitability of difference, in fact, is what marks his most important break with ancient thought – and makes him more relevant than ever today. Montaigne is that rare thing, a philosopher who understood and cherished the limits of reason. His otherwise hopeful position is nuanced by a constant mindfulness of the difficulty in making any connection at all, let alone a fully rational one, between one person and another. Not for him a picture of politics as a smooth working-out of reason's inner logic.

With the possible exception of Epicurus and his followers, the ancient Greek philosophers, whatever their differences on questions of essence and method, all held to what we might call *the uniformity of reason*. That is, they did not accept that people could behave with impenetrable irrationality or disagree beyond the reach of argument – indeed, this belief in the power of reason is what made them philosophers. Socrates went so far as to say that vice itself was really a form of ignorance, for if someone really knew the facts of the case, that person would no longer be able to do the wrong thing.

Plato's moral psychology was more complex, making room for weakness of the will – what the Greeks called *akrasia*, knowing what is right but failing to do it. But even Plato trusted that illumination, and hence agreement, was possible. (For those incapable of being illuminated, there was always the justifiable force and deception practised by those who were wiser and knew better.) And Aristotle, though he remarks wryly in the *Nicomachean Ethics* that Socrates' reasoning about vice being ignorance does not seem to square with the evidence, is convinced that virtue is purchased, in part, through the exercise of *orthos logos*, right reason. In an unfortunately typical piece of special pleading among philosophers, all three famous figures from Athens argued that philosophical contemplation was the highest form of life, necessary to direct the irrational emotions — or, if that was not possible, to suppress them.

This unreasoning commitment to reason's power endured through the centuries to Montaigne's time, and it has not entirely disappeared in our own day either. For example, it is a prominent feature of those political thinkers, mostly modern liberals, who believe that all differences between people can be ironed out by appeal to some form of higher rationality, or through meta-vocabularies of pleasure, preference, and economic utility. This drive for a common language of political discussion is in some ways admirable, since it seeks to resolve disagreements rather than simply eliminate them, but at a fundamental level it is misconceived. Some ethical and political differences simply do not go away; some conflicts can never be resolved, only managed. Moreover, people often act for irrational reasons, reasons that cannot really be illuminated through further reasoning. If I am being irrational, it usually does no good for me to be told that and given the many reasons why I should not be so. At such a point, reasons fall on deaf ears, and only some form of therapeutic intervention, perhaps a certain kind of philosophical criticism that helps to reveal my inner conflicts, may eventually allow a more rational discussion to resume. But even then, there will be motives and beliefs ever in play that will not, try as we might, come into rational relief.

Curiously enough, therefore, and contrary to the explicit desires of most philosophers through the ages, we make a strategic error when we look to rationality as the means to realize justice. We should look rather to *desire*, to what we want – and to the limits of getting what we want given the presence of other people with their own desires. We have to be careful, however. Desires are not mere preferences, and they do not arise to consciousness fully formed and obvious in themselves. Sometimes they hide, or take on strange forms, or displace themselves into other things. Sometimes they make themselves known only in the less illuminated places of the human mind, in dreams and wishes that seem alien but cannot be – for they too come from within us. It follows that commonalities and divergences in human affairs, and the political demands they make on us, are not *discovered* through pure acts of intellection or insight but rather *made* in the grimy workshop of coexistence. Citizenship is less an intellectual achievement or state of illumination than it is a way of carrying on, a form of action. It is a way of finding ourselves, or at least enough of ourselves to make do, within the complicated, cross-hatched world of our shared dreams.

Montaigne senses this complexity in the matter of human desire, and his discussion of friendship suggests his own misgivings about the philosophical confidence that life will surrender to plain reason. Most associations between persons, he notes, are actually pragmatic. "As familiar company at table, I choose the amusing rather than the wise; in bed I prefer beauty to goodness; and for serious conversation, I like ability even combined with dishonesty; and similarly in other things." One person is loved "for his beauty, another for his ease of manner, another for his liberality, this one for his paternal affection, and that one for his brotherly love, and so on." These ties are limited by circumstance and need. We do not care about the doctor's religion, only his skill; the footman's chastity is not at issue, just his duty; and the cook may swear as much as he likes, so long as he can make a soufflé that rises well.

Virtues and affections are relative to context, in other words. Goods are plural in number and variable in extension, because only the demands of what is needed – of what works – can determine what is good. And this awareness of the plurality of goods is essential, since it means we can begin to navigate in and through our routine differences with something more like peace. In a genuine friendship, it is true, these differences may ultimately disappear and issues of "benefit, obligation, gratitude, request, thanks, and the like" fade from view. But this form of perfect friendship is so unusual that we should see it not as a goal but, like universal human rights, as a kind of *regulative ideal*: a distant and all but unreachable prospect that may nevertheless, in its perfection, guide and shape our lesser associations.

A *perfect* society would be one in which, as Aristotle argued in his version of the political virtues, all citizens were friends with one another. But that is not actually possible, given what Montaigne's experience (and ours) teaches. We often have genuinely irreconcilable differences with those who share our political fate. We may dislike those we have to live with, or simply be indifferent to them. And yet these divergences will not surrender to reason, no matter how assiduous and extensive our attempts to resolve them in that way. Tolerance and sensitivity, civility and respect – these emerge as the distinctive virtues of a diverse political order. Citizens must build character more than intellect if they are to take up the challenging task of political commitment; they must be good citizens rather than simply good maximizers of self-interest or good generators of individual preferences. It is not that self-interest or preference are inimical to justice, only that in themselves they will not secure it. Therefore, the good citizen must nurture an attitude of hopeful pragmatism, must cultivate the specifically political virtues of negotiation and acceptance, as well as the more searching virtues of love.

Significantly, Montaigne ends the essay on friendship – the first substantial one he wrote, and the one in which la Boétie figures most prominently – by referring to his own political situation. Here we see how his idea of friendship meshes with the defence of the political virtues, together providing a sense of what he thinks constitutes a well-lived life. He had planned, he says, to attach in the volume a version of la Boétie's tract, the argument against tyrants that first drew the two together. But he had discovered that it "has in the meantime been published, and for disreputable purposes, by men whose aim is to upset and change the form of our government, without the least care whether they improve it or not."

He means the Huguenot subversives then rampaging through the countryside, towards whom he was not wholly unsympathetic, but whose violent methods he deplored. He acknowledges that the Huguenots' annexation of his friend's views is not altogether strange, for if la Boétie "had had his choice, he would rather have been born at Venice than at Sarlac; and with good reason" – that is, would rather have been citizen of a republic than subject of a king. "But he had another maxim deeply imprinted on his soul: that he must most religiously obey and submit to the laws under which he was born. There was never a better citizen, nor one who cared more for his country's peace; no one more hostile to the commotions and revolutions of his time."

That is Montaigne's political credo, always derived more from experience than from first principles. Loyalty is a virtue, in the citizen as much as in the friend: the rule of law, as Socrates taught, must be observed if there is to be a state at all. But loyalty is not unreasoning, and it is not uncritical. Tyranny is abhorrent, freedom benefits all, whereas violence benefits no one for long. Being a good citizen is as much a matter of cultivating the self as of discerning philosophical truths. Probably more so, in fact, because all that remains when contradictory arguments and ideological disputes burn themselves off is a residue of commitment, one person to another. Lacking that commitment, we lack the possibility of justice. And then no amount of argument will save us. Citizenship, like friendship, is a fragile combination of opportunity, commitment, and constantly renewed regard. Without it, we are not fully human, not fully ourselves.

Challenges to Virtue

What has become of political virtues in the time since Montaigne? How have we fared in making citizenship a matter of character? Well, consider a prominent if dispiriting recent trend. Far from the civic republican conception of political virtues offered by Montaigne, it is the bourgeois-puritan virtues that have lately received the most political attention, especially from conservative social critics such as David Frum, Irving Kristol, and William Bennett. While these writers usually resist an easy identification with moralistic Republicans, who want to mould citizens in their own clean-cut Christian image, when push comes to shove they offer a familiar catalogue of virtues for American citizens: thrift, diligence, prudence, sobriety, fidelity, and orderliness.

Kristol, his original spirit of youthful rebellion spent by early middle age, devoted himself from about 1985 to writing essays that offer an unreflective defence of the bourgeois virtues of self-reliance, hard work, and the family. That these virtues might be experienced by many as repressive, thus offending the liberty that Kristol himself argues is at the heart of political life, seems not to have occurred to him. His wits likewise desert him when he confronts the realities of a changing world in the 1990s. Multiculturalism, he says in one notorious article in the journal *Commentary*, "is a desperate . . . strategy for coping with the educational deficiencies, and associated social pathologies, of young blacks." Or, in another: "One of the reasons homosexuals are so much more vulnerable to the AIDS virus is that, for reasons that remain unclear, homosexuals tend to be significantly more promiscuous than heterosexuals."

Frum is not so obviously bonkers, but the twist in his version of these virtues is that the way to make the American people better is not to give them education vouchers or high-minded art. No, the royal road to moral improvement is actually economic. If we could only roll back the welfare state, dismiss nannyism, and put the free-market *risk* back into life, all the rest would follow. Victim politics would wither on the vine, crazy Parisian ideas would be driven out of the universities, and slackers would leap off the welfare rolls and into minimum-wage service jobs. They would work because the alternative was not a monthly government cheque but starvation. "We cannot rescind the emancipation of appetite," Frum concedes grumpily, "but we can make its indulgence riskier by cancelling the welfare state's seductive invitation to misconduct." This is a form of bourgeois "virtue" that Benjamin Franklin, for one – or that great poet of genuine self-reliance, Emerson – would not have recognized as valid.

Undefended in these arguments, but of course crucial to them, is a crudely Lockean belief that there is a *natural right* to property and the political bargaining that such a right leads to. This conception of political virtue loses the nuance of Montaigne's alternative to politics-as-bargaining, instead substituting simple moralism as a top layer on an uncharitable every-man-for-himself political theory. From this vantage, you have what you have by right, and the government should damn well keep its grubby mitts off what's yours, and stop redistributing a quarter of the nation's wealth (or whatever scary figure is currently in vogue). "Federal spending will keep on growing, and therefore federal taxes will keep on rising," says Frum, "until a president is elected who does not hear every pathetic anecdote as proof that money must be lifted out of the pockets of Mr. Rodriguez to give to Mr. Gonzales."

Never mind the lack of *noblesse oblige* in this brand of winners-win/losers-die conservatism. Focus instead on the possibility, here studiously ignored, that personal economic success might be possible *only because society as a whole exists*, or that justice might demand that social inequality be balanced out precisely by doing our best not merely for ourselves but for the least well-off. This fragile but essential idea – that justice is not a superfluous addition to economic success, but instead a direct moral entailment of it – is more than ever in danger of going out of political fashion in a world of massive personal wealth and almost unbridled growth. In our time, wealth has become its own, free-floating standard of evaluation. Witness, for example, the weirdly defensive arguments offered recently by some political economists that democracy might just be as good at generating wealth as authoritarian governments – as if there were not independent and overwhelming moral arguments in favour of democracy, all wealth levels aside.

Though significant in their influence on recent political dis-course, these conservative efforts at defending political virtue are at best incomplete or confused, and at worst mad or cruel. Most importantly, as Montaigne's concerns remind us, the list of citizens' virtues needs to be expanded well beyond the instrumentally rational norms of getting and spending that dominate most versions of the bourgeois code, especially in the current gospel according to globalization. Being a good citizen cannot simply be a matter of the productive selfishness that most contemporary conservatives (who are really classical liberals) consider adequate. Furthermore, we need to supplement any account of citizens' virtues with another account, concerning the virtues of political leadership – something the right-wing virtue theorists conveniently ignore, as if the need for political leaders, like intrusive government itself, would simply atrophy if people were more rational and self-disciplined. But where do we begin in such a massive task as putting the character back into citizenship?

———

Civility has become the political virtue of choice for more thoughtful political theorists, and with good reason. It has a central role in recent attempts to enrich the idea of citizenship in the face of excessively bargain-driven conceptions of politics. Indeed, civility has been defended by everyone from the liberal eminence John Rawls, who lists it along with tolerance, reasonableness, and fairness as the cornerstone virtues of liberalism, to the moderately conservative Stephen Carter, whose defence of it included what is now a standard-issue lament about the decline of manners in American culture.

These laments, meanwhile, *de rigueur* but invariably ineffective, can be read everywhere from campus speech codes to the pages of *Sports Illustrated*. The story is always the same, involving some sketchy anecdotes about instances of bad manners, coupled with naked nostalgia for a notional golden age of good behaviour, always just out of reach – the 1950s, when our parents were young, when Emily Post lived, and so on. Such complaints misconceive the relationship between manners, which may vary greatly over short distances, and the deeper political virtue of civility, which involves a broader commitment to social good.

Still, the real trouble is not these nostalgic uses of the idea of civility, but rather that not even the subtle political theorists can agree on what civility is. They simply seem to kick the political disagreements civility is supposed to manage up to a higher, more theoretical level. That is, they replace disagreements among citizens, which the virtue civility might be thought adequate to address, with disagreement among theorists about what this virtue is. These theoretical disagreements can only be addressed by reason – and then only imperfectly. Thus we are faced with a host of competing definitions of civility, each more complex than the last and none commanding the straightforward assent of actual citizens.

The legal theorist Leslie Green, for example, defines civility as willingness to tolerate imperfections in public institutions and in the application of the law. But Carter defines it as "the sum of the many sacrifices we are called [upon] to make for the sake of living together," indicating the virtue of respecting a diversity of thought and morals in everyday life. Rawls at one point saw civility as Green did, but then decided that it also involves a commitment to give publicly intelligible reasons for the political principles one held to. The conservative thinker Michael Oakeshott sees civility as part of the crucial preservation of the civic republican tradition, embodied in the unspoken norms that function alike in parliamentary procedure and a complex game such as cricket. Benjamin Barber, a civic republican of a different stripe, views civility as part of a strongly participatory ideal of citizenship, complete with compulsory national service, active community associations, and frequent plebiscites. In my own writing, I defined civility as the willingness to participate in a public dialogue of legitimacy – to give and receive arguments about the way a society is grounded.

Academic discourse typically focusses on such disagreements, and there is indeed much to be made of them. But let us ask the more basic question instead. Why should we care about political virtues at all? Beyond an antiquarian interest in Aristotle or Montaigne, or a scholarly interest in contemporary philosophical debates, what difference do they make?

Well, here is my answer. We should care about political virtues because these qualities can be associated with a political role that is also an ethical role, that is, the role of *the good citizen*. They give us a textured way of thinking about what it means to be political, to occupy what I called Role Seven. They also save excessively abstract political theories, especially the dominant forms of universalist liberalism, from familiar charges that they deracinate, flatten, or empty individuals of moral content. Here citizens are not merely the "punctual selves" of rational choice, not simply the blank bearers of rights imagined by a legalistic definitions of citizenship. Instead, there is a concrete and detailed character to which they can aspire. The political virtues, we might say, put our political rights into action – make them concrete in the character and deeds of actual citizens.

How should we pursue this lead? Not with more abstract theory. In this regard, the philosopher Stuart Hampshire's book *Innocence and Experience* contains the following relevant charge. "Most Anglo-American academic books and articles on moral philosophy," he says, "have a fairy-tale quality, because the realities of politics, both contemporary and past politics, are absent from them." Philosophers, says Hampshire, have on the whole failed to take up *Machiavelli's problem*, which is to say, "the relation between gentleness and integrity, virtues in the private lives of persons, and the hardness and deceit that seem to be necessary in government and in the retention of power and effectiveness in public affairs."

In this they are not alone. Many people, not just philosophers, find it hard to accept that the successful practice of politics may on occasion demand what are, from a purer point of view, unpleasant traits. Educated and critical citizens have been very successful in avoiding what we might also call *Plato's dilemma*: the dire choice between accepting rule by those less worthy and taking on the difficult business of ruling oneself. Most of us are never called on to serve in public office. Few of us seem to possess the peculiar talents and drives that make for success in politics, and of those who do, many yet prefer the safety of sideline criticism and fear the corrupting influence of direct power. And so the field is left to the mediocre and the ambitious. The agonies and dilemmas of the philosopher-king are with us still, a constant feature of democratic citizenship, where each one of us is responsible for the legitimate state, each one of us feels (or anyway should feel) the constant duty of critical engagement.

The first thing to accept, then, is that political virtues are necessarily two-sided. Both leaders and led must exhibit certain qualities for the hard realities of politics to tend towards justice. And because, in a democracy, every one of us may be considered a potential leader – at least in theory – the problem of the political virtues is now more acute than ever. We struggle to find a character for political commitment, to make our procedural and juridical commitments concrete, because rights and duties are not enough to secure justice. They must be made part of our deeper selves. Our current attitudes about politics obscure this crucial point. That is evident as much in the moralistic attitude citizens take up to the personal qualities of their leaders as in the contempt leaders sometimes feel for their citizens.

To remedy this situation, we have to understand the nature of political virtues more vividly and in greater detail. And to do that, we must examine three kinds of challenges that must be acknowledged if we are to make specific political virtues viable in our sometimes overheated political culture. They are (1) the temptation to ask too much of citizens, by identifying private and public virtue too closely; (2) the temptation to hold politics to a perversely negative standard, as in some forms of nasty political realism; and finally (3) the temptation of aloof moral purity, which simply rules political necessities out of moral court. We might call the first temptation Aristotelian, the second Machiavellian, and the third temptation Christian.

To get a better sense of what political virtue entails, therefore, let us begin with what we might think of as Aristotle's political idealism.

Unlike the purity of civic commitment we saw defended by Socrates in the *Crito*, there is no simple identification of public and private virtue in the political thought of Aristotle. He does not see virtue as all of a piece, or moral expertise as leading inevitably to perfect citizenship. Instead, in a manner perhaps more familiar to us, with our multiple social roles and personal identities, important divergences remain between his notions of the good person and the good citizen. That is one reason Montaigne finds him congenial. Yet he is not by any stretch of the imagination a thinker given to the modern idea of a fractured and layered self.

Aristotle makes a point of saying, in a famous passage on citizenship in the *Politics*, that "it is possible to be a good citizen without possessing the excellence which is the quality of the good man" and "the excellence of the good citizen cannot be identical with that of a good man." His argument is that the standards for citizenship may vary (with particular constitutions, for example), while those for the good man are everywhere the same. Only in an ideally constituted polis, the political organization to which our nature fundamentally directs us, would there be a factual convergence of the two standards in the figure of the leader.

This is a little tricky, and scholars have argued about it at length. Aristotle does not say that every good citizen will likewise be a good man, and vice versa. But he does presume that those qualities that make for human flourishing generally (ethical standards) will necessarily include, or be related to, the social dimension of flourishing together with others (political standards). This is so even when we accept, as he concludes in the *Nicomachean Ethics*, that the highest ethical life is one of contemplation, not one of ethical or political action; for even here a political association is necessary to provide the enabling conditions – the food, drink, and shelter – necessary for the contemplative life.

So there is not for Aristotle, as there may well be for us, a presumed *conflict* between ethics and politics. Or, to put it another way, in his view there should be no hard choices between the private and the public exercise of virtue. On the contrary, his theory is a strong defence of a mode of life in which too wide a divergence between those realms is evidence of failure in virtue.

Aristotle states in the opening parts of the *Ethics* that his aim is to find "the ruling science," the science of "the highest good" – namely, happiness understood as *eudaimonia*, or rational satisfaction with how one is faring. Because this happiness concerns humans, and because humans are "by nature an animal intended to live in a polis," the proper science of human flourishing is therefore political science. This is "the most controlling science, the one that, more than any other, is the ruling science, . . . for though admittedly the good is the same for a city as for an individual, still the good of the city is apparently a greater and more complete good to acquire and preserve." Further, the notion of human happiness is never complete if pursued outside the context of political association.

The metaphysical priority of the city is thus established as an enabling condition of human flourishing. "The polis exists by nature and . . . is prior to the individual," Aristotle continues in the *Ethics*. "The man who is isolated – who is unable to share in the benefits of political association, or has no need to share because he is already self-sufficient – is no part of the polis, and must therefore be either a beast or a god." There is a presumption here of possible harmony between the aspirations of the individual, primarily his desire to be happy, and the needs and possibilities of the city. The city makes flourishing possible, not in the modern liberal sense of providing a background network of negative liberties – ruling out various forms of government or neighbourly interference, say – but by being the site of true happiness, for it is here that we find friendship and practise the exercise of virtues towards others.

The virtues Aristotle discusses, and the way of life he celebrates, are probably unfamiliar to our own ways of thinking. Many of his virtues of sociability – temperance, mildness, friendliness, wit – are ones we rate rather poorly, or anyway without much sense of ethical and political seriousness. And the aristocratic imperatives of this form of life sit uneasily with us, especially those concerning the disposition of wealth and honours. Lavish outlay is certainly practised today, for example, but is not often considered a social good; nor do we think of the magnanimous person as Aristotle did: "one who thinks himself worthy of great things and is really worthy of them." In fact, we might regard instead the virtue of modesty – a quality of self-deprecation that Aristotle and his students would have considered a vicious weak-heartedness.

Even friendship, the central theme of the *Ethics* and the virtue allied most closely with justice and the pursuit of civic flourishing, is something we nowadays tend to detach from the political. If we did not, there would be no sense in E.M. Forster's celebrated challenge about friends and country. There is for Aristotle no choice to be made (and therefore no issue of courage or "guts") between my friends and the civic body to which I belong. Particular friendships may be, as Aristotle says, "subordinate" to the larger community, but without community there is no friendship. "There is nothing for which nature seems to have given us such a bent as for society," Montaigne chimes in many centuries later. "And Aristotle says that good law-givers have paid more attention to friendship than to justice. Of a perfect society friendship is the peak."

Of course by Montaigne's own argument, true friendship on this model is an extremely rare and difficult thing in any case. His friendship with la Boétie, he avers, is without equal in perhaps three centuries. How can we make sense of friendship *between citizens* if the model of friendship is so demanding and unusual that most of us fail to achieve it? There is a lurking paradox here between the call for friendship as the basis of any legitimate political body, and the stipulated rarity of "true" friendship. The paradox is resolved, or might be, with the understanding of true friendship as a regulative ideal on the virtues of citizenship.

In any event, the tension is present in Aristotle, too. Friendship demands, in his discussion, a host of obligations and duties that are unfamiliar to our notions and practices of friendship. Most of those associations we call friendships are defective in Aristotle's view, incomplete associations based on pleasure or service. Montaigne's explanation of the point is lucid: "Generally speaking, all those relationships that are created and fostered by pleasure and profit, by public and private interest, are so much the less fine and noble, and so much less *friendships*, insofar as they mix some cause, or aim, or advantage with friendship, other than friendship itself. Nor do the four kinds recognized by the ancients — natural, social, hospitable, and sexual — separately or in combination, come up to it."

Indeed, the reason Aristotle can say that justice and friendship have the same scope and extension is precisely that the series of relationships that make up the good life – together with their rewards and responsibilities, and the character traits associated therewith – are exactly what he defines as justice: the complete exercise of virtue with respect to another. The true friend becomes, in a sense, another myself. We are not unlike a single soul in two bodies, reminiscent of the sundered roly-poly people described by Aristophanes in Plato's *Symposium*, ever destined to seek their other half in a restless search for completion. It is not just that Aristotle's virtues seem distant to us, in other words; his very notion of friendship as virtuous – a notion Montaigne champions for his own purposes – is foreign in tone.

Nowadays we tend to see the relationship between justice and friendship very differently, and we have largely lost the sense of close connection between the two terms. Treating our friends (merely) with justice seems churlish, like asking for money after offering drinks at a party. Where is the exclusive love and loyalty they deserve? Friendship may be, indeed, the complete exercise of virtue towards another, but this is not something we typically view as political. From the other side, asking us to be friends with our fellow citizens may be asking all too much. We have trouble making room for the idea of virtue in politics, and never in the same way or to the same extent as in private associations. For us, virtue is most often thought of as a private matter, not a public one. We may agree that justice is the ruling principle of the public/political sphere, but only insofar as it is more or less divorced from our idea of friendship.

These divergences may indicate that we have an impoverished view of both friendship and justice. But the main problem is that Aristotle addresses himself to a political association that is, by our standards, tiny, exclusive, homogeneous, highly privileged, and rigidly like-minded. He faces no difficulties of the kind associated with the politics of pluralism; the demands of necessarily fractious politics, what Hampshire calls "justice as conflict," are absent from this idealistic account of virtuous political life. There is therefore little sense, in Aristotle's discussion of *eudaimonia* and the qualities necessary to secure it, of the prospect of unresolvable political disagreement. Given the standards of human flourishing, evident in what the philosopher Alasdair MacIntyre calls "Aristotle's metaphysical biology" – a naturalistic account of human life, which contains within it normative precepts about how to live – ethics becomes for the Athenians a simple matter of *getting it right* with respect to the single true standard embedded in their nature.

This is a serious blind spot, and it complicates our thoughts about Aristotle's account of political virtue. Aristotle's conviction that there was, and had to be, one correct answer to the question "What is human flourishing?," especially when combined with the priority of the polis, prevents him from considering why citizens and leaders might come to value traits concerning compromise, suspicion, ruthlessness – not to mention tolerance and civility. In short, he did not see in the *Politics* the need for politics, because, like many philosophers, he was too confident about the role that rationality plays in human affairs. Not only does his notion of rationality define who counts as a citizen – notoriously excluding women, slaves, Metics, and barbarians – it also suggests, very much contrary to political experience, that each of these citizens is rational all the time: an error that many contemporary political theorists, borrowing little else from Aristotle, also make.

———

Nobody could accuse Machiavelli of excessive idealism about political virtue, but he does have a theory of citizenship, one that is impossible to ignore as we attempt to flesh out our commitments as citizens of a complex, sometimes violent world.

Machiavelli's famous political primer *The Prince* defends a certain conception of human flourishing, we might say, which points to glory and the personal aggrandizement of the ruler. Of course this cynical political manual does not portray Machiavelli's republican views, which emerge only in the more balanced *Discourses*, but the sharp political realism of *The Prince* represents an important problem for a consideration of the less-desirable demands of politics. Whatever we may say about *The Prince*, its continuing influence illustrates a stark, if unwelcome, point: politics often demands, and facilitates, people and traits that are morally unpleasant.

Unlike Socrates' or Aristotle's, Machiavelli's conception of political life begins with disagreement as a central fact. Indeed, this is the kind of violent disagreement that leads to habitual assassination and purges. The reason Machiavelli poses such a deep challenge to ethical and political theorists is this willingness to distill the essence of this chaotic world into strong realist drink. The result is not to everyone's taste. The virtuous prince of his imagination has an apparently overwhelming imperative to gain, consolidate, and maintain political power. This strikes many people as dangerous, if not insane or simply evil. If politics lies only in this, what becomes of conventional morality? But for the Machiavelli of *The Prince*, that question is not so much difficult as simply irrelevant – where, that is, it is not actually dangerous: thinking too much about morality is exactly the sort of self-indulgent weakness that leads to rulers losing their power.

One of Machiavelli's express aims in *The Prince*, therefore, is to plot the relationship between politics and morality by offering a version of the then-popular discussion of such issues, that is, a table of princely virtues. Courtly manuals were all the rage in Renaissance Europe, offering educated nobles a means of improving their standing by improving their manners. Machiavelli criticizes this humanist tradition of the courtly manual, with its detailed cataloguing of the character traits necessary for gentlemen and leaders, by means of vicious ironic imitation.

The satirical success of *The Prince* is frequently underestimated. Whatever else it is, Machiavelli's little book is a masterpiece of mockery, skewering the pretensions of the many manuals then purporting to teach virtue by rote. This "mirror of princes" tradition, idealistic and underwritten by theologico-metaphysical commitments Machiavelli certainly did not share, had already raised the implicit central question of *The Prince*. When, and how, is princely morality different from ordinary morality? Are there virtues possessed by a prince that are not to be found, and not to be looked for, in a citizen?

The discussion of political virtues in *The Prince* forms a self-contained whole, a compact unit of investigation that runs for five closely argued chapters. It succinctly destroys the idealism of the mirror-of-princes writers who were Machiavelli's near-contemporaries. In contrast to these immediate Renaissance forebears, Machiavelli presents not a sketch of an idealized super-personality, a kind of philosopher-king, but instead a portrait based on a close study of the laws of history. This entails recasting many of the traditional princely virtues such that they begin to appear vicious. By the same token, some of the traditional vices gradually acquire in Machiavelli's sly hands a sheen of perverse virtue.

Throughout, Machiavelli agrees with the humanists on at least this point: the virtues of the prince must be conceived differently from those of the ordinary citizen. When fate marks one for great things, certain qualities of no utility in private life – perhaps of active disutility there – begin to acquire a central importance. But by so obviously imitating the accepted form of tabulating the traits necessary for a ruler, Machiavelli offers a brisk and devastating refutation of the humanist tradition's idealism. And in doing so, he clarifies for us, in a way impossible for members of that tradition, the problem of relating morality and politics. The Machiavellian virtues of the prince do not pose a problem of *extension* (how do we add princely virtues to the discussion of workaday morality?) but rather a problem of *separate spheres*: how can we call good princely qualities "virtues" at all?

The general statement governing Machiavelli's discussion is the following, which begins with a brief claim in favour of moral skepticism and moves quickly to separate politics from traditional morality:

> Any man who tries to be good all the time is bound to come
> to ruin among the great number who are not good. Hence
> a prince who wants to keep his post must know how not to
> be good, and use that knowledge, or refrain from using it, as
> necessity requires. . . . For if you look at matters carefully, you
> will see that something resembling virtue, if you follow it,
> may be your ruin, while something else resembling vice will
> lead, if you follow it, to your security and well-being.

Notoriously, Machiavelli thinks the thesis of this general statement is sanctioned by historical study – a study most philosophers have foolishly ignored, preferring the allegedly stronger sanction of first principles. But history teaches better than reason, and its lesson is that there is a necessary connection between virtue and consequence, a connection that must serve to revise our notions of virtue. Philosophers may attempt to convince us otherwise, as Socrates famously did with Plato's brothers Glaucon and Adeimantus in the *Republic*, but the prince pays attention to that sort of advice only at his peril. And hence the reversal of the traditional conception of morality. With the imperative "Keep the state" foremost in mind, the table of praiseworthy qualities is necessarily recast. Indeed, it is reversed.

Thus the qualities of liberality, kindness, honesty – the traditional virtues of kings – do not, according to Machiavelli's analysis, pose good cost/benefit prospects for the prince. A judiciously cruel ruler, one who stops short of wantonness but makes his willingness to punish known, can command where a more lenient one is overrun. Nor should the prince hesitate to break promises, despite the advice of classical authors. Conspicuous generosity is a good idea, but liberality can easily lead to higher taxes and a taste for riches among subjects, both risky developments when it comes to holding on to power. (Or, as the recent satirical volume *A Child's Machiavelli* says more simply: "When you take over some place, kill off everyone who's against you, pronto, then act really nice to everyone left. If people're scared of you at first, you can boss 'em around easier later." And: "Only give things away when people are watching. If you wanna give presents to people, make sure it's other people's stuff. If you're not a Boss but you wanna be one, make sure you trick everyone into thinking you're a really generous guy.")

"Doubtless if all men were good," Machiavelli notes, these deceptions "would be bad; but since they are a sad lot, and keep no faith with you, you in your turn are under no obligation to keep it with them." In general, an appearance of virtue is politically useful, but actual virtue can lead to political ruin, for "hatred may be earned by doing good just as much as by doing evil."

"In actual fact," Machiavelli says,

> a prince may not have all the admirable qualities we listed
> [in the traditional catalogue], but it is very necessary that he
> should seem to have them. Indeed, I will venture to say that
> when you have them and exercise them all the time, they are
> harmful to you; when you just seem to have them, they are
> useful. It is good to appear merciful, truthful, humane, sin-
> cere, and religious; it is good to be so in reality. But you must
> keep your mind so disposed that, in case of need, you can turn
> to the exact contrary.

The qualification is important. Machiavelli's worldliness does not lead – even in *The Prince* – to an extreme version of moral skepticism but a rather modified one. Though *seeming* and *appearance* can indeed do most of the good of the traditional virtues, it is nevertheless also good actually to possess these virtues. Yet they must not lead the prince away from his main objective, to secure and maintain power. The prince "should not depart from the good if he can hold to it, but he should be ready to enter on evil if he has to."

So Machiavelli does not attempt to deny the existence of traditional virtues, or standards of justice, as the sophist Thrasymachus does in his famous pro-realist argument with Socrates in the first book of Plato's *Republic*. Thrasymachus takes the very modern view that justice is no more than the benefit enjoyed by the stronger in a political struggle – only to be bogged down immediately in some confusing objections from Socrates about when and how anyone actually knows what is to their advantage. Because he avoids this pitfall, Machiavelli does not face the difficulty of relying on precisely the virtues or standards he is criticizing in order to make his point – a reliance that, when exposed, led Thrasymachus to his doom in the face of Socratic challenge. But neither, from the other side, is Machiavelli a *perfected* Thrasymachus, the sort of stick-to-your-guns political realist who systematically denies any standard of justice beyond the advantage of the stronger.

Unpalatable though they may be, these points make it clear that Machiavelli should not be included in the cynical sophistical tradition of Callicles and Thrasymachus, as many people think. He is rather of the mind of the young Adeimantus, in Book II of the *Republic*, who cannot help noticing the alarming tendency for actual justice to be punished, while injustice *combined with a reputation for justice* reaps rewards. Unlike Adeimantus, however (and probably unlike us), Machiavelli does not believe this problem can be solved with a better definition of justice.

Contrary to reputation, Machiavelli is not attempting to erase the distinction between good and bad. He is instead attempting to say how the distinction must fare when faced with the new and peculiar imperatives of politics. His experience tells him that his citizens' enmity is as often earned by attempts to do the right thing as by attempts to act for advantage. And so "a prince who wants to keep his state is often bound to do what is not good." It is that challenge to political virtue that we cannot ignore.

We should not consider the matter at all settled by these reflections, of course. Machiavelli is not the last word on the demands of political power. But neither can Machiavelli's argument simply be avoided: he *is* the first word. Indeed, the tenaciously maintained hope that the Machiavellian challenge to political innocence *can* be avoided is one large element in the philosophical naiveté that gets us nowhere in the actual political world. We may seek refuge in the idea that politics and morality have nothing to say to each other, occupying separate and incommensurable realms, but this sort of defeated political realism, often combined with assumed moral superiority, leads only to smugness and impotence. Innocence is just the flip side of extreme Machiavellian cynicism, and neither achieves much for those of us trying to realize justice within politics.

It would of course be fortunate if the imperatives of politics merely concerned, as they appeared to do for Aristotle, an institutionalization of the imperatives of ethics. But Machiavelli does not believe this is, or is any longer, the case in a modern world of conflicting values – and we must acknowledge the force of that claim, for what was true for Machiavelli is doubly true for us. Politics is not quite a mug's game, as defecting citizens and cynical electors so often say; but it is a game with tricky rules and many pitfalls. A leader who believed with Aristotle that ethics and politics will naturally converge would be imprudent as well as factually mistaken. He would make easy pickings for his rivals, even if he had not already sown hatred and contempt throughout his citizenry.

That consequence would be bad both for them and for him, and for anyone to pretend otherwise is mere sanctimony. Machiavelli wants us to face the problems of political virtue as dispassionately as he himself did. There is no avoiding the necessities of politics, and even in democratic states we must have leaders if we are to enjoy the freedom to pursue divergent goals, which is the point and legacy of the great modern movements of emancipation. Leaders are not always nice people, and so the need for leaders may well involve serious revision of the traditional virtues – and not only for the leader himself. The citizens who depend upon an elected representative to secure their peace and flourishing will also have to acknowledge their place in the political order and the traits necessary to make that order work. The virtues of citizens and the virtues of leaders are intimately related.

Machiavelli's recasting of the traditional virtues in *The Prince* has been much remarked, of course. What has not been so remarked are the implications for citizens of this recasting. The crucial point for our present purposes is that an unwillingness to face the second half of this equation – the demand that political virtues concern both leader and citizen – too often leads merely to the pure-as-snow moral disapproval of leaders. It can in turn lead to, or underwrite, the *habitual* disapproval citizens feel for those who rule them, a disapproval that sometimes descends into bare contempt in democratic societies. Here leaders feel the compulsion to justify themselves to the citizenry in the shadowy, and in practice unverifiable, terms of "mandate" and "popular will" – even as they act to reinforce that cynical status quo in which money, and money alone, can purchase an election victory.

It is as true in politics as elsewhere that familiarity breeds contempt, but this does not go the whole distance in explaining the bitter contempt many citizens these days feel for their elected leaders. The contempt indicates a deeper issue: the acute discomfort many citizens have about the demands of politics, and about the people who seem to come forward to meet them. This discomfort cuts both ways. Leaders who must exhibit yet cannot defend themselves in terms of (realistic) political virtues find that they earn only their citizens' disregard. And citizens who discover that they have no stomach for the occasionally nasty realities of politics retreat from the issues because the traits necessary in good citizens sometimes sit badly with the (innocent) moral virtues they are presumably trying to cultivate in their private lives – or anyway holding other people to.

The result is a polity racked by hypocrisy and willful blindness, in which the disapproval of leaders and led becomes mutually reinforcing: on the one hand, a pervasive and unquestioning distrust of elites, matched by an equally pervasive but mostly unspoken contempt for an ignorant and close-minded electorate. In such a situation, what hope can remain for justice?

The Pact of Civility

In politics today no less than in centuries past, what we desperately need as citizens is an effective response to the three challenges I have called Aristotelian, Machiavellian, and Christian. Here Montaigne points a useful way forward, giving us the keener sense we seek of the possibilities of citizenship under conditions of ethical or cultural disagreement – conditions that are now, in virtually every corner of the world, inescapable.

We can never let Machiavelli determine the bottom-line political virtues, even when the proximity of conflict between citizens might seem to make that tempting. His emphasis on the cynical virtues of the ruler is as one-sided as the philosophical purity that holds itself aloof from politics. That is why Montaigne – especially the politicized

Montaigne who emerges from the formative encounter with a republican sympathizer like la Boétie – turns out to be one of Machiavelli's ablest opponents. Montaigne's humane skepticism, his insistence on "putting cruelty first," his skeptical regard for the rule of law, distinguish him as a thinker willing to meet Machiavelli on his own ground. In defending the political virtues, we must do the same. Montaigne plots a persuasive course between the single-minded and brutal republicanism of Machiavelli and the self-interested conflict politics of classical liberalism, where politics is always a clash of appetites.

This may not be immediately obvious. We may be inclined to say that with Montaigne innocence is being served once more, for Montaigne's *Essays* indeed seem to defend the moral virtues of honesty, kindness, and tolerance. But the important feature of this defence is its basis. Montaigne is tolerant and kind because he is hard-headed, not soft-hearted. His forbearance is a direct result of his ethical non-cognitivism, part of a larger epistemological modesty evident throughout the *Essays*. He will not lay down the law because he knows, even better than Socrates perhaps, the extent of his own ignorance.

"[R]eason has taught me," he says in one well-known passage,

> that to condemn anything so positively as false and impossible is to claim that our own brains have the privilege of knowing the bounds and limits of God's will, and our mother nature's power. I have learnt too that there is no more patent folly in the world than to reduce these things to the measure of our own power and capacity.

"It is a dangerous and serious presumption," the same essay continues, "and argues an absurd temerity, to condemn what we do not understand. For, having by virtue of your excellent intellect established the boundaries of truth and error, and found yourself compelled to believe stranger things than those you deny, you are then obliged to abandon those boundaries."

Precisely because Montaigne believes no knowledge of ultimate truth is available to the human mind, he moves in strikingly modern fashion to adopt a position of ethical and political tolerance. What we cannot finally know, we cannot pronounce final judgment upon, and that includes crucially the question of the proper routes to salvation and whether, for example, the Eucharist involves consubstantiation or transubstantiation. Being thus unable to judge, and rejecting the bloody (if popular and effective) expedient of eliminating all competing positions, we have no rational choice but to adopt a position of accepting and even embracing difference.

I say "embracing," and that is indeed a kind of ideal of the process, but far more likely is ongoing uneasiness, dislike, even hatred. Tolerance does not provide a means to eliminate these facts of political life, only a way of managing them. And, as numerous recent well-meaning attempts show, tolerance cannot be legislated. Think, for example, of the campus speech codes and politically correct workplace directives of recent decades. It is worth remembering that virtue, the political no less than other kinds, rarely can be enforced.

Montaigne's pragmatic form of tolerance, a pillar of emerging liberal thought, would not receive its more influential defences until a century later – and would not expose its deepest difficulties until another century after that. Those seventeenth-century defences of tolerance, especially Locke's *Letter on Toleration* (1689) and Spinoza's *Tractatus Theologico-Politicus* (1670), are the first great works in the liberal tradition, and if Montaigne is not quite a liberal simply by judging that cruelty the worst thing we do, he is at least an attractive kind of proto-liberal by anticipating the need to accommodate disparate positions in diverse polities. Like the early modern liberals who come after him, Montaigne believes we must secure conditions of just coexistence without insisting on a single answer to the question of how one ought to live. He does so, moreover, *without* adopting the reductive, market-driven view of the human person that now dominates many liberal states, especially in the post-industrial West.

Thus does political virtue go beyond the self-interested bargaining of the marketplace, finding in the character of the citizen a deeper form of moral commitment, one person to another. I rarely find myself in agreement with the conservative *Spectator* columnist Peregrine Worsthone, but not long ago he had the key insight about Montaigne's possible influence on our current political predicament. "If Montaigne could persuade the French aristocracy that it could afford to show mercy to the enemy on the battlefield," Worsthone wrote, "surely some latter-day Montaigne should be able to succeed in persuading the contemporary business class that it can afford to get its snout out of the trough." The language of political virtues insists on something that the interest-oriented discourse of political and economic rights cannot; namely, that *privilege confers obligations on those who enjoy it*. That there is moral duty to act not only for one's own benefit, but for the benefit of others less able to fend for themselves. *That's* citizenship in action.

———

Montaigne's habitual pose of haphazard musing, so charming and so often applauded, is in fact highly calculated, and the *Essays* reveal themselves upon close study as finely constructed and polished literary creations. But the appearance of casualness remains, an enormously winning quality that also contains an important methodological commitment. Unlike previous writers, Montaigne is not going to appeal to iron-clad rules of logic, or even to the sort of hard historical determinism that Machiavelli claimed for himself, in pursuit of his political insights.

Instead, and consistent with the image presented to the reader – the image of a writer slightly bemused and uncertain, who knows no more than the reader – Montaigne states that his "sole aim is to reveal myself; and I may be different tomorrow if some new lesson changes me. I have no authority to exact belief, nor do I desire it, for I do not feel myself to be well instructed to instruct others." This personal focus leads to a standard of evidence that is some large distance from Machiavelli's discernment of historical necessity, even more from Aristotle's standard of functional necessity revealed by reason alone. Montaigne will even commit the scholarly sin of heeding whatever he chooses to believe. "In this study of our manners and behaviour that I am undertaking," he says, "fabulous incidents are as good as true ones, so long as they are feasible."

That might sound a little shaky, even to readers well disposed to the writer. Surely fantasy cannot be as good as fact when it comes to argument, even if example and anecdote may convince as much as argument? But why not, exactly? Montaigne is on firm ground when he discusses the role of worldly experience in moral education. "Human society," he says, "is wonderfully adapted to [learning], and so is travel in foreign countries . . . for the principal purpose of discovering the characteristics and customs of different nations, and of rubbing and polishing our wits on those of others." Experience of difference, in other words, is improving not only in widening one's horizon but in instilling almost instinctive openness: a cognitive virtue that is also a political one. "Mixing with the world has a marvellously clarifying effect on a man's judgment," he continues later, for "this great world, which some still reckon to be but one example of a whole genus, is the mirror into which we must look if we are to behold ourselves from the proper standpoint."

The images employed here are significant, anticipating a discussion of the political virtue of civility that would occupy a central position in the Enlightenment two centuries later and recur in our own day, as political theorists struggle to cope with burgeoning social differences in multicultural states. Joseph Addison and Lord Shaftesbury, among others, speak in the 1770s of the moral and political role of the virtues associated with civility. Here the importance of being *reflected* in our social encounters with other citizens assumes a distinctly moral tone. Montaigne, adding in the 1580s to the book of manners tradition of the Renaissance, provides an important bridge between the straightforward early manuals of social propriety – Giovanni della Casa's endlessly diverting *Galateo* (1558), say, with its injunctions against scratching oneself or drooling at table – and the more broadly conceived and systematic discussions of the Enlightenment thinkers.

It is in Addison's *Spectator* essays that we observe the eighteenth century's first serious consideration of the improving and socially necessary capacities of politeness. Addison's easy and felicitous style, to which Dr. Johnson would later refer any writer desirous of a suitable model, might seem an unlikely vehicle for serious moral and political instruction. Yet it is the genius of these essays that, like Montaigne's before them, their witty and diverting discourse on manners and morals is ultimately more instructive than any project of grim correction. "I shall spare no pains to make [my readers'] instruction agreeable, and their diversions useful," Addison says in *Spectator* No. 10 (1771). "For which reasons I shall endeavour to enliven morality with wit, and to temper wit with morality, that my readers may, if possible, both ways find their account in the speculation of the day." This famous statement of intent then continues in a vein Montaigne would have found congenial: "I shall be ambitious to have it said of me, that I have brought Philosophy out of closets and libraries, schools and colleges, to dwell in clubs and assemblies, at tea-tables, and in coffee-houses."

The governing conceit in Addison's public-spirited philosophy of manners is an awareness, derived from the Latin root of the word "politeness," that social concourse is essentially a matter of one citizen *polishing* another: polishing, that is, not only so that rough spots and edges may be removed, but also so that one may begin to reflect another in the common social project of public life. Politeness therefore takes on a democratic and pragmatic meaning not typically available in its most obvious manifestation, the cultivation of manners. (Dr. Johnson, in a 1773 edition of *The Spectator*, noted that "all works which describe manners require notes in sixty or seventy years or less.") Politeness as Addison finally understands it – what we should really call the virtue of civility – is much more than correctness and propriety in behaviour. The latter notions may indeed vary over relatively short distances in time and space, and will always be subject to the whims and lightning changes of social fashion. They may also, insofar as they become an object of attention in themselves, deflect people from virtue: nothing is no more viciously exclusive than modishness for its own sake or excessive regard for the arcane details of manners.

But underlying modish manners is a more solid aspect of civil behaviour, and the only aspect of politeness that can sensibly be allied with morals and the larger concerns of society. This is the political aspect of civil behaviour. Better understood, this sort of civility entails consideration of the interests of others, coupled with a willing restraint on the expression of my own interests. The polishing we render unto each other is a function of a two-sided social orientation, in other words: in conversation with our fellow citizens, we must be willing both to listen and to respond. Together, in a general conversation governed by civility and restraint, we make and hear the claims of which society is composed. Together, then, listening and responding, we forge a fragile social identity. We come to reflect one another as part of the general interpretive project we call social life, and in so doing attempt to create the political order that will serve to hear and answer the various claims we all wish to put in play.

As an essayist, not a political philosopher or moral psychologist, Addison had a notion of politeness that must remain suggestive rather than definitive, casual rather than systematic. It would be left to the likes of Adam Smith to complete the task, which he had begun, of plotting a more complete moral psychology suitable to the demands of a rapidly changing social world. But there can be little doubt that Addison's view of politeness included a sense of its cultural power. In the *Spectator* essays, says the historian J.G.A. Pocock, "*politeness becomes an active civilizing agent.* By observation, conversation, and cultivation, men and women are brought to an awareness of the needs and responses of others and how they appear in the eyes of others; this is not only the point at which politeness becomes a highly serious practical morality. . . . It is also the point at which Addison begins to comment on the structure of English society and the reconciliation of its diverse 'interests.'"

In other words, politeness so understood has moral and political implications – implications at odds with the dismissiveness towards politeness that has become the norm in most social philosophy. Civility, so far from being a weapon of exclusion marshalled by the rich or well-born to preserve social distinctions, is here elevated into an active democratizing force. Indeed, understood as an awareness of others' interests and views, civility is an essential element of any defensible political order, that is, one founded on the values of pluralism and tolerance and tending towards justice. More deeply still, civility provides a way of conceiving the social pact as more than a fractious state of suspended war, the uneasy social contract of the Hobbesian imagination.

Like Addison, Montaigne is not afraid of the world's lessons. Indeed, he does not think a compelling moral vision can be articulated without them. Experience makes us tolerant because it widens the horizons of our knowledge and demonstrates the plurality of answers to the vexed questions of how to live and worship. Yet Montaigne, once more like Addison, thinks the same experience teaches us some basic lessons concerning human behaviour, and these are not subject to relative variation. Like the claims advanced in the Universal Declaration of Human Rights, they articulate a form of universalism upon which certain tentative conclusions can be raised.

"[N]o man's brain has yet been found so disordered as to excuse treachery, disloyalty, tyranny, and cruelty, which are our common faults," Montaigne says in his essay "On cannibals." Taking seriously this rare opportunity to put ourselves in question before the example of a radically different form of life, Montaigne insists that these lessons are obvious. Modern society – that is, his society of the early modern period – is racked by both large- and small-scale nastiness. It is sick at the core. We must therefore try to eliminate the "common faults" or (in Judith Shklar's more engaging translation) "ordinary vices" of humanity, especially lying and cruelty.

"I am an enemy to all subtle deeds of deception," Montaigne says, "and I hate to take part in trickery, not only in sport but even to obtain an advantage; if the action is not wicked, the way to it is." Moreover: "Lying – and in a lesser degree obstinacy – are, in my opinion, the only faults whose birth and progress we should consistently oppose." Matters are likewise with cruelty. "Among other vices, I cruelly hate cruelty, both by nature and judgment, as the worst of all vices," he says in the essay "On cruelty," which also contains his general discussion of virtue and vice.

Montaigne begins that essay, one of the most sustained and successful in the collection, by stating that virtue must be "both something else and something nobler than the propensity towards goodness that is born in us," and goes on to allude to the importance of learning and character formation in the exercise of virtue. As elsewhere, there are strong Aristotelian echoes throughout the discussion. Virtuous actions are ones that are right, but also done for the right reason. "Firmness in the face of danger – if firmness is the proper word – contempt for death and patience in misfortunes, may arise in men – and often does – from an inability to judge events correctly and realize their actual nature," he says. "This failure of apprehension and stupidity sometimes disguise themselves as valorous actions; and I have often seen it happen that men have been praised for deeds that really deserved blame."

Montaigne even chastises himself for his own failures in virtue.

His friends call him prudent when he is no more than lucky. "I am so far from having attained that first and most perfect degree of excellence, in which virtues becomes a habit. . . . My virtue is a virtue that could be more properly called a casual and fortuitous innocence." There is irony here, for obviously Montaigne's innocence is not casual and fortuitous, but instead studied and purposeful. It is also a direct and considered reaction to the pervasive cruelty of his historical context. "I live in an epoch," he acknowledges, "when, owing to the licence of our civil wars, we abound in incredible examples of this vice: there is nothing to be found in ancient histories more extreme than what we witness every day. But this has by no means reconciled me to it."

And we admire him for saying so. Unfortunately, this is not yet a complete answer to the Machiavellian temptation, for the peculiar imperatives of politics are not being addressed here. Montaigne is now retreating a bit into his innocence, into a private realm of moral virtue in which a blanket condemnation of cruelty is possible. This is a long way from the ends-means flexibility of Machiavelli's analysis, and it is enormously attractive. Yet there is a need for more nuance to make the position fully viable.

Indeed, one has to pause and wonder how Montaigne, the landowner and politician, can fail to acknowledge that deception – if only of benign kinds – is not simply inevitable in political life, but indispensable there. In politics, after all, one sometimes does have to be cruel to be kind, and the sort of pure ethical vision pursued by Montaigne – at least in the context of these *Essays*, where he does not ignore the world so much as sometimes view it through rose-tinted glasses – could only lead finally to political disaster. Machiavelli might wonder, and so might we, how Montaigne managed to survive for even five minutes, let alone two terms, as mayor of Bordeaux.

With these thoughts in mind, the focus of our present task is sharper. The difficulties are likewise clearer. How can we offer a comprehensive list of the political virtues that fight off Machiavelli without succumbing to a simplistic identification of ethics and politics or to an equally unhelpful triumph of innocence? Can Montaigne's worldliness speak to us after all? How, in short, is character related to action in the peculiar dispositions we call political virtues?

Let us begin with basics. There are at least three structural features common to any account of praiseworthy character traits — whether we mean the traits of the Homeric heroes, the early Christians in Rome, Ben Franklin's Puritans, the post-revolutionary Jacobins, or the tart Christian ironists of Jane Austen's novels. The three common features are (1) a *telos* or end for all human activity, which specifies the point and nature, the ultimate goal, of human life; (2) a social role or roles so that people within a shared context can find an identity that helps them fulfill this end; and (3) a cluster of institutions that back up the social role and thus reinforce the existence and coherence of the *telos*. With these three elements in place, we can also expect to find a more or less coherent practical discourse that supports a tradition of philosophical inquiry concerning virtuous action and judgment.

That inquiry, in turn, has a structural function. If healthy, it will uncover other essential components of virtue as they apply to individuals. There must be, for instance, a sense of narrative continuity, such that individuals taking up the social role in context — say, the role of "good citizen" — will find ready materials that allow them to tell a coherent story about a life so lived. They have to make sense of themselves, as citizens, within the larger narrative demands of life itself. And so there must be, in addition to handy narratives, a coherent list of the relevant virtues — which is to say, a list of the traits or "internal goods" necessary and sufficient for human flourishing within the given context. (Internal goods are goods, either prerequisites or rewards, without which a practice could not maintain

itself; they are distinct from external goods, which merely super-
vene on the practice. Thus, to take a trivial example, footspeed is a
virtue in — a good internal to — the practice of football. Multimillion-
dollar salaries are not.)

I emphasize these structural elements of virtue, after the manner
of Alasdair MacIntyre, in order to make a suggestion concerning
specifically political virtues. Is it possible that politics creates its own
context of human flourishing, a distinct human practice complete
with its own ends and social roles and, hence, a list of the relevant
internal goods or virtues? Is it possible, further, that this one is neither assimilable to any wider one (as in Aristotle's political idealism)
nor, on the other hand, so influential that it threatens to overturn
other kinds of virtue (as in Machiavelli's political realism and the
flip-side notion of political innocence)?

The first strategy, the strategy of assimilation, is enormously
attractive to a certain kind of ethical thinker who believes there is
one, and only one, answer to the question of how humans should
flourish. But precisely therein lies its danger. As long as a given society fails to converge on a single answer to this question, the practices of politics will not be susceptible to standardized virtue of the
Aristotelian kind. Indeed, the imperatives of governance may make
such talk seem irrelevant even in very coherent social contexts.
Neo-Aristotelian idealism about politics as human flourishing will
then begin to sound naive, even ridiculously hopeful. Thus the triumph of innocence in another form — a form that may lead, in turn,
to its own kind of cynicism. Ethical discourse may soon be relegated
to a disused corner of political life, to be trotted out only for instrumental show. Examples of this cynicism are all too easy to find,
especially in an election year.

If, responding to this familiar situation, we instead adopt a neo-
Machiavellian strategy of redescribing virtue to suit the imperatives
of politics, we face the opposite danger of devaluing the other kinds
of virtues in our social context. Even if "everything is political," the

practice of politics is never all there is to life, and to grant it uncon-
ditional priority in all aspects of human affairs is to risk the cynical
glory-seeking of the Machiavellian prince. Montaigne does indeed
plot a useful middle course here, both between the Aristotelian and
Machiavellian temptations *and* between republican and liberal versions of political virtue. But there is still a little too much innocence
clinging to him, as I have suggested. Montaigne was right that being
cruel is the worst thing we can do. He was wrong in thinking that
we must respond to that fact on a purely ethical level. The peculiar
virtues of politics – distinct from those of individual moral life – can
help us find a way forward.

To see what they might be, consider the structural analysis of
virtue in a context of political activity. The *telos* of politics, according to the Machiavelli of *The Prince*, is glory. That is a controversial
definition of the end of politics, but let us accept it for the sake of
argument: politics is about the glory of peoples as they come together
in community. But, as Machiavelli himself knew very well, there can
be no political glory without political survival, and so the first duty
of any prince was to stay in power. He must keep his subjects happy
enough and loyal enough to ward off his own demise without giving
them so much that they became soft, lazy, or complacent. The glory
here is not personal, since it depends on others; and it is not simple,
since it depends on the ongoing good will of the people. This is not
quite the way we usually think about politics, but it possesses an
important kernel of truth. Without stability there is no community
at all.

Let us therefore call this the political *telos* of social stability.
Machiavelli went too far, for most of us, in maintaining that such stability was merely instrumental to the maximization of princely
glory. That kind of thinking is exactly what accounts for the continuing misconceptions about a thinker who was, in fact, a committed
republican. In any case, we should rather say that the creation and
maintenance of social stability in politics should serve the ends of

justice, and of inclusiveness, not those of the individual who happens to be in power. Those in power must be aware, even more so than Machiavelli's prince, that their well-being and success depend on a happy citizenry. That, to put it bluntly, is the essence of democratic politics. We can shift the balance, then, and democratize the sophistication of Machiavelli's analysis without simply dismissing his insight: we seek not glory at the expense of the people, but justice for the people consistent with the pursuit of glory.

Of course, what justice means, precisely, especially in a diverse society, is going to be subject to a lot of debate, possibly with little if any prospect of final agreement. That should not worry us unduly. Indeed, the idea of *final agreement* may be deleterious to the debate, since conflict among citizens is not so much a problem to be solved as a basic fact of any kind of social coexistence under conditions of diversity. So we must rephrase the issue of the political *telos* on a meta-level and say something like this: the end of politics is the creation and maintenance of social stability, such that a vigorous debate *about justice* is possible, because only such a debate gives us the enabling conditions of general inclusiveness and welfare. We cannot say in advance what justice will mean to citizens; only that they must be engaged in a discussion of what it means in order to be citizens at all.

The social roles specified by this kind of conception politics are obviously two, those of leader and citizen. I have already suggested the dangers of Machiavelli's one-sided emphasis on the princely role, with citizens relegated to a background chorus of venal, lying, and self-interested clamouring. To balance the picture and the practice, we need to say more about the citizen as a positive social role, and the leader as a social role subservient to the desires of citizens. There is nevertheless an important asymmetry between these roles. One of the benefits of democratic citizenship in complex states — and surely necessary in any conception of citizenship that hopes to universalize across social conditions — is that we don't all have to be involved in the business of governance. We want to be free to get on with our other projects, the demands of Roles One through Six. To accommodate this means ceding power to a minority of governors, and the minimal danger of creating self-serving elites is part of the harsh bargain we strike in being left to ourselves most of the time.

Without a means of controlling that danger, of course, democratic politics loses its legitimacy: witness the very urgent problem of global accountability. That is why the institutions of politics, finally, must be numerous and complex: parliaments, voting procedures, courts, civic action, all the venues of public discourse. The crucial evaluation concerning these institutions will be: do they contribute to the goals of the practice, and do they foster the social roles of citizen and leader?

In sum, there is no reason we cannot view politics as this kind of human practice, a context susceptible to ethical analysis. There is, therefore, no reason we cannot find within its rather special version of human flourishing a list of relevant character traits that underwrite politics. There is furthermore no reason that this conception of politics should ever be limited in scope. That is, because it addresses politics as a basic fact of social life, rather than as part of specific ethnic or national history, and does so without demanding virtues that are excessively particular in origin, it remains open-ended on the crucial issue of extension. It could provide a blueprint for citizenship on a global scale.

Having said all that, what is a list of relevant political virtues for this conception of politics? With some trepidation, I provide a provisional list here.

CITIZEN	LEADER
love of self	love of honour
civility	courage
decency	prudence
fairness	compromise
limited self-interest	opportunism

suspicion	appropriate ruthlessness
tolerance	charisma
reasonableness	unsentimentality
sensitivity	sensitivity
respect	respect

The listed virtues of the leader may look at first blush pretty Machiavellian, including as they do some rather negative qualities. But an important measure of balance is achieved by the virtues of sensitivity and respect: the willingness to listen to the claims of all citizens, and treat them all as equally valid in terms of their ability to make claims. A leader must be opportunistic not for personal gain but in order to maximize the available solutions to political disputes. He or she will use the means that are available, consistent with the other virtues. Sentimental appeals are rejected not because sentiment is valueless but because political decisions must be made on a basis that can be reasonably defended to all citizens, not only those of a particular disposition. Sometimes, finally, this need to forge compromises and make hard choices will require a measure of ruthlessness, courage, and charisma.

The "hard" or "realistic" virtues of the leader are also importantly balanced by the matching virtues of the citizen, especially in his or her critical and suspicious aspects. Citizens must be vigilant and aggressive in their assessment of leaders' actions; they must be, equally, vigorous in their demands for accountability. Yet suspicion is not all the citizen must exercise. He or she must also exhibit sensitivity to the claims of fellow citizens, even while pursuing self-interest so that personal goods can be maximized, consistent with the pursuit of those goods by others. This kind of citizen is actively participating in politics, though not always in governance *per se*. That is, because the political discourse of justice is central to the end of politics as defined earlier, all citizens are here understood as participants in that discourse. That, indeed, is what their citizenship consists in.

We need not demand that citizens become strong republicans on the ancient model, united around a shared conception of the public good. Any dangers of homogeneity aside, that notion simply will not apply very well to our multiplex world. But citizens must participate to the extent of feeling a duty – moral, not legal – to make their justice claims known, and to listen to those of others. (Also, where relevant, to *help* those who cannot make claims easily or at all, as, for example, in the duty to insist that education and literacy are fundamental to democratic politics.) By no means does this duty to listen rule out the insight that citizens' interests may be determined only through interaction with fellow citizens, or that some differences will remain after, may even be exacerbated by, much public discussion. Civility, conceived as openness to the arguments of others combined with a measure of restraint on my own arguments, captures the necessarily deliberative elements of inclusive political life.

There are at least two *prima facie* problems with these lists of virtues, of course. First, I do not know whether they are complete. Second, I do not know the precise hierarchical relationship among these traits, if there is one. (In my own defence, Aristotle was weak on this point too, when it came to his list of ethical virtues.) Still, there will be relationships of priority we can discern. For example, the leader's love of honour represents his commitment to the idea of a just society and his willingness to work for it. That will place some kind of effective constraint on the exercise of other, less attractive virtues like appropriate ruthlessness and coldness, even if it does specify a relationship of necessary priority.

The virtues of the leader reflect the role of a mediator between conflicting citizenly interests. At the same time, the citizen watches the leader intently, and, while willing to tolerate imperfections in both government and other citizens (hence the virtues of tolerance and reasonableness), he or she must be vigilant and vocal if the leader is to be kept in check (hence the virtue of suspicion). The shared virtue of respect, which like sensitivity appears on both lists, suggests a shared commitment to the idea of political association combined with a recognition that other citizens are partners in that commitment.

The details of a political context may also vary in such a way that we might want to add or subtract one or two of these traits. Though there are arguably some Aristotelian and republican elements in it, this list reflects a conception of politics that is significantly social-democratic. Which is to say a conception in which politics is viewed as an important aspect of a fully human life but also as a means to higher ends, namely, the ability of individuals to pursue their divergent visions of human flourishing with a minimum of interference and a maximum of social harmony. This conception of political virtues suggests that Role Seven is crucial, arching over the other roles we might inhabit. It does not suggest that Role Seven is the only role, and any other human activity of lesser value.

Insofar as politics serves an end beyond itself and the leader's love of honour is instrumental to that end, I suppose this vision of the political virtues may seem more pre-modern than modern. All the same, such a conception of politics incorporates modern political realism, takes stock of it, we might say, to the extent that we do not, under this conception, despise the ambition of political animals. Instead, we exploit that ambition to larger and better purposes, and keep our leaders in check so that our interests and desires are always in play. As citizens we recognize, in a fashion more Aristotelian than Machiavellian but somehow a mixture of both, that the love of honour in proper measure is no bad thing, is indeed an appropriate and important virtue. In that subset of citizens who take on the business of government, it is an indispensable one.

Now, this may suggest a picture of politics that is no better, in its optimism about political power, than any fairy tale. Politics, some will say, is always about the creation of group interest and, in contemporary electoral politics anyway, the existence of party machines and dollar-pumping business interests that systematically exclude citizens from the decision-making process. Hence the common defection of ordinary people from the duties of citizenship, including the minimal one of voting. But the cynicism behind such a view of politics is part of what makes its hold on our political system so tenacious: this is part of the dominant rhetoric of inevitability, which robs us of more agency by the day. Without a sense that citizens can do more than they do now, can make the world responsive to their desires, there is no reason for them to consider trying. I do not wish to give the impression that creating virtuous democratic citizens and leaders will be easy, especially as the political forum we must deal with expands in scope. Rather, I am suggesting what we need to understand about ourselves as citizens before we can even set about that task.

Even Plato, who appears to drive a wedge between the honour-lover (the timocrat) and the philosopher, in fact supports the view that the timocrat's love of honour is an effective aristocratic curb on tyranny. Tyranny gains a foothold, in Plato's famous political pathology in Book VIII of the *Republic*, not in timocracies but in democracies. Here the love of honour has degenerated first into love of money (plutocracy) and then into aimless love of freedom (what Plato means by democracy). Now the private pursuits of citizens create an atmosphere in which political ambition is despised and power is pursued only by that dangerous criminal lunatic, the tyrant.

The honour-lover, by contrast, though he falls short of the philosophical life, is at least oriented to goods: his pursuit of honour is achieved, as in Machiavelli, only by securing peace, security, prosperity, and liberty for his citizens. He cares about justice not, perhaps, because he has a vision of its eternal Form, but rather because he struggles to put it in political practice. Indeed, because the timocracy is the first degenerate form after the ideal city, and the strong subtext of the *Republic* is that this ideal city will remain impossible, we might go so far as to suggest that Plato believed the timocrat would be, here and now, the best available ruler. The philosopher might know – as many of us today profess to know – how *best* to rule; but he lacks the peculiar ambition, the willingness to go public, to force and cajole, as well as persuade, a sometimes reluctant electorate to do what is in their own best interest.

An honour-loving leader requires, significantly, a certain kind of activist and participatory citizen. These citizens – critical but civil, committed but never devoid of self-interest – are precisely those who can demand and accept the leader of specifically political virtue. Here the idea of political virtue is fulfilled, because it is neither an unrealistic account of angelic democratic citizens nor an unpleasantly realistic account of vulpine politicians and their vegetating charges. Recent conflicts between citizens and their leaders show that these countervailing virtues are not flourishing. We have no lack of critical citizens, certainly, but they are sometimes unwilling to give their leaders the ability to perform the tasks set for them. Instead, the leaders are ruthlessly evaluated according to a standard of private virtue that, inconsistent with their public role, they routinely fail to meet.

The so-called character issue in American politics, or the well-worn claims about public distrust of "political elites," are instances of this confusing insistence on the private realm's relevance to politics. We are here once more falling into the temptation of innocence, and doing so in a way that merely distracts attention from the real issues of global governance. So long as we judge our leaders according to the standard of purely ethical virtues and not political ones, they will be hamstrung, unable to take up the roles for which we have elected them. So long as we merely despise the elites we have ourselves created, the elites necessary to the task of governance, our political life will be systematically unstable. It may even, as Plato suggests, create an atmosphere of public chaos, the legacy of democratic desire, that will allow shadowy tyrants a foothold in our society. Power may become invisible and therefore unaccountable.

What I am arguing, then, is that we need to rehabilitate the virtues of politics on both sides. The idea behind any idea of political virtues is, as the philosopher John Rawls puts it, "that without a widespread participation in democratic politics by a vigorous and informed citizen body, and certainly with a general retreat into private life, even the most well-designed political institutions will fall into the hands of those who seek to dominate and impose their will through the state apparatus." Therefore, "the safety of democratic liberties requires the active participation of citizens who possess the political virtues needed to maintain a constitutional regime." I am working with those ideas foremost in mind.

Civic instability, our self-created confusion concerning the democratic and aristocratic elements of our political structure, reflects an ongoing crisis in political life, and one that will not be settled without a measure of self-evaluation. Certainly one reason we sometimes handle our elected leaders so harshly is that we cannot come to terms with our own complicity in their natures as negotiators and facilitators of our diverse interests. And, to be sure, many cynical people take advantage of this upon entering politics. Our discomfort with the quasi-Machiavellian virtues of leadership is a reflection not only of the kind of leader created, but of the kind of citizen presumed. We attack them because they are creatures of our own making, and we will continue to do so as long we fail to accept our necessarily political natures — even if those natures are not all, or the best, of what we consider ourselves.

From the other side, of course, the reactions of political leaders have themselves contributed to the atmosphere of distrust between leaders and led. From Plato onward, leaders have felt themselves to be special, the chosen few set apart for great things by fate or birth. Even in democratic nations, where we actively discourage such thoughts, our leaders sometimes betray an arrogance about themselves, coupled with a contempt for the electorate, that undermines the democratic process. In more extreme cases, this leads to paternalism, delusions of grandeur, and a sense that one is above the law. In benign cases, it leads to such things as "leadership studies," which preach the gospel of leadership as technology, something for the gifted to take up, like chess or crossword puzzles. Finding themselves judged by what they consider an inappropriate ethical standard, leaders then make self-serving appeals to morality as a means of duping an electorate for whom they have little respect. Finally, mistaking the political imperatives of social stability and justice for a personal imperative of re-election, they subvert all their leadership roles to the narrow one of protecting the incumbency.

Clearly this situation is socially unhealthy, but it is not inevitable. An emphasis on political virtues gives us the means to ameliorate it, for it clarifies the citizen's role in the creation of leaders and their peculiar standard of evaluation. Leaders are, and must be, judged in their purely political actions by a different, let us call it higher, standard than are private citizens. But these citizens also have a public responsibility that is different from their private ones, and we cannot afford to forget that when we think about our citizenship. In politics, especially in trying to make this into a world we want, we must think beyond ourselves; we cannot simply reproduce the thoughts that come to us in our other roles. Indeed, in rare but crucial periods of social restructuring, these politically virtuous citizens may take on an even more central role, no longer content to let the professionals thrash out the business of governance, but instead taking the society's basic assumptions back to the debating table. That is the highest duty of citizenship, one for which we must always be ready.

Some thinkers, and some citizens, believe the political virtues may be too demanding of ordinary democratic citizens. They argue that we should reserve our calls for virtue only to rare but important periods of deep debate, periods where the very idea of a nation is in question. They think we will be called to participate fully only once in a lifetime, if that. Yet this asks too little of democratic citizens, for it leaves governance open to the aspirations of rascals and demagogues, if not outright lunatics. And every nation is currently in question, if we only pay attention to the changes in the structures of global money and power. Our very *readiness* for such times of deep political debate is part of our duty as citizens; and a citizenry too much accustomed to letting government govern unopposed will not be able to rise to the higher challenge of expanding the very notion of what constitutes a society.

This is now the constant challenge before us. Far from being in play only during periods of radical reform, the political virtues facilitate a constant willingness to speak and act. Citizenship has periods of greater or lesser demand, certainly, but even for loosely organized democratic citizens of a post-national world it must be a central role, a focus of desirable and important virtues. Indeed, the more variable the structures of old-fashioned governance – the more current nation-states are subject to the influence of corporations and trade organizations – the more necessary it is that we see ourselves as citizens of the world, as sources of the only possible sovereignty in an expanding social universe of growing cultural diversity and threatening economic determinism. This is not the end of the matter (or the present argument). We must continue to exercise our citizenship wherever it is most effective, and remain mindful that social conditions are always changing in jagged and unequal ways. A virtue account can help to create the conditions of its own success, in a sort of virtuous circle where each action adds a brick to the public square that supports such actions; but it cannot, by itself, analyze the larger social forces that often act to constrain and distort our actions. For that we need to examine the details of our engagements with the materials of everyday life.

Does this mean, finally, that we are going to be friends with all our fellow citizens? Well, yes and no. We may dislike those to whom we owe a citizenly duty, and sometimes talking to them will only make us dislike them more. That does not diminish the duty, or the virtues that nurture its exercise. The relationship between citizens is friendly in the sense of feeling obligation and commitment to others — obligation and commitment that go beyond the abstract legalism of rights, using the faculty of imagination instead to make a connection between people united by, if nothing else, their human vulnerability. This kind of connection, which grounds the larger goals of inclusiveness and justice, is a significant achievement. It is certainly a great deal more than we now have, when we often simply refuse to see in another person the same aspiration to belong, to be at home, that we know we feel in ourselves.

How can we go on refusing? Our deeper, more personal friendships are a clue to what citizenship demands on the larger scale. In particular we remember the insight that not every form of social commitment is ruled by bargaining and exchange. We do not give gifts in order to receive them in return. A friendless person would by the same token be a deficient citizen, not because such a person would be bereft of sense or reason, but because he or she would not understand what it means to care beyond personal advantage, beyond the bargaining of naked interest in a cold, exchange-dominated world. By a delicate mutual reinforcement, the healthy political realm is also the place where deeper friendships may find a ready soil. To that extent anyway, Aristotle was right: we are only fully ourselves in a thriving polis. The nature of that polis is now — or, rather, once more — in deep question.

We are never citizens only, but in the world as it is developing we must be citizens always. Are we equal to that challenge?

Chapter 4

SPACES AND DREAMS

In the flâneur, one might say, is reborn the sort of idler that
Socrates picked out from the Athenian marketplace to be his
interlocutor. Only, there is no longer a Socrates. And the slave
labour that guaranteed him his leisure has likewise
ceased to exist.

—Walter Benjamin, *The Arcades Project*

In the Arcades

There is, first of all, the matter of the mysterious briefcase. When Walter Benjamin killed himself in September 1940 in the small Pyrenees village of Port Bou he was, according to the woman who helped him across the mountains to reach the Franco-Spanish border, carrying "a large black briefcase." It was filled, he told her, with "the manuscript that *must* be saved."

Benjamin, on the run from the German authorities and already the veteran of two internments in camps near Nazi-occupied Paris, had apparently lugged the case all over southern France. Now, even with his bad heart and crippling chainsmoker's lungs, he was prepared to hoist it out of the temporary refuge of Marseilles and up through the nearly vertical vineyards and mountain paths that led over the mountain and into Spain. "You must understand that this briefcase is the most important thing to me," he said. "I cannot risk losing it. . . . It is more important than I am."

After nine hours of climbing and a night spent exposed on the mountainside, Benjamin reached Port Bou with his two travelling companions, a woman called Henny Gurland and her teenage son. There he discovered that the Spanish authorities would not allow him passage without a French exit visa. The affidavit he had from Max Horkheimer in New York, the scrap of academic letterhead with his name included as a research fellow, were not enough to let him through and on his way, eventually, to the United States. That meant an immediate return to France and, sooner or later, further incarceration by the Germans. Benjamin despaired. He could, *Casablanca*-style, hang around Marseilles until another route presented itself, as when, with his friend Dr. Fritz Fraenkel, he had absurdly disguised himself as a French sailor. But he was fifty-eight and getting too old for that kind of jape, not to mention too tired to make the arduous mountain crossing again.

He had told Lisa Fittko, his mountain guide, that "he had enough morphine on him to take his life several times over." The main thing, he said, was that the manuscript should be safe, out of the reach of the Gestapo. "Today," Fittko wrote forty years later, "when Walter Benjamin is considered one of the century's leading scholars and critics — today I am sometimes asked: What did he say about the manuscript? Did he discuss the contents? Did it develop a novel philosophical concept? Good God, I had my hands full steering my little group uphill; philosophy would have to wait till the downward side of the mountain was reached."

On September 25, 1940, the day of his death, Benjamin wrote his last letter. It was addressed to his close friend Theodor Adorno, then in New York, having left his research post in England the year before to aid Horkheimer with the American version of the Institute for Social Research, which the pair had founded in Frankfurt a decade earlier. Henny Gurland copied out the letter in her own hand and then destroyed the original to protect the dying Benjamin. "In a situation presenting no way out," Benjamin wrote to Adorno, "I have no other choice but to make an end of it. It is in a small village in the Pyrenees, where no one knows me, that my life will come to a close. . . . There is not enough time remaining for me to write all the letters I would like to write."

The last line is especially poignant, since Benjamin's epistolary prowess was renowned among his friends, who included most of the leading French and German intellectuals of the interbellum years. His courtly letters were part of a vibrant cultural conversation that included Horkheimer, Adorno, Gerschem Scholem, Siegfried Kracauer, Hannah Arendt, Raymond Aron, Georges Bataille, and dozens of lesser lights, and that provided the displaced Benjamin with the intellectual community and solidarity the crumbling European world of the 1930s could not. Benjamin is often identified with the Frankfurt School of critical social theory, and his work indeed began appearing in their house journal *Zeitschrift für Sozialforschung* in the early 1930s. But his interests ranged wider and were vastly more eclectic. He flirted with kabbalistic mysticism with Scholem, discussed film theory with Kracauer, and fell under the influence of Bertolt Brecht. He was a Berliner by birth and temperament, yet he spent the bulk of his mature working life exiled in Paris, writing and speaking in German and French and, at the end, in preparation for his American life, in English.

He was, in short, a child of his times – a citizen of a shattered world. And he died by his own hand just as that world fell into deep crisis.

As a German stylist Benjamin possessed great charm and precision, and he wrote profusely for scholarly journals and newspapers alike. (An early attempt to secure an academic post was blocked, putting him in the good company of the philosophers Hume and Spinoza, among others, in making his intellectual way without benefit of a university position, by his literary efforts alone.) His diary of a visit to Moscow in 1926 is justly celebrated, and his memoirs of his childhood in Berlin around 1900, when he was eight, and another depicting his young adulthood in the city, are works of singular power. All his writings show a man consumed by minutiae, the bits and pieces of everyday life: coins and stamps and things lying on shelves, the gloves and dolls and buttons for sale on the street.

He is melancholy and enthusiastic in almost equal measure, and as his little book of sketches and aphorisms, *One-Way Street* (1928), amply documents, he could be wry and funny about the sad lot of the writer and intellectual in a world ruled by philistines and complacent academic drones. "Principles of the Weighty Tome, or How to Write Fat Books," he writes there: "1. The whole composition must be permeated with a protracted and wordy exposition of the initial plan. 2. Terms are to be included for conceptions that, except in this definition, appear nowhere in the whole book. 3. Conceptual distinctions laboriously arrived at in the text are to be obliterated again in the relevant notes." Already, in that early work, he saw the street as a metaphorical space, a scene of political discovery through signs, advertising, stamp shops, and displays of mechanical toys.

At his very best, Benjamin is a writer to bear comparison, in tone, with his hero Kafka and, in close attention to the texture of daily experience, with another of his idols, Proust. He could be as tart as the Viennese satirist Karl Kraus, whom he greatly admired. (Among other virtues, Kraus was responsible for labelling the proto-Nazi camp followers of Oswald Spengler's *The Decline of the West* – in German, *Der Untergang des Abendlandes* – the "untergangsters.") Benjamin's prose, especially early on, is oblique and witty, two traits almost wholly absent in the other associates of the Frankfurt School. He has a talent for pith almost on the level of a sprightly Nietzsche, another exile from academe – though Nietzsche's was self-imposed. Susan Sontag has aptly described Benjamin's style as "freeze-frame baroque." He loved compact, shimmering sentences, arresting but sometimes elaborate metaphors, and he practised the aphoristic form as a matter of both inclination and method. "All the decisive blows are struck left-handed," Benjamin writes in *One-Way Street*. "Ambiguity replaces authenticity in all things." We understand most when we have not set out to achieve understanding.

But Benjamin is most famous today for two works, one a relatively short article and the other a mammoth project, uncompleted at his death and perhaps, in its nature, impossible to complete. The article is "The Work of Art in the Age of Mechanical Reproduction," a widely influential argument about the way multiple copies or broadcasts of a given work dispel the "aura" of bourgeois sacredness that falls over art in high capitalism. Much anthologized, much disputed – these days mechanical reproduction seems simply to create a different sort of aura, the kitschification of art into cheap gallery-shop gewgaws that, in another mood, Benjamin would have enjoyed picking through – this article shows Benjamin the social and cultural philosopher working near the top of his game. It lacks the warmth and humanness of his earliest work, perhaps, but it is that rare thing, a wholly accessible original argument, novel theory advanced with ready examples and a salutary absence of jargon.

The book, the monumental *Passagen-Werk*, or *The Arcades Project* – first published in German in the 1970s as part of Benjamin's collected works, and available in a complete English translation only in 1999 – is, by contrast, an intellectual folly, a massive and spectacular ruin. (Architectural images are common in describing this sprawling, challenging work.) An ambitious, even grandiose, reading of the logic of capitalism through the Arcades, the covered walkways that had been such a prominent feature of mid-1800s Paris, the *Project* had occupied Benjamin for thirteen years and had grown into an overwhelming obsession during the last decade of his life. For Benjamin, these little urban spaces where Parisians daily (and nightly) strolled to view luxury items, posters, panoramas, and each other, are the master trope in a close archaeological reading of modernity, his *Urgeschichte* or primal history of the late industrial age. Organized into numerous subject-driven mini-albums called "convolutes" (the irony is intended), the *Project* aims to be a comprehensive illumination of the daily life of an era, when Paris was, as he put it, "capital of the nineteenth century." Everything from boredom to fashion to political revolution is covered, everyone from the *flâneur* to the cocotte to the utopian anarchist walks out of the gaslit dimness of the nineteenth-century Arcades and into the light of Benjamin's probing, fascinated gaze.

It would be fittingly romantic if the heavy black briefcase Benjamin carried across the Pyrenees had indeed contained the voluminous notes and papers of *The Arcades Project,* snatched from the Gestapo with a singular man's last ounces of strength. But in truth the materials for this monumental work remained in Paris where Benjamin had laboriously compiled them. Georges Bataille, then working as a librarian at the Bibliothèque Nationale, Benjamin's habitual place of work, hid them from the Nazis for the duration of the war and sent them on to Adorno after 1945 when Paris was once more in French hands. Remarkably, nothing further was ever heard of the mysterious briefcase, or the important manuscript it supposedly contained. Benjamin's final possessions, listed by authorities upon his death, include "a man's watch, a pipe, six photographs, an X-ray picture, glasses, various letters, magazines, and a few other papers whose contents are unknown." The briefcase has to be accepted as an enduring mystery, or perhaps it must be reinterpreted metaphorically: a token of everydayness carried improbably into a death zone, the banal symbol of a desperate man's intellectual burdens, now gone forever, its purpose served.

Benjamin's death might perhaps have been avoided — what suicide might not? — but it is not quite the tale of noble sacrifice for philosophical truth that some *post facto* romantics have wanted it to

be. The very day after he overdosed on morphine, the order nullify-
ing refugee visas was rescinded, and Benjamin's companions were
allowed to leave France. Complaints, prominently from Hannah
Arendt, that more could have been done to help him over the border are understandable but apparently misplaced. So this is, rather,
the painful story of a good man caught up in the political events of
his time, unable or unwilling to adapt to circumstances ruled by
deception, slyness, and double-dealing. "You had to learn to slip
through holes, to turn, to wriggle your way out of this ever-changing
maze, if you wanted to survive," Lisa Fittko wrote of what things
were like in the south of France with the Nazis in Paris, the French
state transplanted to Vichy, and the Gardes Mobiles all over the border countryside. "But Benjamin was not a wriggler."

He was not. Stateless, a citizen of the republic of letters but of no
other when membership mattered a great deal, Benjamin succumbed to the forces of history. Perhaps Arendt is right that his
Institute friends could have rendered more concrete aid than a letter
of affiliation, could have exerted themselves more thoroughly from
their comfort in New York. But the evidence shows they were help-
ing Benjamin for months, were eagerly awaiting his arrival. Perhaps,
sadly and more likely, Benjamin made his too-hasty exit with a
resigned sense that life and work had overtaken him, rendering him
too weary to continue. As with the briefcase puzzle, there are no
answers to these mysteries now. Like the briefcase, and like so many
other desperate people in that short autumn of 1940, Benjamin
leaves the stage with the scene unfinished, the project incomplete.

———

Benjamin's basic plan for *The Arcades Project* was a stroke of genius,
his life's Big Idea. In an early letter to Benjamin, an enthusiastic
young Adorno called it his friend's "destined contribution to *prima
philosophia*," his major undertaking, and it can hardly be surprising

that the work occupied the older man for thirteen frustrating years. Benjamin actually made two runs at the *Project*, the first in 1927 when he was planning a newspaper essay on the subject, and then again in the early 1930s. What began as a nice idea for a medium-length essay had by that time become, as Benjamin put it, "the theatre of all my struggles and all my ideas."

The dandy, the *flâneur*, the collector, the gambler – these figures parade through the Arcades, and *The Arcades Project,* bestowing a strange form of immediacy on the world Benjamin struggles to bring to life. Here long-forgotten minor revolutionaries rub up against the insistent respectability of petit bourgeois shopkeepers, together forging, sometimes bloodily, a modern republic in the long wake of 1789. Early photographic pioneers like Nadar and Bisson and Daguerre, writers like Verlaine and Laforgue, construct the challenging, unignorable aesthetics of modernism. A long section on Charles Baudelaire, using him as a lens on modernity, is a book in its own right (and has been published as such). Benjamin's purpose is not merely historical or literary, however. It is only through a devoted attention to the details of objects and faces in the modern urban scene, he argues, that the commodity fetish of capitalism can be effectively dispelled.

And only thus that a certain kind of emancipation is possible: use value and exchange value make way for connoisseur value. Collecting is the tactic of choice for a new kind of revolutionary, according to the man who hoarded books and bibelots, who scribbled incessantly in notebooks (collections of notions, quotations), and kept a numbered list of every book he had ever read. "The collector dreams his way not only into a distant or bygone world but also into a better one," Benjamin writes, " – one in which, to be sure, human beings are no better provided with what they need than in the everyday world, but in which things are freed from the drudgery of being useful." Collecting and connoisseurship, perhaps unexpectedly, prove to be politically effective.

Many features of everyday life presented themselves to Benjamin's fascinated scrutiny as he attempted to work out the logic of these transformations. And many metaphors have been employed to describe the resulting pile of quotations, annotations, aphorisms, and miniature essays. Benjamin was influenced by modern poets and early film pioneers, especially the Surrealists, and claimed to be seeking something of the dislocating effect of montage. Breton's *Nadja* and, even more so, Aragon's *Le Paysan de Paris*, taught him to see the city in a strange, diffuse light. But the voices of the various historical figures are too clear for montage to adequately describe the sheafs of material that he arranged in a peculiar alphabetical sequence. A better image is that of the dream, or the phantasmagoria, itself a persistent theme of the *Project*. The Arcades are a kind of social dreamscape, not least in the forms of phantasmagoric popular entertainments that occurred within them: the illuminated dioramas and magic lantern shows and spinning zoetrope projectors – all the early precursors of moving pictures. So it is no surprise that Benjamin saw in the jumbled pieces of Arcades life the residue of a collective dream, and attempted, despite objections from Adorno and his more orthodox Marxist colleagues, to offer a psychoanalytic interpretation of that dream.

Here, as understood in traditional Marxist critique, the surface experiences of everyday life are a "superstructure" riding atop the material conditions and relations of production characteristic of an age. The scenes and images of the Arcades are clues to what lies beneath. "The economic conditions under which society exists," Benjamin says, "are expressed in the superstructure, precisely as, with the sleeper, an overfull stomach finds not its reflection but its expression in the contents of dreams, which, from a causal point of view, it may be said to 'condition.'"

That social dream was actually a form of somnambulism, because in everyday life we always walk as well as dream, and the site of our collective sleepwalking was of course the street. "Streets are the dwelling places of the collective," Benjamin writes in one version of his introduction to the *Project*. "The collective is an eternally wakeful, eternally agitated being that – in the space between the building fronts – lives, experiences, understands, and invents as much as individuals do within the privacy of their own four walls." Years earlier, in his memoir entitled *A Berlin Chronicle*, Benjamin had described his own education through the "dreamy recalcitrance" of his walks in that city's centre. Now he sees that "[m]ore than anywhere else, the street reveals itself in the arcade as the furnished and familiar interior of the masses." Here people stroll and shop, slowly moving between the tasks of mundane life; or sometimes, more significantly, strolling becomes an end in itself. Thus the importance in this streetscape of the *flâneur*, the strolling idler. "For the *flâneur*, a transformation takes place with respect to the street: it leads him through a vanished time. He strolls down the street; for him, every street is precipitous," Benjamin writes. "An intoxication comes over the man who walks long and aimlessly through the streets. With each step, the walk takes on greater momentum; ever weaker grow the temptations of bistros, of shops, of smiling women, ever more irresistible the magnetism of the next street corner, of a distant square in the fog, of the back of a woman walking before him."

Yet within this transforming excitement there is, too, a kind of languor, a pose of habitual and superior ennui that is worn proudly and ostentatiously, like an expensive cloak. "Boredom is a warm gray fabric lined on the inside with the most lustrous of silks," writes Benjamin at one point in the brilliant convolute on boredom, revealing himself as the most acute philosopher of the condition since Schopenhauer. "In this fabric we wrap ourselves when we dream. We are at home then in the arabesques of its lining." The stroll and this cultivated listlessness are thus intimately related, the slow pace the outward sign of the *flâneur*'s inner grace. "*Flânerie* is the rhythmics of this slumber," Benjamin concludes. "In 1839, a rage for tortoises overcame Paris. One can well imagine the elegant set mimicking the gait of this creature more easily in the Arcades than on the boulevards. Boredom is always the external surface of unconscious events. For that reason, it has appeared to the great dandies as a mark of distinction."

Fittingly, the major literary success of the *Project* is its ability precisely to induce in the reader a peculiar oneiric attention, a watchful dreaminess – even a sort of illuminating boredom. Details wash past in waves; quotations loop in and out of the elliptical, jagged arguments; polished sentences pitch up from the morass like foil-wrapped sweets discovered on the beach. (In *One-Way Street*, Benjamin had written: "Quotations in my work are like wayside robbers who leap out armed and relieve the stroller of his conviction.") The best comparisons are not really to other books that work the same kind of ground, like Roland Barthes's *Mythologies* or Marshall McLuhan's *Mechanical Bride* – both collections of short meditations on the detritus of everyday consumer life – but rather to works of visual art: Peter Beard's overwhelming pastiches of image and text, for instance, everywhere scribbled with notes and comments and revisions; or, maybe better, Joseph Cornell's meditative, surreal collisions of disparate objects within the conventional, even banal, medium of the box. Like them, *The Arcades Project* spills out of its container to induce a weirdly vertiginous response in the viewer. It is a cabinet of wonders that ever threatens to burst the confines of two covers, to become instead a three-ring circus of the mind.

This is not, to be sure, quite what the Institute for Social Research had in mind when they initially agreed to finance Benjamin's work on the *Project*. When Adorno convinced Max Horkheimer to put Benjamin on a kind of academic retainer – he was scraping by in Paris on a thousand francs a month or less, constantly asking, in the most cultivated ways, for more money – he wanted Benjamin to, as it were, get serious. Adorno and Benjamin had been friends since the late 1920s, and in 1929 Benjamin had travelled to Frankfurt and Königstein and read to Horkheimer, Adorno, and

Adorno's future wife, Gretel Karplus, some sections of the work he was then calling "Paris Arcades: A Dialectical Fairyland." These sections, which survive as notes on expensive handmade paper, plus a short and even earlier essay written as a draft of the original newspaper article, are the earliest versions of the *Project*. There Benjamin was thinking of the work as, in spirit, a continuation of *One-Way Street* and the prose has his unique signature.

"In the crowded arcades of the boulevards, as in the semi-deserted arcades of the Rue Saint-Denis," he writes in the newspaper draft, "umbrellas and canes are displayed in serried ranks: a phalanx of colorful crooks. Many are the institutes of hygiene, where gladiators are wearing orthopedic belts and bandages wind around the white bellies of mannequins. In the windows of the hairdressers, one sees the last women with long hair; they sport richly undulating masses, petrified coiffures. How brittle appears the stonework of the walls beside them and above: crumbling papier-mâché! 'Souvenirs' and bibelots take on a hideous aspect; the odalisque lies in wait next to the inkwell: priestesses in knitted jackets raise aloft ashtrays like vessels of holy water. . . . Over stamps and letter boxes roll balls of string and of silk. Naked puppet bodies with bald heads wait for hairpieces and attire. Combs swim about, frog-green and coral-red, as in an aquarium; trumpets turn to conches, ocarinas to umbrella handles; and lying in the fixative pan from a photographer's darkroom is birdseed."

This delicious jumble of Magrittian images – sacred cigarette ashes, swimming combs, metamorphosing seashell-horns – is the opening flourish in what would prove, over time, an impossible task. "These items on display are a rebus," Benjamin told the group in Frankfurt, "and how one ought to read here the birdseed kept in the fixative pan from a darkroom, the flower seeds beside the binoculars, the broken screws atop the musical score, and the revolver above the goldfish bowl – is right on the tip of one's tongue." Benjamin wanted, as we all do when something is situated there, to get

that reading off the tip of his tongue and out into the world of discourse. His colleagues wanted it too, perhaps even more than himself; in the beginning they were enthusiastic and, what's more,
prepared to offer money. But, like grad-school examination boards
everywhere, they wanted more theory, more direction, more *work*.
They could see the charm and potential of the "Arcades"; what they
could not see was the political theory. What was the solution to the
rebus? In response, Benjamin proposed the notion of the *dialectical
image*. In the spirit of Marxist *Kulturkritik* and *Ideologiekritik*, he told
them, he would read the images of the Arcades as part of a larger
social process.

Even so, he could not quite part with the notion of the dream.
"The new, dialectical method of doing history teaches us to pass in
spirit – with the rapidity and intensity of dreams – through what
has been, in order to experience the present as a waking world,
a world to which every dream at last refers," he wrote later. "It
is at this moment that the historian takes up . . . the task of dream
interpretation."

Energized and with a measure of financial security from his initial
sponsorship, chastened a little by the demands of his colleagues,
Benjamin now returned to Paris and began work on the new,
expanded version of the *Project*. What he did not anticipate, perhaps,
is the fecundity of dreams. Dreams are evidence that we are creatures who produce more meaning than we can ourselves understand. They are surplus texts squeezed out of the unsealed edges of
consciousness. In addition to this, though, dreams are mercurial and
wispy: there is so much to them that we cannot bring within even an
adept interpretation, even given world enough and time. Who has
not had the experience of relating a dream to someone – professional
listener or generous friend – only to realize that the story being

related is just one tiny part of a whole epic narrative, which is quickly drifting out of the mind's reach or changing under the pressure of our telling into something not quite what it was before?

Benjamin had of course sensed these difficulties with the prospect of interpreting the dreamscape of an entire social epoch, even before he had immersed himself in the *Project*. "The narration of dreams brings calamity," he had written a half decade earlier in *One-Way Street*, "because a person still half in league with the dream world betrays it in his words and must incur its revenge. He has outgrown the protection of dreaming naiveté, and in laying clumsy hands on his dream visions he surrenders himself." Benjamin's suggested antidote there: always eat breakfast before attempting to recount a dream. You will be sufficiently diverted by the pleasure of food to allow the dream to drift away and dissipate, as it should. But this bluff, ironic advice is nowhere to be found now that Benjamin is sitting down with his piles of quotations and historical anecdotes, his images and sheafs of everyday details, to tackle the *Project*.

"One can easily imagine that he approached their composition as he would a festive occasion," the Benjamin scholar Rolf Tiedemann writes of this stage of the *Project*, perhaps overestimating a little the average writer's level of glad confidence. "But he did not get very far. The discrete texts, whose sequence he did not establish, are soon interspersed with and finally overgrown by quotations and bibliographic notes, and in places with commentary." Benjamin could not always let the quotations speak for themselves, but neither could he confine himself to a traditional essay on the topic of the Arcades. As with Montaigne's *Essays*, the watchful and deeply engaged author was never long absent from his text. Benjamin does not speak of himself, as he did in earlier works, but he cannot forbear from more and longer additions. Like Montaigne, his obsession makes ultimately for the creation of a new literary form, in this case the essay-in-fragments, a huge fractured poem. "The fragments of the *Passagen-Werk* can be compared to the materials used in building a house, the outline of which has just been marked in the ground or whose foundations are just being dug," Tiedemann notes. Though he hardly realized it, Benjamin was in the process of realizing one of his own aphorisms. "It is common practice in baroque literature to pile up fragments incessantly," he wrote in the 1920s; this is how allegory works, and "allegories are, in the realm of thought, what ruins are in the realm of things."

None of this halts him in his endeavours – on the contrary. Benjamin, as his friend Scholem once noted, is the most patient of men, and he now embarks on a decade of work, sifting and collating and commenting, during which he is forever in the position of waiting for crucial details to fall into their proper place. He becomes a supplicant before his own work. The dream of the Arcades stands before him like the rich history of Paris, the acknowledged world capital of the industrial age, like the materials of a house waiting to be built.

Key elements seem to stay relatively fixed in that dream house, all of them significantly spatial or architectural. They are the importance of ironwork and glass as building materials characteristic of the age, technical innovations that made the Arcades possible, not to mention the Crystal Palace and the Eiffel Tower; the role of gaslight, plush fashions, and sumptuous furniture coverings on the languorous attitude and slow pace of *flânerie* in the crowded streets; and the boulevard scheme of Baron Haussmann, which erased whole sections of Paris in the new grand prospects of the modern city – and, incidentally, made barricades that much more difficult to realize in street fighting. ("With the Haussmannization of Paris," remarks Benjamin, "the phantasmagoria was rendered in stone.") But as time passes Benjamin begins to add new elements to the structure as well: large chunks about the political visionaries Saint-Simon and Fourier, long excursions into the 1848 uprising and the bloody Paris Commune of 1891, close reading of the dozens of partisan newspapers and *feuilletonist* serial publications of the century's highly charged second half. The convolutes multiply, the stacks of apposite quotations grow, the *Project* expands, sprawls, splits, and recombines.

Adorno, meanwhile, is increasingly insistent with his demands to know how the work is progressing. The correspondence between the two men, which spans the lifetime of *The Arcades Project,* is marked by a scholarly formality that hides a fierce intellectual struggle. They are "Herr Benjamin" and "Herr Wiesengrund" (Adorno's other surname) to each other until late in 1936, when they have been writing and visiting each other for almost a decade. Even after that Benjamin consistently addresses his friend "Teddie" with the formal German pronoun *Sie*. By contrast, Adorno, in his early to middle thirties during the time of their most important exchanges, is hardly deferential to a man eleven years his senior and already an established and widely successful writer. He is forever taking Benjamin to task in the most appalling way, and has the rigid arrogance of a young man certain of his own brilliance. He imperiously demands Benjamin's support in various projects of his own and, beneath a measure of evident respect, treats him with a genial familiarity that borders on contempt. "I feel that our theoretical disagreement is not really a discord between us," he explains to Benjamin after a lengthy and scathing letter about a draft of the Arcades essay, "and that my own task is to hold your arm steady until the Brechtian sun has finally sunk beneath its exotic waters." Benjamin, ever polite, replies with "thanks for your lengthy and instructive letter."

Adorno was concerned about the negative influence of Brecht and others on Benjamin, seeing them as enemies of the *Project*'s true nature. He was a vicious and remorseless judge of people and work, and his letters are filled with compact denunciations of Benjamin's friends: Scholem's woolly mysticism, Ernst Bloch's self-cancelling cleverness. Adorno's habitual pseudonym in the *Zeitschrift für Sozialforschung* from these years, adopted to protect himself from the German authorities during his own exile in England, is unintentionally apt, indeed unimprovable: he called himself Hektor Rottweiler.

When Siegfried Kracauer published a book on Jacques Offenbach and his circle in Paris – a book quoted a number of times in the Arcades materials – Adorno writes to Benjamin that it is so bad they must seriously consider cutting Kracauer from their acquaintance altogether. The book, he says, is "crassly erroneous," its preface "shameless and idiotic," the social observations "no more than old wives' tales" full of "foolishness and superficiality." Indeed, "the piece is so irredeemably terrible that it could easily become a best-seller," and "if Kracauer really does identify with this book, then he has definitely erased himself from the list of writers to be taken at all seriously." Benjamin replies that, yes, the book is bad, "nothing but a messy box of chocolates," but gently suggests that a policy of total ostracism is probably impractical.

Benjamin himself was surprisingly unperturbed by Adorno's attack-dog mentality and near-constant cavilling, especially about the lack of dialectical precision in the new version of the *Project*. Henri Lonitz, who edited the first published version of the correspondence between the two thinkers, speculates on the roots of connection binding exiled German intellectuals to one another in these trying times. "The correspondence reveals the enormous significance of the practical and cultural solidarity which Benjamin and Adorno shared with one another during the period of their intellectual isolation," Lonitz argues. Both were, for various reasons, enduring a period of social and cultural exile during the 1930s. Neither had been accepted by the academic establishment within Germany. (Adorno failed to land a university position too, despite a good dissertation in his original field, musicology.) With one, Benjamin, an "alien body" among the French intellectual elite in Paris and the other, Adorno, slogging away on a supplementary philosophy qualification at Oxford, the two agreed that "maintaining a vital outlook" was essential. It was, Lonitz acknowledges, an outlook "which a conventional middle-of-the-road wisdom would easily interpret as one of ruthless critique."

Adorno's ruthlessness sometimes approached malice. Were the stakes really high enough to justify it? Lonitz thinks so: "This ruthlessness with regard to the essential questions – and the authors regarded every one of their individual works as a contribution to a shared project of theoretical importance – expressed precisely that form of criticism which is equally and simultaneously a form of intellectual self-criticism." It was not simply that the pair found themselves distant from friends and family and routine academic security. They were also conscious, as they had to be, of the profound and alarming changes that were sweeping through Germany and the rest of Europe in the thirties. Leftist intellectuals like themselves could feel the ground shifting beneath their feet. Worse yet, they were Jewish. In such a context, Benjamin and Adorno, beset by hostile or indifferent external forces, watching the armies of darkness gathering on the horizon, were doing nothing less than trying to save their cultural and political world, a world of clear intellectual distinction and defensible aesthetic standards.

In any event, it was clearly as part of this mutual critique in the spirit of learned community that Benjamin submitted to what is, taken in total, a barrage of harsh and negative judgment. He had already, after the readings given in Frankfurt and Königstein, abandoned what he called the "romantic form" and "rhapsodic naiveté" of the original version of *The Arcades Project*. Perhaps stung by Adorno's comment that one could hardly write a history of the nineteenth century without mentioning Marx, he had begun a close reading of *Das Kapital*, a work which to that point he knew only through the rather tendentious interpretation of Georg Lukács, in his book *History and Class Consciousness*. In this often obscure work Lukács argues that the "reification" of objects and ideas as commodities is inevitable under capitalism and can only be opposed by creating general class consciousness, a sort of unified front of ideological resistance. Now, as Benjamin struggles to realize the original plan within a larger theoretical structure, he is sometimes flailing. His thoughts and annotations spread in a dozen directions. And Adorno is forever at his elbow, the sharpest of sharp critics. Is he a muse, calling out the best in a gifted but undisciplined writer? Or is he a *bête noire*, tirelessly finding fault with every hard-won piece of progress?

Adorno is not a doctrinaire Marxist – he mockingly says his objections to Benjamin's methods are not about "laxity and eclecticism," standard charges of the Third International. But he is a committed theoretician, and he wants Benjamin to deliver the goods on the spirit of modernity in the form of precise theory. At this time he is himself moving away from the traditional musicology of his early career and, together with the other Frankfurt theorists, hammering out in bits and pieces a complex social theory of our cultural experience under conditions of mass production. In the early 1930s Horkheimer had published an article sketching the difference between traditional and critical social theory, the latter aimed not simply at analyzing existing social relations but at dispelling ideology and fomenting social transformation. This article is considered the founding statement of the Frankfurt School, as they were later known, and the distinction between traditional and critical theory became the unofficial manifesto of the group. It is, indeed, the basis of activist critical theory still.

But theory has its limits, especially to a writer like Benjamin who was so taken with detail, whose stated aim is "to assemble large-scale constructions out of the smallest and most precisely cut components. Indeed, to discover in the analysis of the small individual moment the crystal of the total event." *The Arcades Project* is best conceived not as social theory at all, whatever the degree of precision, but rather as a complex kind of monadology, a cultural hall of mirrors in which every surface, however small, reflects all the others. For Benjamin, a single effluvium of everyday life could contain in its essence the whole of the relations of production. In *One-Way Street* he had defined imagination as the ability to "interpolate into the infinitesimally small." It is in the land of imagination that Benjamin wishes to dwell.

That was too dreamy for Adorno. Two of his letters to Benjamin from the latter half of the 1930s stand out from the usual mixture between them of running commentary, gossip, travel plans, discussions of money, and complaints about publishers and editors – the standard fare between writers who are also friends. One, from 1935, is Adorno's lengthy response to an exposé of the entire *Arcades Project*; the other, from 1938, is a request, more in sorrow than anger, that Benjamin seriously revise an essay on Baudelaire, drawn from the Arcades material, which he had submitted for publication in the *Zeitschrift für Sozialforschung*. Both are filled with intricate but fundamental objections to Benjamin's work.

"If you transpose the dialectical image into consciousness as a 'dream,' you not only rob the concept of its magic and thereby rather domesticate it," Adorno objects in the 1935 letter, "but it is also deprived of precisely that crucial and liberating potential that would legitimate it in materialist terms." Analyzing the Arcades images as if they were elements of a dream is not sufficiently rooted in the bigger picture, a picture that can only be sketched with more robust theoretical materials, in particular a social theory of how things are produced and make their way to market in the first place. Three years later, discussing Benjamin's remark that Baudelaire's poem "L'ame du vin" had been prompted by a new duty on wine, Adorno makes a similar point: "I regard it as methodologically inappropriate to give conspicuous individual features from the realm of the superstructure a 'materialist' turn by relating them immediately, and perhaps even causally, to certain corresponding features of the substructure. The materialist determination of cultural traits is only possible if it is mediated through the *total social process*."

Beneath the tortured Marxist rhetoric, Adorno's worry is simple. He thinks Benjamin is too taken with his bits and pieces, his jumble sale of images and caricatures. *He is not being sufficiently dialectical.* "If one wanted to put it rather drastically, one could say that your study is located at the crossroads of magic and positivism,"

Adorno tells his beleaguered friend. "This spot is bewitched. Only theory can break its spell." He reminds Benjamin that in the essay on mechanical reproduction he had himself argued tellingly against aesthetic aura, the halo of approval that clings to A-list works and figures. Adorno turns the tables on Benjamin now. "How," he asks, "does your critique of the auratic dimension relate to the auratic character of your own writings?" What had Benjamin produced except another dream, as opaque and fetching – but also as politically null – as the shadow-plays of the Arcades themselves?

Post-Cultural Identities

That is a genuine worry, for ourselves as much as for Benjamin in his struggle to complete *The Arcades Project*. It is a worry at the root of our constant engagements with the products of everyday life, the cultural and material achievements of the world in which we live. Do these engagements allow us to form an emancipatory consciousness, interpreting our dreams in the manner Benjamin suggested? Or do they simply bewitch us with their slick loveliness, leaving everything around them untouched and unthematized? More deeply, how could we ever translate a virtue account of citizenship into action if the social conditions of its realization are either absent or obscured by constant consumerist distractions and the illusion of freedom? Let us pursue these worries further, but with a slight change of direction. Consider for a moment a more contemporary reading of our cultural experience, two passages from Don DeLillo's 1985 novel *White Noise*.

The first is from the book's opening pages, where the narrator, a troubled professor of "Hitler Studies" at a midwestern American

university, describes the caravan of station wagons that bring privileged college students back to their dorms for the start of a new
autumn term (today the vehicles of choice would of course be Mer-
cedes suvs and Range Rovers):

> The students greet each other with comic cries and gestures
> of sodden collapse. Their summer has been bloated with
> criminal pleasures, as always. The parents stand sun-dazed
> near their automobiles, seeing images of themselves in every
> direction. The conscientious suntans. The well-made faces and
> wry looks. They feel a sense of renewal, of communal recog-
> nition. The women crisp and alert, in diet trim, knowing peo-
> ple's names. Their husbands content to measure out the time,
> distant but ungrudging, accomplished in parenthood, some-
> thing about them suggestive of massive insurance coverage.
> This assembly of station wagons, as much as anything they
> might do in the course of the year, more than formal liturgies
> or laws, tells the parents they are a collection of the like-
> minded and the spiritually akin, a people, a nation.

There is no clearer statement of the complicated weave of cultural
identity in the world of late capitalism. Here posture itself, the
details of physiognomy and grooming, rather than anything so vul-
gar as the colour of one's credit card, is the marker of class membership. This tribe's belonging is effortlessly sketched in gesture and
expression.

Now compare a second passage, later in the book, where the
narrator catches sight of the students themselves, scattered in the
library, and considers the value of the tuition, $14,000, necessary to
attend his elite institution:

> I sense there is a connection between this powerful number
> and the way the students arrange themselves physically in the

reading areas of the library. They sit on broad cushioned seats
in various kinds of ungainly posture, clearly calculated to
be the identifying signs of some kinship group or secret
organization. They are fetal, knock-kneed, arched, square-
knotted, sometimes almost upside-down. The positions are so
studied they amount to a classical mime. There is an element
of overrefinement and inbreeding. Sometimes I feel I've wan-
dered into a Far Eastern dream, too remote to be interpreted.
But it is only the language of economic class they are speaking, in one of its allowable forms, like the convocation of station wagons at the start of the year.

This studied casualness, this topsy-turvy disdain for the standard
operating procedures demanded by chairs and tables, is more than
youthful awkwardness. In fact, its outwardly awkward aspect actually hides a deep comfort level, a claim on understanding the way
things work, a long acquaintance with the inner machinery of entitlement.

If you travel to the right parts of the northeastern United States,
or a few places in North Carolina and Michigan and northern California, it is possible to observe these scenes still, every September, as
the air gets crisp and the leaves begin to turn. I saw them myself during the years of graduate school, when I apprenticed at one of those
institutions where the annual tuition constituted what was, by any
measure, a "powerful number." But nowadays, these two passages,
and the distant, powerful reality they illuminate, come to mind
every autumn in a different way when I return to my own institution
of higher learning and confront a much different spectacle.

The students I see there have no easy sense of superiority. Their
posture, far from loose-limbed jangle of monied confidence, is
instead diffident, inward, uncertain. No one leans against anything
with a suggestion of massive insurance coverage. The students stand
with genuine awkwardness, facing in different directions. In many

cases, their parents have made the trip alongside them, and uncomfortable on a university campus, they hang back with unease. The faces are many shades of colour, there are turbans and headscarves, and the clothes are a patchwork of branded urban cool, logo-heavy bagginess, high heels, and tight sweaters. There is ravewear, Gothic makeup, athletic gear of every imaginable make, the occasional displaced nerd in corduroys and a button-down shirt.

On the surface, these students send a message no less powerful than their homogenized cousins in the less diverse, more exclusive institutions to the south. They appear to be the avatars of the New World Order, the very picture of those happily diverse global teens, the marketing masala, depicted so vividly in *Colors* magazine or the ad campaigns of Benetton and the Gap. They appear to be, in short, representatives of the current fantasy of a post-cultural future, a generation emancipated from tribal particularisms to create a world where skin colour and religious background have no bearing except in finding matching clothes, because the shared values of shopping and hanging out and being cool trump everything else. There is even a measure of truth in this appearance, for these students will tell you that the most important thing is *not to judge anybody else*, and they will speak of tolerance without hesitation, viewing it (as the political theorist Alan Wolfe has neatly put it) as their Eleventh Commandment.

But on closer inspection, the cheerful picture of multiracial harmony quickly begins to dissolve. For some of these mix-and-match teens, for example, the first Ten Commandments actually matter a lot more than any notional Eleventh. They will apologetically inform you that however much they like you, it is a sad fact that you are going to hell because you will not accept their deity. Others will preach the gospel according to tolerance so energetically that they create a whole new form of intolerance. Many of them soon display all the vicious cliquishness and exclusionary disdain of street gangs, refusing to consort with anyone who is not a Sikh, or not an East Asian Christian, or not a black Christian, or not from the south side of Markham. Partly this is just adolescent posturing, of course, the way we all struggle to define ourselves by drawing lines between Us and the Others. But these emergent tribalisms, especially in the context of a university's vaunted claims to foster open-mindedness and free inquiry, are more than simple disputes about style or comportment. Those things, crucially, are the first line of recognition; but the real conflicts in play here run much deeper. They will not be outgrown by a change of clothes or a change of neighbourhood.

Occasionally, in the time-honoured fashion, a common enemy can create common cause even among the divided. Often enough, in the first-year philosophy classes I teach, I have seen the enemy — and the enemy is me. The reason for this is simple and instructive. When they are done properly, introductory courses in philosophy are systematically unstable, given as they are to asking uncomfortable questions about the nature of pre-reflective beliefs. Not surprisingly, students usually have had little prior experience with the peculiar disruptions of the Socratic *elenchus*, where one is asked, over and over, to defend something that is taken for granted — say, one's acceptance that the external world is real. Nobody likes too much of this, as Plato's dialogues amply demonstrate. There, various characters — Cephalus and Thrasymachus in the *Republic*, Euthyphro in the dialogue bearing his name — make off with some haste when the questioning gets too rough. Students sometimes forget that they, too, can leave whenever they want to, rather than staying to have their nascent world views exposed in all their fragility.

But stay they often do, and sometimes because they feel there is an important victory there to be won. The crucial moment often comes when what is at stake is the divine. It is my experience over a number of years now that the status of knowledge in general, even the ethical question of how one ought to live, does not move first-year philosophy students nearly as much as the issue of God's existence. Which I, for my peculiar purposes, choose to deny.

You have to imagine it. The tall arrogant Sikh in the back row, the one who always saunters in late and never deigns to take a note or even turn off his cellphone, is joining forces with the eager Taiwanese-Canadian true believer in the front row. The two of them are being egged on by an evangelical young black woman off to the left who, until now, has not said anything or shown any indication whatsoever that the class diverted her attention more than a reasonably competent nature documentary. *They are all right, and I am wrong! Of course God exists!* But which God, I ask them. Whose God? No, never mind that, they tell me. For now, they have to defeat the unbeliever who stands before them, uttering these unreasonable demands for more argument, more reason, more articulation. If nothing else, the vehemence of these objections bespeaks a concrete need to believe that is far from the depressing portrait of a generation without goals or judgments. And that is all to the good. As Socrates knew, you can work with a dogmatist. It's the bored nihilists, too cool to argue, who defeat the philosophical project before it has begun.

At that moment, their excitement is the goal, and any teacher would happily sacrifice himself on the point of their convictions. Socrates was likewise right that pissing people off is how we first, and maybe best, go about the business of provoking thought. We are, at least partially or occasionally, rational creatures and so we want to overpower the other who challenges our beliefs in argument, not just in battle. Power is power, and philosophy is usually no match for it when push comes to shove. The pen is not mightier than the sword in any direct confrontation, unfortunately. But power ultimately needs justification as well as sheer victory, and conviction sooner or later craves legitimacy as well as certainty. It is not enough simply to shut someone up, as the Athenians did to their most famous citizen. To achieve a real victory, you have to shut him up *with reasons.* Socrates knew this, knew it far better than his willing executioners.

The thing is, once you open the door to reason's own kind of power, things swiftly become much less clear than they were before.

When philosophical disputes spill out of the classroom, or make their way to the shopping mall or back to the parental dinner table, back to the outside world where other kinds of power hold sway, previously robust commitments begin to lose their solidity under the persistent drip of interrogation.

The students who come to my institution, in their various colours and their awkward postures, are a mass of contradictions and conflicts. Their identities, their very bodies, are battlefields in the modern culture wars. They come from many places and traditions, and they enter a world with its own traditions, some of them bizarre, but still held loosely together by the idea that rational inquiry is basic to human life. Here they put themselves on the line, trying to juggle the mass of criss-crossing, cancelling signals – the sometimes undifferentiated white noise – of modern life. Religious belief. Linguistic habits. Consumer pressure. Family demands. Market constraints. And, perhaps, an emergent kernel of self-regard that rises free of all the rest. Out of these materials, shifting and variable, they must construct something called an identity.

This cacophony of signals is modernity's double-sided legacy to them. Working with more options than they can reasonably process, under constant pressure to be themselves despite a conspicuous lack of concrete social roles or widely accepted virtues, they must each sculpt an identity from the sharp rock of possibility. Individuals on the verge of entering the world have, for several hundred years now, faced this kind of challenge to the prospect of finding out who they are. But these young people, so apparently rich in possibility and so obviously immersed in liberating choice, are something else again. They are the test cases of a new task: that of finding meaningful roles to occupy in a complex global world where consumer choices loom larger than ethical ones, where brand loyalty counts for more than political fealty, where purely personal projects of comfort and success seem to push all other forms of value to one side.

Together with their older counterparts, the young jet-set, dot-com executives who get creamed off the top and begin their transcontinental migrations from start-up to start-up, from one venture opportunity to another, are the canaries in the coal mine of a fast-changing social milieu. If we want to understand the world we are fast creating, we must, like Benjamin reading the strolling migration of the Parisian *flâneurs*, study the details – the toys and tools, the pleasures and frustrations – of everyday life in the new global arcades. How do we begin that new project of dream interpretation?

———

Both cultures and individuals are subject to the pluralistic conditions typical of late modernity. Indeed, one feasible characterization of what we can still usefully call the modern condition is that it is a program of deliberate breaks from tradition or inherited stability. (In this sense, the postmodern tendency in thought or art, favouring irony and self-reference, is just an extension of the larger modern project, not a decisive break with it.) Ezra Pound's imperative "Make it new" is only the most succinct expression of this desire, so peculiar and so powerful still. This freedom from the past has, notoriously, both costs and benefits. Definitions and singleness are thrown over in favour of fluidity and provisionality, but this is a toss that unsettles as much as it liberates. We are forever in danger of losing perspective in a relentless demand for speedy novelty, coupled with its unlikely twin, the superior insouciance of the jaded aesthete – or, nowadays, the overstimulated consumer.

Consider. When Proust says of his character Albertine, in *À la Recherche du temps perdu*, that she "is no longer a woman, but a series of events," he expresses something crucial about the dawning sensibility of the new century – a dawning precisely dated by Virginia Woolf as occurring in December 1910, when an episode of drawing-room frankness about casual sex convinced her that traditional morality was over. Joyce's Bloom, walking through the crowded landscape of a single day's consciousness, maps the same terrain, and gives some sense of modern art's struggles to slow down, in imperfect media like language or pigment, that quickness that is the new century's soul.

Proust proposes attaching to Albertine "a sign corresponding to what in physics is the sign that indicates velocity." She is no longer a person, as that notion was once understood by moralists and philosophers; she is now instead, as the critic Peter Conrad nicely puts it, a *vector*, a trace of speed in a continuum of indeterminacies as complex as anything sketched by the special theory of relativity. She is, too, the fractured face of Cubism, the meaning-making soul on overdrive, fashioning more language and imagery than it can understand, as diagnosed by Freud. She is modern. The world no longer means what it did, and the people within it, if they are able to shore up their fragments against the wrack of change, are no longer the same creatures as their pre-modern forebears. Character, in the sense of the well-formed disposition to act with integrity – a word whose etymology invokes the oneness of the integer – gives way to a layered and complex selfhood, the "multiple subject positions" of more recent theory.

This shift is real and its consequences but poorly understood even now, ten decades later and more. At its banal end, it makes for individuals who are reduced to clusters of spending patterns – the annihilation of self in the steady, dead-eyed gaze of the demographer or corporate-financed cool hunter. These are the anthropologists of the new global market, who no longer perceive persons with stories to tell but only pathways traced from door to product; no longer see individuals but only half-formed nodes in the culture/cash nexus. Even in a more reflective part of the spectrum, plurality is likewise endemic, retaining its unsettling force in the demands of multiple conflicting values or norms: duty to country over duty to self; the value of loyalty as against the value of honesty; family tradition over individual ambition.

These deeper conflicts, while not entirely unknown to the premodern mind, nevertheless attain a greater force when the project of personal self-fulfillment, abetted by the democratization of leisure and art, begins to vie in importance with more traditional social roles. Now individuals face a set of challenges that their forebears in traditional hierarchical societies did not. It is only in a modern world where everyone is expected to be the artist of his or her own life, in other words, that some of the deep conflicts of our recent experience become possible. It is only when we are constantly told that we must create a unified identity out of the shored-up fragments of diverse experiences and materials that we see just how fractured our identities really are. As ever, modernity generates its own self-destructive crisis. And whatever was true in this vein a hundred years ago is doubly true now that the scope of the challenge has passed beyond the limits of a single society or even continent.

Often such conflicts are characterized, especially in our own day, as battles *between* self and culture, as if one were constantly attempting to shake off the bonds of expectation, perhaps in the manner of that powerful late-twentieth-century creation, the teenager. But to what extent is culture itself reworked and relativized here, made a fetish object or cheap form of *aide-mémoire?* We tend to think of the banalization of culture as a recent blight, what with our multi-ethnic celebrations of food and clothing or our commodification of foreignness via tourism. But the evidence indicates a much longer timeline. Indeed, it suggests that cultures begin to lose their integrity at just the same time individuals do, namely, when the unstable consensus of the industrial age, with its reliance on print technology and the primacy of the nation-state, is plunged into turmoil by the advent of new technologies, new mobilities, new forms of both belonging and alienation.

Karl Kraus captured the problem with characteristic economy: following Robert Musil's coinage, he called the Austro-Hungarian Empire "Kakania" in a scatological play on Emperor Franz Josef's ubiquitous *K. und K.* (kaiser and king) symbol. "In Kraus's view," writes Peter Conrad, "Kakania gave the rest of the continent a lesson in falsity. Europe, he thought, had become a cheap and nasty variety shop. The states which emerged from that world-ending war covered up their political duplicity and economic distress by selling tawdry souvenirs to tourists – the papier-mâché helmets of London policemen; dwarfed Eiffel Towers; perhaps (for connoisseurs) a silver rose in plastic. . . . Culture was merely a costume party, and the purpose of travel is to try on funny hats."

On both sides of the individual/cultural divide, then, the effects of this ongoing revolution in sensibility are palpable, and not always positive. Variety in materials and options, as any shopper well knows, can lead as much to the tyranny of choice as to a sense of freedom. Fluidity in one's personal identity can just be another word for confusion. It is therefore no surprise that the story of modernity, our continuing story, now exported to the whole world, is one of simultaneous promise and ennui. For every enthusiast like the Futurist Emilio Marinetti, who saw swift machines releasing us from our servitude to the vile earth, there is a countervailing languid Wildean aesthete or *weltschmerzlich* Schopenhauerian nihilist, who finds superiority instead in a been-there, done-that boredom with everything new or fast. The postmodern cool of a figure like the avant-garde architect Rem Koolhaas – as persona, if not necessarily as designer – might be considered a contemporary fusion of these two attitudes. He is at once drawn to innovation and technology but projects a disdain for everything meaningful or ordered. He celebrates "the city as unauthorized event" even as urban landscapes sprawl out of control and concentrate wealth and power in tiny nodes. Such a combination is inherently unstable. For every cultural innovation that promises a more fulfilling and liberating sense of personal identity, there is a mass-produced hat or parodied dance craze that makes cultural belonging an empty gesture, akin to joining a hobby club or reading the books recommended by Oprah Winfrey.

In the field of intellectual life, meanwhile, much of the contemporary theorizing simply has not helped us get a grasp on the rich dilemmas of our particularity. For every open field of possibility, which seems to offer a glimpse of ourselves as freely created artworks in progress, there is now a corresponding form of reductionism: materialist accounts of emotion, demographic accounts of reason, psychotherapeutic accounts of motivation. These attempts to explain the whole intricate world with a single theory, however grand, end up robbing us of agency and spinning us back into an ethically and politically vacuous world of random mutations, rotating atoms, and unquantifiable risks. Multiple subject identities, meanwhile, are not proof against the really powerful forces of our altered world, old-fashioned things like concentrated wealth or rearguard essentialism about human nature's limits.

Under these conditions cultural defence too often becomes a kind of fetishism, and identity declines into nothing more than the time-worn chauvinism of excluding the out-groupers. Excessive regard for national sovereignty now means that our hands are tied when it comes to passing judgment on, say, the systemic murder of Kosovars in the Balkans, labelling it a civil war and engaging in an extended moral debate that contrives to leave everything very much as it is. For every apparent gain, in short, we now observe a balancing danger. This is the world we have created, the world that creates us.

We cannot address the political emptiness of our de facto global culture by simply continuing the talk about nations and their laws; or by allowing local debate to continue as if political choices were *not* conditioned by, and implicated in, complex events around our fast-shrinking globe. Such moves are misleading, and ultimately futile, sideshows to the real political debate shaping our collective future, a debate too often held not in public spaces, among citizens, but in small-scale conversations among the clever and the privileged. Pursuing outdated forms of political protest or argument is worse than useless. It simply surrenders the larger field to the power of quick-response corporations and high-speed capital to create and dominate markets, to rape the environment, and to amass profit without regard for the labour that actually generates wealth.

So much is obvious. What is not obvious to many people is what, precisely, we can do about it. The task for any useful theory of citizenship now is to provide a sense of meaningful political activity in a world where such activity is ever threatened with meaninglessness. We have to press the internal commitments of globalism rather than retreat from it. We have to make the new cosmopolitan ideal not just a marketer's dream or an image from a Gap ad campaign, but a political reality. We must, furthermore, create a new, and newly complex, sense of belonging that embraces differences as well as transcends them, that forges commitment across boundaries without erasing the things that make those boundaries interesting in the first place. Already it is impossible to travel the world without coming across a Disney store or a Nine West outlet in some public square. We could hardly count it a victory if we simply reproduced that deadening sameness at the level of the citizenry.

A tall order. The persistent challenge set political theory by diverse cultures is how to find a degree of political substance that is sufficient ("thick" enough) to bind citizens, but at the same time sufficiently flexible ("thin" enough) to allow them to pursue their life projects without undue interference. This challenge holds whether we are confining ourselves to a single nation-state like Canada or the United States, or attempting to speak boldly of a larger transnational sphere. When we consider the difficulties that beset even these lower-level political bodies – the enduring conflicts between French and English Canada, for example, or the sharp divides and threats of separatism still afflicting blacks and whites in twenty-first-century America – it may seem bizarre to attempt a move to a higher plane. Is there, could there ever be, a single conception of citizenship that would answer to the needs of those living in Germany as well as those living in Indonesia? Is anything that could be intelligible in both places, and in a hundred more besides, going to be much better than an empty form?

Legitimate concerns. To get this argument off the ground, however, we have to narrow our search parameters somewhat. The simple answer to the former query: no, there is not a single conception of citizenship equal to the diversities of current nations. For one thing, most of them (Germany is a good example) are rooted in nineteenth-century ideas of the nation as *ethnos*, as a body of racially similar people. In contrast to earlier notions of the nation as *demos*, a body of politically linked people, these ethnic nations have a built-in charge of malignant bigotry. Hence the gradations of citizenship offered to people who enter contemporary Germany, from the lowly *Gastarbeiter* – the guest-worker, modern-day equivalent of the Metics found in ancient Athens – to the literally full-blooded citizen. Nor is this even an extreme example of political exclusion based on race. For that you have to look to the southeast, to the Balkans; or to central Africa, in Rwanda.

If we dwell too long on these depravities, our confidence that anything may be said or done begins to wane. They are a necessary curb on flights of political fancy, perhaps, but they cannot be allowed to dominate the field of our awareness. Still, the violent fervour of the sense of belonging at work in these tortured places would seem to mock the attempt to create a more inclusive form of citizenship. In the language of thick and thin, how could any thing capable of stretching across the range of political contexts be anything but thin to the point of transparency, a flimsy sheet of political naiveté?

What we seek is a form of universalism, and because that has become a danger word in recent political discourse, we must articulate a universalism that will not raise the hackles of those who note, rightly, how most forms of universalism have had oppressive effects. However much we may believe in their validity, we cannot simply elevate our own commitments to universal status and call it a day. For those even a little unlike the white male rationalists who first defended universalism, indeed, the attempt to rise above particularity in search of some higher identity has meant only systematic denigration of their very real struggles for minimal identity: as women, as gay men, as people of colour. The dominant notions of universal rights have not adequately accommodated such specifics as wanting to hold hands in public with a same-sex partner or wanting consideration of child-rearing as work. The philosopher Iris Young has expressed the problem succinctly: "[I]n extolling the virtues of citizenship as participation in a universal public realm, modern men expressed a flight from sexual difference, from having to recognize another kind of existence they could not entirely understand, and from the embodiment, dependency on nature, and morality that women represent."

But there is an important difference between *covering-law* universalism and *reiterative* universalism – a distinction first employed in the matter of justice by the political theorist Michael Walzer. Covering-law universalism takes a single conception of X, in the present case of citizenship, and imposes it everywhere, without regard for local conditions or needs. This is what most people think of when they call something universal, and it is indeed the dominant conception, from ancient philosophy to our own day, of what it means to move beyond the particular. As a consequence of its top-down character, however, it is likely that *this* version of universal citizenship would be experienced as alien, even actively oppressive, by those on the ground. Reiterative universalism recognizes, by contrast, the pragmatic limits on both philosophical inquiry and political action: it works from the bottom up, sensitive to variations in local context. It asks not that a single conception, ever unaltered, make way in all cases; only that every case, whatever its particularities, find a way to express a version of the universal value.

So, to take a prominent example, the current culture of science, at least in its unreflective forms, is ruled by a conception of covering-law universalism. This is the idea that claims made under the rubric of scientific investigation are expressions of lucid natural truth, valid in themselves regardless of one's culture or context, almost like laws of logic. It doesn't matter what language you speak as you make such a claim, or what city or nation you were in when you ran the experiment, because here, as people often say, the facts speak for themselves. The universal validity of scientific truth is supposed to drape over those differences, rendering them irrelevant. Granted, this is merely the ideal version of the situation. As recent debates about the social status of science have amply shown, there are many caveats to offer on such a brief characterization of a complex human undertaking like science. And it is likewise true that the articulation of covering laws has always been subject to ruthless challenge within science. Nevertheless, this kind of universalism is still favoured in the scientific world. In this realm a claim is valid precisely by being available for proof, no matter what the surrounding cultural, linguistic, or political conditions.

But at other times and in other places, science has displayed a much more reiterative form of universalism. At one point, not long ago in the history of our detailed investigation of the world around us, a number of relatively isolated pockets of empirical investigation were each trying, in its own idiosyncratic way and with varying traditional backgrounds, to speak a kind of scientific truth. Sometimes investigation was coloured by religious or spiritual commitments, sometimes guided in part by what we would consider aesthetic or traditional values. And yet, the notion of scientific truth still functioned as a universal value, governing each instance of the same kind of investigation but with a degree of difference that would seem odd, if not dysfunctional, to someone reared in the fluidly global scientific culture of our own day. It was not dysfunctional, however, just locally variant. The local variations posed no philosophical threat to the value of truth as it then ranged across the different contexts. Hybrid forms are common, even typical, in such circumstances; elements of the universal value mingle with local customs and eccentricities. The value moulds itself to the peculiar shape demanded by the local conditions, without entirely losing its coherence – and, importantly, without losing its connection to other iterations of the same value in other local conditions.

Lest you think it is an implication of this example, let me hasten to add that we need not claim a form of reiterative universalism must "mature" into a covering-law universalism in order to be fully valid. Science works better because of the extensive communication across other boundaries, it's true, and it has successfully developed its versions of (always provisional) covering laws in the form of the best explanation so far. But citizenship, like justice or other less empirical concepts, may not possess the same kind of potential to generate covering laws – and may not have to. Certainly there have been many thinkers, past and present, who believed citizenship required a universal articulation in order to achieve full validity. But that aspiration is neither politically necessary nor, in present circumstances, very desirable. Such theory-driven desires can only cloud our judgment about what is possible, and destroy the value of this important distinction by rank-ordering the two forms of universalism, such that the real victory of reiteration is lost. Pragmatism in politics demands a corresponding pragmatism in theory, in other words. We must remain agnostic on the question of whether citizenship will ever achieve the kind of universalism that is currently enjoyed by scientific discourse, and we can do so happily. Our real achievements in building citizenship, not some elevated external standard, must be our measure of success.

What this means in practice is not something I or anyone could hope to say in quick detail, for it is work not yet done. Nevertheless a few modest claims can be made already. It does seem unlikely, as I have been suggesting throughout this discussion, that *essentialist* notions of citizenship will help us navigate the challenges of an interdependent world. It is very likely, instead, that they will simply continue to bolster and justify the kinds of bloodline or basic-trait barriers that have too often made citizenship brutally punitive. And yet the standard solution to that impasse, which involves shifting thoughts about citizenship to procedural or constitutional ground, has displayed only limited success. The modern discourse of rights has given us a tool kit of valuable ideas and arguments, but it has not helped with the more basic political difficulty, getting citizens to care and listen and act in the first place. It has even, in some recent cases of constitutional challenge both in Canada and the United States, fostered a litigious and uncooperative form of special pleading that undermines community. What the focus on political virtues in the previous chapter suggests is this: citizenship can function only if it is perceived and inhabited as a political role, which is to say as *a concrete disposition to act*.

I wish I had a program that would solve these difficulties, an algorithm of citizenship. But there is no such thing. What I am noting is, instead, just how deep the challenge to act goes, and how difficult the political task before us remains. For, as Benjamin's engagements with the world of things constantly remind us, constructing a stable identity in the dreamscape of the Arcades is a project fraught with overdetermination. There are always, as my ultracool post-cultural students well know, too many options, too many choices. Paradoxically, the problems of politics often arise today not in the form of a problem of *scarcity*, but as one of *abundance*. We have too much, too many things to choose from, and that effectively distracts us from forming the concrete intentions to address the more basic issue of uneven distribution of things and choices. We are so intent on dealing with our own condition of having too much information and too many brands – for this is a genuine challenge, as we all know in the high-speed first world – that we often miss those who have too little, too few. A surfeit of options may be considered both a blessing and a curse, I suppose. One's attitude to the volume and velocity of everyday life can vary from day to day, and it often depends simply on how fast you like to go, how much of a multi-tasker you want to be. And yet there is one sense in which we have no option. Politically, we cannot begin elsewhere than with the surfeited social-cultural environment that already shapes us – and try to make it better.

That sentiment may sound a little defeatist, given that it begins with something that many people find overwhelming and depressing, namely, the condition of being alive and aware in the current social landscape of websites and shopping malls. In some critics' hands, indeed, I suppose it might be another and more sophisticated form of the same complacency that seems to come over cheerleaders of globalization whenever they put pen to paper. But I am suggesting something far more radical. Here we have to follow Benjamin – not to mention Plato – in tacking along the line where hope meets despair. Without losing the thoroughgoing mindfulness of our own limitations (in foresight and good will, in time and energy), we can perhaps begin to articulate a sort of realistic wishfulness, a worldly utopianism. An action-oriented conception of citizenship is, first and foremost, engaged with other people in the creation of shared social spaces and in the discourse that such spaces make possible. Through participation and conversation, we reproduce our social meanings through time: that is what culture is. Squares and institutions, walkways and stadiums, these are the places where the dreams of a people are realized in stone and iron, glass and air. They are sites of politics, not merely of design or style; or rather, here design and style are themselves aspects of the political.

By the same token, when those spaces are taken away from us, violently or by stealth, we are diminished in ourselves and in our politics. Benjamin, visiting Moscow in 1926, was disturbed by the starkness of the public space. "There are no cafés. Impossible to get a drink," he wrote. "Free trade and free intellect have been abolished.

The cafés are therefore deprived of their public." There were no *flâneurs*, no idleness, no urban contingency, no fun. With their communal rooms, shared child-rearing, and workers' clubs where leisure was cooperative and regimented, the Soviets had allocated fifteen square metres of space to each citizen – and along the way found "a radical means of expelling 'cosiness'" and the cloying sentimentality of bourgeois individualism.

Benjamin was ambivalent about cosiness – the prized bourgeois-interior quality of *Gemütlichkeit* – but we can still hear in his complaint the longing for genuine public space. Revolution has swept away the nooks and crannies, leaving only the vast open squares of a now-empty, even oppressive, triumph. The poet Vladimir Mayakovsky had written of the 1919 revolution that "the streets are our brushes, the squares our palettes," but the result was a canvas of unremitting seriousness. Le Corbusier, in Moscow at about the same time to design Centrosoyuz, the head office of the consumer cooperatives, noted that "the people take things seriously." It is part of the self-chosen task of political revolutions to re-order space and time, to mould them in the image of the serious new order: renaming the months, rewriting history, rebuilding the cities. Sometimes – in Tiananmen Square, say – a formerly glorious revolution is challenged by a new political upheaval on the very same ground that was set aside in celebration of the first, now calcified, act of emancipation.

I have drawn these examples from the revolutionary politics of the Left, and that might seem to cut against the very idea of utopian political action. But my worldly utopianism is not revolutionary in that violent sense: I am not advocating the ruthless elimination of everything existing. It is also worth noting that the very same task of creating social space is just as often – these days, much more often and more pervasively – undertaken by the forces of conservatism, usually with more money and slyness, less violence and noise. Benjamin's example of Baron Haussmann's boulevards in Paris, which tipped the balance away from harrying street fighters and towards mounted cavalry, is to the point. In my own city, there are still intricate cow-gate entrances to certain older public institutions, such as the courts in Osgoode Hall on Queen Street, allegedly constructed to slow down storming protesters who might want to march on the lawmakers and have it out. Free-trade zones and exurban sprawl, even the 33 percent increase in domestic housing size in America, are all examples of a much more widespread and alienating distortion of the built environment than any leftist revolutionary could ever hope to effect.

All social space is suffused with political meanings and agendas, the very stones and walls a kind of testament to the ongoing struggles for liberation and justice. And as with space, so with time. We should never forget that the legal profession has managed what neither the Jacobin revolutionaries nor the scientific community could, namely, to recast time on a functional base-ten model, measuring out advice and influence in six-minute tenths. Nor should we fail to notice that the eternal now of our speedy times is, functionally, a form of forgetting – a way of leaving the status quo mostly intact through the distracting power of constant novelty, and of equally constant nostalgia.

The lesson of the Arcades, whether we are discussing the ones Benjamin depicted so lovingly in his unfinished *Project* or the global and even non-spatial ones we occupy today, points to this: we keep thinking that we can *get home* by going more quickly forward or by retreating more decisively back. And yet, the truth is that neither course will really take us where we want to go. So what will?

Places to Dream

"If I were asked to name the chief benefit of the house," Gaston Bachelard writes in *The Poetics of Space*, "I should say: the house shelters day-dreaming, the house protects the dreamer, the house allows one to dream in peace." The house, for centuries the epitome of privacy, is being transformed under these conditions of rapid social and technological change. It is therefore a key case study in the emergent forms of public and private space, for how we dwell speaks volumes about what we value, how we think, who we are. Our forms of daily living, even more so perhaps than our forms of work, raise the crucial question of civil society, the issue of third-space possibilities – the space between work and home – where citizenship must be enacted.

Take a vivid recent example. The innovative designs collected in "The Un-Private House" exhibition in 1999 at the Museum of Modern Art in New York demonstrate the dialectical playfulness of a younger generation of architects, and dwellers, as they mould the human shelter to new needs and desires, new identities. Inhabiting spaces that are open-ended and ambiguous, with walls that move, massive windows or floors that split into multiple planes, these are identities apparently broken free of the bourgeois, domestic, procreative functions of the standard single-family dwelling (SFD), that basic building block of the modern world. The new houses are open to outside view, smart in their extensive electronic wiring into the Internet and the telecommunications network, tightly hooked up to the fast world that flows always through, never around, this transformed domestic space: a space neither public nor private, but attempting a transcendence of both.

But is this transformation a new liberation, or bondage by another name? Ultimately these un-private houses demonstrate that they are not about moving past the limits of the private, but merely about projecting self-image. They are not really public but instead enact a retreat from the public, even a disdain for it. Real progression in our style and practices of inhabitation necessitates something far more demanding than this new form of supremely elegant, but often banal narcissism. It involves the private realm influencing and transforming the public realm through a sustained critical engagement.

We tend to take the public/private distinction for granted, but it has a particular, and quite recent, history. It is also, like so many taken-for-granted features of our experience, a bearer of ideological value – and one we can no longer reproduce without challenge. The house as most of us know it is a key part of that history. Indeed, it is no exaggeration to twin the single family dwelling with the very notion of bourgeois privacy, the walls and separation facilitating the democratized individualism that begins to take hold of the West in the fifteenth century and reaches its highest early expression in seventeenth-century, especially Dutch and English, visions of the private life. Gone, except in monastic life, was the common house of the Middle Ages. Even the gentry's massive dwellings gradually shed their population of retainers and domestic sycophants, leaving the physical structures but not the political and psychic infrastructures that once made them work. Eventually, labour and education moved out of the dwelling place into other more public spaces – the factory, the office – and the line separating the public and private worlds sank deeper and deeper in the sand of daily life.

This separation of public and private, whatever its many difficulties, works to structure the world of modern experience, creating along the way not only notions of work and rest but also the in-between realm of the third space – not the home or the office but the restaurant, stadium, or bar (the public house) where we repose between public labour and private leisure. Here entertaining and pleasure find a public as well as a private expression, and the line between the daily realms shifts and drifts. The idea of public civility and the rules of etiquette, for example, first codified in manuals by Renaissance Europeans to address a more public and varied world of daily experience and exposure, take on a signal importance as we navigate among the spheres of this tripartite life.

How do we comport ourselves in the office or at the theatre? What parts of the body may be touched, or mentioned, in the bedroom but not the boardroom? Every time we venture out into public, or invite outsiders into the home, we run the risk of doing the wrong thing or making the wrong impression. Etiquette manuals are in part guides for passing gracefully through the rituals of a life that is less and less traditional, and therefore open to variation and confusion; but they are, even more basically, guides for the presentation of self in everyday life, rule books for entering the public eye. It is no coincidence that they gain their first enthusiastic readers at a time – Montaigne's time – when the public/private distinction is acquiring new stability and influence.

The house looms large in this modern economy of public and private because it is a locus for the newly valued bourgeois ends of privacy, quiet, and intimacy – the things the public realm does not, and cannot, provide. Most of us still inhabit some version of the standard two- or three-storey SFD with its two or three bedrooms – even if, as in my own case, it is broken into small, mixed-use apartments with an office in every living room and a television in every kitchen. Eighty percent of the nearly two million housing units under construction in the United States in 1998 were private SFDs. These structures, so prevalent around us, are historical legacies of a particular way of working and living, but they also meet our deep inner needs. Who among us does not cherish the sighing, post-commute drop into the armchair, cool drink in hand; or the secluded garden's retreat from the hurly-burly of city life? Who does not feel, atavistically and maybe mistakenly, that we have not reached adulthood until we own a house?

The traditional pattern of straight, married, child-rearing families is maintained with less certainty today, of course, but the drive to seek domestic privacy continues. (Old ideological structures do not give way as quickly in the suburbs as they do in the university seminar rooms downtown.) Housing developments now bloom not with post-war bungalows and small trimmed lawns, but with chock-a-block monster homes whose proportions demand a vast yet impossible acreage. Gated communities keep the world at bay with electrified fencing and private security guards. So-called stealth houses slide down the sides of ravines, presenting to outside view only an innocuous doorway that belies the opulence of the dwelling space within. Planned towns like Disney's much celebrated (and much criticized) Celebration, Florida, are revealed as exercises in consensual delusion – the ideal community reduced to a literal utopia, a branded corporate no-place of perfect lawns, pastel paint, and artificial main streets. Until, that is, real people move in and begin to complain about the garbage collection or the scholastic standards of the local public school.

This is the confused landscape from which the new un-private houses rise to view. Drawing inspiration from famous see-through structures like Philip Johnson's Glass House or Mies van der Rohe's Farnsworth House, they challenge the ugly developments around them, reflecting a discomfort with available options. They also speak to dwellers' changing desires as the twentieth century breathed its last and we moved into the twenty-first: half the families in the United States today are married couples without children, and a quarter of the total population lives alone, well up from the rate of 8 percent that was standard for most of the century. People are getting married later, or not at all. Young professionals in North America will now change jobs an average of nine times before reaching mid-career. Labour, which now often involves manipulating data rather than materials, is portable and ubiquitous.

The un-private houses limn these changes in their very walls –

or lack of them. Here, at first glance anyway, we observe the public/private line rubbed out, redrawn, even mocked. We see reflected, in the mirrors and shiny surfaces, the changing bodies of our late-model selves, our happily layered and hybrid existences. There are no children's bedrooms here, no traditional dining rooms, no half-finished rec-room basements. Things are not allowed to pile up or collect in jumbles; they are replaced as surely as an old car or last year's fashions. Sleek exercise rooms and offices and gourmet kitchens, complete with granite counters and brushed-steel appliances, reflect the new priorities of a happy self-obsession. Work now invades the home more aggressively than ever, and the wiring of modem-ready phone lines and cable feeds makes these contemporary houses a transparent artificial intelligence – not so much Le Corbusier's machine for living as a machine for talking with, a piece of inhabitable communications technology. Computer screens loom from unexpected corners, televisions and telephones trace their cables through the mutating spaces. In some cases, the house begins to resemble a spaceship flight deck or cutting-edge laboratory, like the Automatic House located in rural northern Italy, where computer technology is, *Star Trek* fashion, seamlessly ubiquitous, summoned from anywhere by casual voice-command.

As the MOMA curator Terence Riley points out in an essay on "The Un-Private House" exhibition, these developments can also bring their nightmare visions: fear of invading technology, total surveillance in the Orwellian vein, ceaseless and frenetic labour, the inescapability of other voices. And yet the dangers do not seem to faze the new inhabitants. They are not afraid of the porous features and built-in uncertainty of their new houses, the way an earlier generation found the Farnsworth House so threatening. "There are no rooms," one happy client said of 64 Wakefield, his loft-style, structure-optional space in Atlanta, "just situations." In the same vein, a successful young designer once told me that the reason she could be happy making mass-produced household objects rather than hand-crafted domestic artifacts was that her company's foot stools and coffee tables were in fact flexible in their potential – stackable, or multi-purpose, or open to modification – so that they existed as variable "characters" rather than as static things.

Well, maybe. Certainly these particular clients had the privilege of getting just what they wanted in a house: the large office/bedroom space for the two stockbrokers, market quotations flashing past; the ultimate workout room in the loft of two gay professionals. This is a privilege denied most of us. But it is also, as Bachelard reminds us in his subtle meditation on spaces, a paradoxical, even dangerous privilege. The dream house, when realized, can be the death of dreaming: the dreams of dwelling harden into thoughts, serious and stiff. Imagination always goes beyond what is immediately given. But that means it must have incompleteness to play with, must have nooks and corners and dark places to explore – or simply to gaze at in apprehension.

So much of our current house fixation seems dedicated to killing the dreamer rather than sheltering him, in other words. The cutting-edge un-private houses are only the avant-garde end of a spectrum that includes, at the other end, the unadventurous designs and deadening sameness of new tract houses, the voracious subdivisions of North America's fast-growing exurbia. To observe this more prosaic version of the dream-house quest, and see its dangers to our larger sense of self, scan the cable channel HGTV, a dedicated home-and-garden fetish-fest, or troll the magazine racks with their visions of domestic possibility. The broadcast schedule and editorial spreads are jammed with the quest for domestic perfection – a quest that becomes a kind of nightmare fraught with disappointment, always falling short of the glossy and elusive ideal.

On the popular show "Dream House," a smiling host introduces us, each week, to a couple struggling to get the house they want. "Budget considerations and your wish list may conflict," the host says one evening. "Compromises and disappointments are inevitable."

Notice the assumed economy of desire and disappointment; hear the chastening, homiletic wisdom of his warning. The clients, building a standard-issue three-bedroom in suburban Minneapolis, heard it. But they have a dream. "Visiting the plumbing supply store helped a lot," aspiring homeowner Jim Sandberg says in his flat Minnesota accent, laid over shots of ranked, gleaming faucets and fixtures. "Seeing all that stuff there. In terms of the dream. Closing in on the dream." But dreams are not prey. Well-being is not for sale. And conscious desires are not always the road to imagination. Granted, there may be a drive for beauty in these expressions of the culture's desire, a need to create aesthetic grace notes in one's environment – this has to be understood if we are to approach these issues – but that drive and that need are often overwhelmed by the imperatives of acquisition and luxury, the craving for something that will engender envy in others. The real house, the house that becomes a home, opens one up to otherness, to possibility. It does not simply manifest, in concrete dimensions, a status-quo personality.

The dream house, in all its guises, both traditional and cutting edge, is therefore always poised on the cusp of its own failure. A house must be a space for dreaming, but not a dream house. It must, says Bachelard, extend vertically from the subterranean mystery of the earth to the wide-open roundness of being in the sky. It must enclose a space that, by its thresholds, defines the shape of the world: it must have a basement and an attic, if only in the figurative sense. The house protects us from the outside, gives us the shivering caveman pleasure of hearing rain on the roof, seeing snow whipped against the window. That is why the house, when it works, is a battened-down ship floating on the roiling sea of life, at once open and closed to danger. This is the same danger that comes when we realize the house-like structure of ourselves within it. "We have long forgotten the ritual by which the house of our life was erected," Benjamin writes in *One-Way Street*. "What things were interred and sacrificed amid magic incantations, what horrible cabinet of curiosities lies there below, where the deepest shafts are reserved for what is most commonplace."

From this subtle point of view, seeing the value as well as the shortcomings of the relation between public and private, the new un-private houses are not so much open as *suffused*. They reek of workaholic anxiety, the fear of not keeping up, with Lazy Working Sofas and Lazy Working Beds that incorporate shelves and files into the furniture of recline, and of insistent and dulling desire to succeed. This desire leaves no room for imagination, for illuminating otherness. The issue is not simple transparency, for transparency can sometimes make dreams possible. Otto Frey's celebrated desert glass house, for example, is a site of contemplation that genuinely engages its hostile, sublime environment. This kind of transparency, open to the challenges of the world it inhabits and therefore transformed by them, is far more profound than the lustrous "scenes for living" provided by these new houses. Its transparency is not glib or trite, its openness not feigned or superficial.

The new glass houses, by contrast, almost make you want to throw stones. Such houses are monuments to work and narcissism and individuality – to a soulless form of privacy dressed up as exhibitionism. Much of the appeal of the new work-suffused home, for example, is surely avoidance of the open-plan, *surveiller-et-punir* offices of the now-omnipresent Dilbert norm. But this attempt to escape is doomed by its own form. In these islands of self-enclosure, so misleadingly open to view, dwellers do not work to live, or live to work. Instead, they work/live in order to live/work, trapped in an unbroken cycle of flat existence. Any house, see-through or opaque, should be itself a liminal space, a structure full of threshold experiences – the way the *flâneur* transforms the otherwise public street into an interior, giving shape to a collective dream house of the outside space. The house is a place of dwelling, and it should make the dialectic of intimacy and solitude possible, not by being an unbroken skin but precisely through its permeability: it should be a cell with absorbent walls.

The real question is not whether to seek engagement, then, but how best to achieve it and what to do with it. These new houses are an important site for our inquiry because they appear to challenge the assumptions of the modern world, putting privacy and domesticity into question; and yet in the end they really just accept the categories in a more subtle, and reactionary, way. All the vectors of change in the house are here conceived as inward: receiving transmissions, accepting signals, opening up the channels. Or, when the vectors are aimed outward, they are vacuous in the extreme – the constant videotaping and broadcast of insignificant daily details, for example, the Jennicam-style project copied by the performance artist Alex van Es in his house in Apeldoorn, the Netherlands, which has direct Internet connections from its doorbell, toilet, and refrigerator so that websurfers can watch his every move in real time.

In both cases, the project is a matter of putting the self on view, of finding the presence of the imagined observer somehow reassuring. "We have become joyful scopophiliacs," Charles Melcher, an academic expert on voyeurism, told *The New York Times* in early 2000, explaining why so many city dwellers lately seem happy to live without curtains on their apartment windows, living and eating and making love in full view of their anonymous neighbours. "We are a society filled with very sophisticated voyeurs or lookers. With the explosion of explicit images on TV and on the Web, our eyes have been trained in a way that didn't exist twenty years ago." But, all appearances aside, this combination of exhibitionist and voyeur is not really an active engagement of individuals with the world outside them; it is not really a transcendence of old norms of privacy at all. It is merely an empty inwardness disguised as engagement, a bland celebration of self that does not succeed in raising any of the hard questions about what it is to be a private person within a public realm.

This can be hard to grasp, especially if we are moved by the apparently liberating possibilities of our now-constant immersion in technology, the sort of transvaluation of traditional values celebrated by Donna Haraway in her 1985 essay, "Manifesto for Cyborgs." Melcher is absolutely right that the presence of all-seeing communications technology has altered our ways of looking, our sense of ourselves; but it is far more complicated than simply opening the drapes and inviting the outside gaze. "The cyborg is resolutely committed to partiality, irony, intimacy, and perversity," Haraway writes. "It is oppositional, utopian, and completely without innocence. No longer structured by the polarity of public and private, the cyborg defines a technological polis based partly on a revolution of social relations in the *oikos*, the household. Nature and culture are reworked; the one can no longer be the resource for the appropriation or incorporation by the other."

Yet we have been slow to accept the alteration of our natures through technology. This alteration is a story that in truth is the story of human history but that tends, in practice, to become the story of the twentieth century. The reason for this truncation in scope is obvious enough, symbolized in a few choice inventions that came into their own during the eventful century: the machine gun, the airplane, the automobile, the telephone, the television, the computer. Mass production and mass destruction are the twinned pinnacles of twentieth-century life, and we still pledge our allegiance to them at every moment.

One consequence of this fact is the inescapability of capitalism — something that is challenged now and then but mostly just accepted, indeed celebrated. Whether we like it or not, our bodies themselves now underwrite the dominance of the market, because every moment of waking and sleeping life is shot through with commitment to the goods and services of the global economy. We are capitalism made flesh. Another consequence is a profound change in our sense of ourselves, a change best caught by the popular but somewhat misleading label "post-evolutionary." Our mastery of technology means we are no longer beholden to the gene pool, which we can now shape and perpetuate independently of natural reproduction, without all the attendant risks and tempestuous emotions. More than this, we are no longer bound by the natural environment itself, which we can also shape – though on the whole we seem bent on destroying it instead. Indeed, the threat of that destruction, only lately made a subject of explicit political debate, is one reason the post-evolutionary label is ultimately misleading: we are still constrained at the baseline by natural facts, even if this baseline is always shifting with our ingenuity and rapacity. Another reason to be suspicious of the label is that we are of course still evolving, if not quite in the manner of crude Darwinian orthodoxy.

What does all this entail in politics? First of all, an additional obligation as citizens, namely to attend to and understand the conditions of our technological existence – however painful that may be. This is primarily a matter of resisting the ideology of *inevitability* that creeps up around technology – an ideology so stealthy and complete, and so intimately related to the very idea of capital, that it is functionally invisible. But it also a matter of plotting connections – connections that are often resisted or simply ignored as people surf on by – between machines and politics. It is common these days for those of us in the privileged world to carry on large parts of our existence via e-mail, creating little virtual agoras out of our far-flung friends, or organizing dissent via the decentralized medium of the Internet. But these ethereal movements must nevertheless issue in the still-indispensable actions of shared space, if they are to be truly effective. For instance, the anti-corporatist protests of June 18 and November 30, 1999, or April 13, 2000, which drew so effectively from otherwise diffuse spatial quarters to focus on Seattle and Washington, would have meant far less if they had not led to forty thousand people occupying the actual city streets, or five hundred of them engaging in the highest form of citizenship, peaceful civil disobedience leading to arrest. (Sometimes, more intimately, a friendship blossoms in the strangely familiar space of e-mail. But it is *complete* only when we are together and my regard for you can register in the vulnerable, subtle media of the physical senses – when I can look into your eyes, see and touch your face, smell your personal perfume, be next to you.)

In the face of rapidly changing technology, there is a deeper obligation still, to reconceive not only citizenship and political commitment, but human nature itself. In 1928 Benjamin noted that technology is not best understood, as people often say, as the mastery of nature; it is, rather, the mastery of the relationship between nature and humankind. ("Men as a species completed their development thousands of years ago," Benjamin writes, "but humankind as a species is just beginning his.") The relationship is now constantly in question, and the question is always in part a political one. Our existence as citizens is ever conditioned, in countless ways both obvious and subtle, by the forms of communications and entertainment technology that trace their way through our daily lives. Technology no longer arises, as it did for first-generation Marxists, as an issue of the mode of production: the developmental level of the machines used to make goods. Now technology is both more important and less discernible: it has become part of us on a deeper level.

That is why Haraway and other Transhumanist prophets are only half right – or rather, more accurately, why we have so far only appreciated half, the unironic and apolitical half, of what they have been telling us. Yes, we are all cyborgs now, mixed human-carbon hybrids with wires shooting through our watery bodies at every angle. But we have not yet realized the political implications of this fact, swept up in the play of speed and pleasure that the wiring makes possible. We are too much taken with novelty and the "loveliness" of our inventions, the pure electromagnetic wave functions of next-generation technology. Technology becomes a sort of generalized deity, a wispy but all-pervasive god. Thus our great avoidance rituals in the face of technology, such that we fixate on the cutting edge and lose sight of the majority stuck on the trailing one. Or, if techno-political issues do come up, we imagine that they are about something like greater access to hardware – when they might really be about greater access to *the human software of literacy*, that indispensable enabling condition of citizenship, that forgotten civil right.

"Our best machines are made of sunshine," notes Haraway. That is both a virtue and a vice. Lightness and invisibility, the traits of the effective guerrilla, also entail, where power is entrenched, lack of accountability. The genuine citizen-cyborg must send out as well as allow in; she must transmit as well as receive. There is no such thing as a one-way communications node. The difficulty with un-private houses and other projects of personal gratification, therefore, the difficulty with all these entertaining machines we keep giving ourselves, is not the old one of folding domesticity and privacy away from the public view, making that realm female and subordinate. It is rather that, in being so *entirely* permeable to the public view, privacy becomes just another opportunity for conspicuous consumption.

This is the final subversion of the spectre of the public as a means of resented surveillance, in fact rendering the threat of surveillance meaningless by offering the world a complete view of everything that goes on in the house. But now the very idea of the polis as a shared space – a space shared for the purposes of discourse about how we may (or may not) all live together, not for the crude insistence on a single vision of the good life – is undermined in an ostentatious display of private enjoyment. The old public/private ideology is not transcended but simply reinscribed in a new, less obvious manner. Here political action is not so much prevented as nullified, made supremely uninteresting compared to the local pleasures of the house. Why should anyone bother with public spaces and the demanding actions of citizenship? Comfort becomes its own answer, shopping and surfing and e-trading their own defence.

This will not do. We need the separate private realm not only to escape the demanding pressures of public responsibility now and then, but also to engage more effectively with the shared, common aspects of life – to make us the sorts of citizens who can actively create and maintain the essential third spaces of civil society when we do enter into them. Whatever its many dangers and shortcomings, a well-ordered private realm makes a just public realm possible. Among other things, it makes the public/private distinction itself a matter for specifically public discourse, a contested border war. For only there can we offer arguments that will be assessed by our fellow citizens. (As Haraway notes, the nature/culture, human/animal, and body/machine border wars are similarly demanding: there is "*pleasure* in the confusion of boundaries," she says, but also "*responsibility* in their construction.")

Importantly, we do not – cannot – any longer expect these conflicts to resolve themselves into some larger notional whole, some form of dialectical completeness or super-consensus that rises above our disagreements. Nor can we indulge the dangerous nostalgic vision of a perfect political harmony that was lost and must be restored. Consensus is not really the goal of political discourse, which necessarily thrives on dissent; and nostalgia is just a comforting distraction we can ill afford. Instead of these escapist options (*above* the fray, *back* to the garden) we must constantly play, in all seriousness, in the ever-present spaces of the political realm. "Unlike the hopes of Frankenstein's monster," Haraway says, "the cyborg does not expect its father to save it through a restoration of the garden."

This form of thinking is utopian but not Edenic. The private realm it calls for need not be stark and sparse, as it was for the ancient Greeks, who viewed it as the site of mere necessity, of physical maintenance for the more important things happening elsewhere. (In taking this view of themselves as citizens, they of course enjoyed the benefit of patriarchy and a slave-based economy, both blithely defended by Aristotle as natural.) But an excessive concern with comfort becomes self-defeating, for it robs comfort of its point, and its potential role in public justification. The private sphere is for solace and rest, to be sure, but at some point these inward projects must be put in service to the larger debate that shapes the whole of social space.

Without that debate, and the legitimacy it alone offers to a specific ordering of space, the private realm is mere usurpation, an act of aggression against those less fortunate. Property crimes are most often motivated by need or envy, but they also sometimes have a deeper political point. In effect the burglar or robber wants to know, Where is the justification for your having so much when others have so little? And that is not a question that can be answered in the comfort of your own home. There is no political dimension left in the current wave of un-private houses and logo-dominated public spaces; no sense of the commitment to a public good – a commitment that the genuinely private house, in its attention to thresholds, actually maintains. Home is a notion that must establish a relationship between private and public; it cannot be an end in itself.

The ideal of the cyborg polis must therefore be pursued in better forms. Such a polis is, in some ways, not unlike the old civic republican ideal of a public space, where every citizen is a model of the whole, a network of common projects: not because each citizen is cleaving to a single notion of how best to live, or how best to enact political commitments, but because no one of us can ever wholly escape the awareness of intricate dependence on everyone else. Nowadays we must be more aware than ever of the things that separate us, that no single picture of citizenship will do. But that otherness itself, and an awareness of how it is tied up with the fate of numerous others, might be precisely the thing that connects us most acutely. Our existing desires alone, so often convergent with other people only on the meanest of material goods or the most limited of life projects, must be tutored by our deeper longings, the things that lie beneath the smooth surfaces of exchange and chatter. And these may emerge only when we are confronted by the unexpected, the unfamiliar, the uncanny: otherness is imagination's best tutor. So far, the reality of the new globalized ordering of space is, instead of this fruitful tension, a triumph of *undirected inwardness* – not a transcendent public realm, in other words, just a ceaseless and complacent celebration of prereflective individual desire.

We need deeper dreams than that. And yet, without the public oneiric spaces of the arcade or the square, without the people who can help us shape and articulate our wishes, we lack places to do our dreaming. We are left without sites on which to engage each another when we awake from that dreaming and try to make our wishes real. We are left without the most basic enabling conditions to create a world worthy of our aspirations.

———

It would be easy, at this point, to tell the rest of this story as one of glories lost, of possibilities gone unrealized: the century in ruins, all hope of political commitment shattered, the globe a jagged map tracing regions of backward isolationism and uncaring luxury. The temptation only grows when we do what Benjamin did so brilliantly, and engage the world of everyday life by walking its streets.

Go strolling in Paris today, and what do you find? The romantic Paris Arcades are long gone, replaced now by rows of cheap souvenir shops along the Rue de Rivoli, and by the ghastly open-air shopping mall near Châtelet des Halles, filled, as everywhere else, with the inescapable signs of McDonald's, Benetton, Pizza Hut, and a faked-up English pub, the Floozy and Firkin, all obscuring the view of beautiful St. Eustache church nearby. In the ranks of shops beside the Tuileries Gardens, near Rue St. Roch or Rue 29 Juilliet, you can find all the miniature gargoyles, novelty watches, Eiffel Tower charms, fake Hermès scarves, postcard sets, plastic swords, china kitsch (figures of love, loss, kittens), bright pennants, T-shirts, wind-up toys, crystal bowls, and dancing pipe-cleaner pets that you desire. Nearby, a massive scaffolding over the Centre Georges Pompidou shows the way our collective imagination now comes branded and trademarked, our public spaces, which should be dream houses of shared life, infiltrated by tired corporate slogans. The museum is covered with an ad for Swatch, proudly praising "Notre Musée" and its new millennial incarnation. And not far from there, a beautiful mural of Pablo Picasso, as big as a couple of football fields, eventually reveals, as one walks out of the Louvre's Cour Napoléon and towards Place de la Concorde, Macintosh's poor grasp of both propriety and grammar. Like everyone else, Pablo says, "Think Different."

In Boston's Newbury Street, meanwhile, or in the urban-mode stores of SoHo and TriBeCa, even along the Burlington and Piccadilly Arcades in London or in Berlin's new Arkaden amid the blandly refurbished modernism of the Potsdamer Platz, the stories – and the stores – are everywhere the same. There is a Tie Rack on every corner, a Body Shop at the end of every prospect: all the world's city centres reduced to the form and the status of an airport duty-free mall. The leisurely *flâneur*, who once lovingly collected his startling urban vistas and stole glances at beautiful strangers, has been replaced by the mall rat and the tourist, hallumping up and down the conventional routes to see the same logoed merchandise on offer in every other destination.

Where once the Arcades bred culture and revolution in nearly equal measure, we now observe the smug conformity of global consumerism, a world filled with the new International Class: mobile, youthful, affluent, and comfortable, wearing their cargo pants, sneakers, and one-strap backpacks, or their basic-black four-button suits and chunky Kenneth Coles, everywhere from Harajuku to the Leidespleine to Ipanema. Metal and glass are still the materials of choice in the architecturally ambitious malls of the world, from Toronto's long-vaulted Eaton Centre to the Crystal Palace echoes of the Trafford Centre in Manchester; but inside there is no dreaming, just another staggering *Dawn of the Dead* sequel.

That story is tempting, but it is misleading. For one thing, the old forms are still present if one knows where to look. Follow the Piccadilly Arcade into the quiet haven of London's Jermyn Street, where handmade shirts and ties, bright braces and gaudy cufflinks, crowd the Victorian shop windows like rows of glossy confections, and you may yet find the dandies of yesteryear, now promenading in handmade two-vent suits and Turnbull & Asser shirts rather than morning coats and spats. Parisians still stroll better than most people on earth, and of a Sunday you may yet observe the fashionable couples with their children pushing boats in the Luxembourg Gardens while Catherine Deneuve walks by, diva-style, with a cigarette in one hand and her little grandchild trailing from the other.

Near the Place des Vosges in the fourth arrondisement you can, in gorgeous little shops, buy exactly the sort of expensive, handmade paper Benjamin proudly used for the early version of his Arcades essay. The Place itself, a perfect four-square covered passageway bordering the Square Louis XIII park, is a testament to art, history, and high fashion, with the Académie de l'Architecture, the Paris headquarters of Issey Miyake and Romeo Gigli, and the former houses of both Victor Hugo and Théophile Gautier on its southern corners. A courtyard on the north side opens onto what may be the most beautiful hotel in Europe, the ivy-covered, four-star Pavilion de la Reine.

You may even stumble on an intact arcade in the old style, like the Galerie Véro-Dodat, which cuts off the corner of Rue du Bouloi in the first arrondisement, not far from the Louvre. This covered walkway, narrow and dimly lit, is the concrete remnant of the many passageways that obsessed Benjamin, the trace of a trope. Constructed in 1826, it is one of the few remaining examples of the site of Benjamin's excavations, among other things the place where the bulk of Daumier's works were first published. Now it houses a jumble of shops and objects that would have pleased Benjamin: broken dolls and doll houses, randomly stacked oil paintings, leather-bound first editions of Oscar Wilde in Japanese and German, one of *The Ballad of Reading Gaol* complete with Surrealist "realizations" of selected scenes, rendered in charcoal on heavy paper. Which, coincidentally, is exactly the medium used by the hyper-cool art students, all with standard-issue nose rings, dreads and torn jeans, who still sketch the high-modern glass-and-ironwork canopy of the Gare du Nord with the same connoisseur's eye that Benjamin brought to those quintessential nineteenth-century materials.

In short, all the glories are not past. More importantly, the true connoisseur of everyday life is always as much interested in junk as in luxury items, as fixated on advertising jingles as on poetry. Every miniature Eiffel Tower has a big story to tell. We make a crucial mistake if we become seduced by the false promises of a better past, a golden age of public life – something that, despite Adorno's misgivings, Benjamin actually saw quite clearly both within the Arcades and in his own compulsive reaction to them. Benjamin's lesson about the dream of history is that we are always beguiled by its strange surfaces and fantastic images. In modernity we are forever bewitched by the new, and this in turn generates a blinding nostalgia about the past. At virtually the same instant, the duality generates an overwhelming and enervating boredom, which we have not yet, despite all our best efforts, learned to understand.

"We are bored," says Benjamin, "when we don't know what we are waiting for. That we do know, or think we know, is nearly always the expression of our superficiality or inattention. Boredom is the threshold to great deeds." But that is true only if our boredom is attended to, not fled in a ceaseless round of empty stimulation by novelty. Indeed, it was precisely to work through this significant double effect of the modern urban experience – to *liquidate* it, in the language he and Adorno shared – that Benjamin embarked on *The Arcades Project* in the first place. Yet he was still caught, as we so often are today, in the sticky grip of the commodity. Even the sharpest cultural critic, if once he gives in to the temptation of the individual object's magic, is bound to feel the pull of fetishism's deep gravity well. Like many of us today, Benjamin wanted to analyze "the lustre with which the commodity-producing society surrounds itself," to read these mundane "wish symbols" as the "residue of a dream world." If he and we are not careful, that dream becomes a nightmare. In assessing the play of desires that capitalism makes possible, we may simply reproduce those yearnings rather than get the better of them: a form of counter-transference. That is what Adorno senses in the "auratic" vestiges still clinging, here and there, to Benjamin's lovingly constructed folly.

The real problem, as neither of them could clearly make out in the 1930s, but that confronts today's consumers on an hourly basis, is that Hektor Rottweiler was wrong: more materialist theory will not serve here. In fact, no kind of theory will really answer. Adorno falls into the ancient Aristotelian trap, the habitual error of the overweening theorist, of thinking that human meaning can be made entirely transparent by consistent application of human reason. He was wrong to think theory could accomplish so much. More precisely, he was wrong in thinking that the kind of theory he himself could marshal would be able to solve the very problems it had set itself. In the end, and despite its best intentions, such an elevated theory of cultural meaning succeeds only in separating itself off from everyday life, condemning those it would claim to liberate to a hell of everyday banality as heinous as any imagined by a cultural conservative lamenting the emptiness of contemporary culture after the style of T.S. Eliot or Hilton Kramer.

Note to anti-communist triumphalists everywhere: this has nothing to do with the fall of the Berlin Wall or the Nazi-Soviet non-aggression pact. It has to do, first of all, with the peculiar Borg-like qualities of consumer capitalism, so good at folding resistance back into itself in ever-faster waves of cool clothes and subversive pop music; and thus with the limits of any cultural theory when it faces off against artfully unfettered human desire. But it also has to do with the more general limits of theory as a way of coping with the constant too-muchness of the world, a world in which there is always more meaning than we can contain in our ready categories of meaning, our (often unconscious) assumptions. Thought is not stable, it is disruptive; and even a superior theory, like a superior mind, is eventually unequal to the task of fully mastering its disruptions. Wisdom lies in accepting this fact, and seeing the possibilities it opens up, rather than trying, usually with mounting symptoms of crabbiness or derangement, to eliminate all trace of the irrational or uncertain from human life.

Adorno and Horkheimer would articulate the first kind of limit with great precision in the work they undertook after the war, in particular with the devastating pessimism of their essay "The Culture Industry," a still-unrivalled indictment of the banality of mass culture. But they could not change those limits, and they could not save their version of critical theory from an increasingly irrelevant and politically empty elitism. Those developments would of course become clear only later, with the benefit of hindsight. In Europe, in the thirties, things were more stark. "The experience of our generation," Benjamin wrote in a late addition to the *Project*, is "that capitalism will not die a natural death." That sentiment may have a quaintness to our ears, but Benjamin's life was lived in a different world, and he had a prescient vision we would do well to recapture in this age of easy cynicism – not as nostalgia but as a survival strategy.

Adorno's urgings were misplaced, not, as some have argued, because critical theory is impossible under capitalism – as if the failure of a given overextended theory undermined, in its specific limitations, the very idea of social criticism. It is rather because he did not see that Benjamin was struggling with the only possible way to theorize capitalism now, namely, by means of a constant critical immersion in its murky waters. We don't abandon the sharp criticisms of materialist analysis – it still matters fundamentally who owns and who profits – but we approach those criticisms from our own experience of daily life, not from some theoretical pinnacle. This is a dangerous and constant task, a task that necessarily goes unfinished; it is also a task full of optimism. It is, without exaggeration, the task of every committed citizen. Of these two great thinkers, Benjamin is the one who dies unnaturally, who seems to be mired in despair. Yet it is Benjamin who actually possessed the greater stores of hope – who, though so often charged with an excess of whimsy or charm rather than of materialist precision, exhibited the more serious commitment to political change.

Benjamin once complained to his close friend Scholem that he would rather read three lines of Proust than all of what passed then for materialist analysis, and this is the clue to his unfinished story. He could say to the Jewish mystic what only brought fierce objection from Adorno: that he sensed, in the Arcades, a moment of illuminating tension between past and present. Here the "trash of history" could be collected and "redeemed," and the historian, working in this "dialectic at a standstill," this catastrophic present, could assume an almost messianic status. Here, reading the archaeology of the collective unconscious, we "engender, through interpenetration with what is new, the utopia" that "has left its trace in a thousand configurations of life, from enduring edifices to passing fashions." Utopia, if it is to have the positive impact of what Bloch called "the principle of hope," should not be carved out of the thin air of reckless speculation; it should be recovered from the dream materials of life as we live it. And this, in its way, is the *tikkun* of the Lurian Kabbalah.

Benjamin wanted *The Arcades Project* to be the history of an era, but he failed to complete that history. He failed, in another sense, to complete his life. These failures indicate, paradoxically, the success of his dream being our dream still. There is a collective Arcades Project that, like Benjamin's, is forever incomplete; a project of continual resistance in a world where resistance is so often considered futile and money's triumph inevitable. Benjamin's book is not, finally, the history of an era. It is instead the history of a moment – the moment of Benjamin's dream, of the bad dreams we need to wake up from, and of the dreams of a better world that maintain a wispy, beckoning presence even in the most banal fashion trend or pop song. We must always be ready to go astray. "Not to find one's way about in a city is of little interest. But to lose one's way in a city, as one loses one's way in a forest, requires practice," Benjamin says in *A Berlin Childhood*. "I learned this art late in life: it fulfilled the dreams whose first traces were the labyrinths on the blotters of my exercise books."

What are we looking for when we enter the somnambulant world of the shopping mall? What do we hope to find in the trite tourist haunt? What is our vast intercontinental boredom, so persistent and recurring, trying to tell us? That the city is a collective dream house. That its strollers are the agents of a fertile, connective imagination. That the new global arcades are a social critic's dream, a vast text crying out for illuminating interpretation. Read your cultural experience as Benjamin did, savouring the prosaic yet finding the traces of Arcadian desire that point beyond the way things are. Open every mysterious briefcase you find, enter every dim passageway. Your deeper self, perhaps a better world, is waiting there.

Chapter 5

THE WORLD WE WANT

When the Dow Jones industrial average topped the 10,000 mark in March 1999, the market triumphalism that is so common in these cyberspace-bubble days reached a peak of self-congratulation rarely seen even on the confidence-fuelled streets of the Manhattan financial district. "There's a widespread belief," said Bill Meehan, chief market analyst with the New York brokerage firm Cantor Fitzgerald, "that we're in the best of all possible worlds."

The best of all possible worlds? You certainly couldn't argue with the figures. In the spring of 1999, the American economy was booming as never before: ninety-three consecutive months of expansion, with an annual growth rate of 3.9 percent during 1997 and 1998 and rates above 4.0 percent in 1999; unemployment at 4.3 percent, the lowest it had been since 1957; and inflation running, depending on the measure, between 1.0 and 1.6 percent, the lowest mark in decades. Real hourly wages were up by 2.5 percent, consumer spending was up by 4.8 percent, and savings rates were down to 0.5 percent – the lowest mark since 1933. Crime, welfare, and infant mortality rates were all falling. Average life expectancy was seventy-six years, and rising.

Setbacks to the Dow in the first quarter of 2000, together with some alarming fluctuations and sharp drops in the "new economy" tech stocks of the Nasdaq index over the same period, complicated the picture a little, of course. On Friday, April 14, 2000, as inflation rose and profits were taken, the Dow fell a steep 6 percent and the Nasdaq more than 15. The day capped a 25.3 percent drop on the week for the Nasdaq, and it was the single worst day for combined market losses since the Black Monday crash of October 19, 1987. It seemed as though the bubble might finally have burst: the long bull market had gone bear.

And yet, the setbacks did little to dampen the enthusiasm of those who still find themselves on the upside of the emerging global and Internet world. The losses were small compared with several continuous years of growth, after all: the market was just "adjusting" or "correcting" itself. In northern California, twentysomething millionaires are still thronging the martini bars and Asian-fusion restaurants of San Francisco, transforming the hills above Oakland into forbidding enclaves of wealth, remaking the old working-class towns of the valleys north and south of the Bay into upscale havens. West Vancouver is thick with conspicuous, youthful wealth. Their counterparts on the right coast are having the same enlivening effect on Ridgewood and Westchester, Arlington and Somerville, even the refurbished warehouses of King Street West in Toronto. The American South is booming, the Midwest is booming, everywhere is booming. And the best part is, everybody's happy about it. In turn-of-the-century North America, more people are making more money and buying more stuff than ever before. They're living longer, building more houses and filling them with more consumer durables. They're eating out more, going away more, borrowing more, spending more. Gourmet groceries are available on every corner, luxury car dealerships on every other block.

This is the strongest peacetime American economy of the past century, maybe of the country's entire existence. Things have never been better, and there doesn't seem to be an end in sight. Amid the usual pro forma warnings that the world economy should cool off a bit to avoid a hard future downturn, the International Monetary Fund noted with pleasure in April 2000 that the global growth rate for the year, led by the Americans, was likely to be around 4.2 percent, the highest since 1988, and that the global boom would continue even as the economy slowed slightly – good news, really, since that would forestall any sudden changes for the worse – to a healthy growth rate of 3.9 percent in 2001. Even sluggish Canada, beset by massive foreign holdings and falling median income rates relative to the rest of the industrialized world, could not entirely miss the knock-on effects as the new millennium dawned, racking up quarter after quarter of growth in its own right. People on this continent, people all over the place if they know what's good for them, have never had it better. Happy days, it seems, are here again.

Meehan probably didn't realize it, but he was unwittingly quoting the German philosopher G.W. Leibniz (1646–1716), whose doctrine of *theodicy*, or God's justice, is what originally gave us that familiar expression of optimism, "the best of all possible worlds." Leibniz's theodicy was based on a simple but powerful argument. First of all, he said, though there is only one actual world, there are many possible ones. Therefore it is metaphysically conceivable for the world to be other than it is: there are other worlds available out there, feasible at least in theory. And because there are these many *possible* worlds, it follows, it could be the case that the world we have is not actually the best one to be found among the pool of going options.

Yet, appearances of imperfection aside, this is not so. Because God created the world, and God is good, we can be confident that this actual world is not just *one of* the possible ones, but the *best* of all possible ones. God would not – could not – do anything less than call into existence the superior available option in the array. To do so, even among all the many options metaphysically available, would be for Him to be less than God. And that is metaphysically impossible, a contradiction in terms. So yes, there may be wars, pestilence, cruelty, torture, and injustice, but we can nevertheless remain supremely confident that things could not be any better, they could only be worse. Why? Because God created them, and He could not have done otherwise. *Quod erat demonstrandum*.

This ingenious argument struck many people, notably the satirist Voltaire, as patent nonsense, intellectually scandalous. Writing the proto-novel *Candide* (ironically subtitled *Optimism*), Voltaire's inspiration was the Lisbon earthquake of 1755, which killed thousands of innocents. He was likewise mindful of the territorial wars of the early 1700s, which had ravaged much of Europe by looting and pillaging as well as battle, not to mention the everyday suffering that was the lot of most people in his era: the hunger, cold, illness, and early death. In the course of the book, the young anti-hero, Candide, staggers through a multifaceted horror show of suffering, from torture and dismemberment to leprosy and starvation, only to be told at every moment by the eternal optimist Dr. Pangloss, a Leibnizian mouthpiece, that everything is working out for the best – because it must be so in God's best of all possible worlds.

In effect, Voltaire says, Leibniz's theodicy is scandalous because it simply evades the challenge posed by the presence of evil in the world. If God is perfect, that challenge goes, He must be omniscient, omnipotent, and omnibenevolent: the so-called triangle of perfection. And yet there is certainly evil in the world – that cannot reasonably be denied. Indeed, evidence for the proposition that the world contains evil approaches an overwhelming level. Evil is both present and apparently ineradicable. Therefore, all issues of human ignorance aside, one corner of the triangle of perfection must give. God is either deficient in knowledge (He would and could do better, but doesn't know how), lacking in power (He would do better, and knows how, but can't), or worst of all limited in goodness (He can do better, and knows how, but just doesn't give a damn). And those are the only options. Any way you slice it, evil in the world means an imperfect God.

But of course here Leibniz replies, once more: no, no, the problem is with the world, not the God who created it. Or, more precisely, the problem lies with those of us who have the temerity to assess the world or God from within our mortal limitations. Theodicy does not deny the existence of evil. It says instead that evil is merely an appearance, or is all in the service of a greater good not obvious to us. God's perfection is metaphysical bedrock: everything else follows from that, evil or no evil. That holds as a matter of logic, not experience. Any confusions that arise on this point must therefore be the result of our restricted human viewpoint, and the limits of empirical knowledge. We are still prisoners in the Platonic cave of sense perception. But unlike Plato, who at least thought we had a human duty to make our way painfully out of that imprisonment, theodicy assumes that our incarceration is permanent.

It's a neat trick. And there is something increasingly familiar about that style of reasoning as we make our way around the new globalized world, though the talk is no longer of God and evil, but of the Market and its mysterious adjustments or downturns. The Bill Meehans of the world say, based on high growth rates and low inflation, that things have never been better – and imply thereby that they *cannot* be better. They also cheerfully, even unthinkingly, accept that the notions of "better" and "best" they employ are the only valid ones. Leave aside for the moment concerns that even the Dow and Nasdaq combined are not identical with the entire marketplace of exchange, or legitimate worries that these latest climbs may just herald a sharp future downturn: the dreaded "hard landing" of any boom economy, especially one based so heavily on technology companies without real products or assets. For the moment, notice only how we now have a form of capitalist theodicy that, as much as Leibniz's theological one, brooks no rational challenge. It's not a position, it's a religion.

In fact, the capitalist version of theodicy may be even more self-protecting than the religious one. Thus charges that a market-driven economy, even a wildly successful one, is indifferent to disparities in wealth or the great volume of human misery around the world are greeted with a chorus of incredulity. Indications of the potential evils of unbridled growth, the scattered and unaccountable machinery of a hot economy taking over our very ability to make decisions, are waved away as lacking in sophistication. Worries that massive disparities in wealth pose grave risks to peace and security are dismissed as scare-mongering, usually emanating from ignorable third world quarters. But worse than all of this is theodicy's basic defensive posture: any claim of a cautionary kind is met not with counter-arguments but with charges of hypocrisy – as if pointing out that someone must shop for clothing or earn a living means any criticism of capitalism they may offer is irrelevant. Any questioning of the ultimate *point* of all that economic growth is answered not by argument but with a barrage of personal invective.

Such self-serving emotion always betrays a deeper anxiety, something that the original criticism has provoked into a displaced pain, the way a probing tongue can make a toothache the source of irrational rage. These breaks in the smooth self-congratulation of the world as we find it are crucial; they reveal what is really going on beneath the happy triumphalism and the routine enjoyment of life's highest pleasures by an elite few. The emotion is an indication that the challenge comes from within us, not from without: we are in the position of Athenian citizens confronted by a relentless Socrates who wants to know how we can go on living the way we do. We may eliminate him, but we cannot eliminate the question. In this case, of course, the most disturbing thing about the new market theodicy is that it is just as self-protecting and blinkered as the old theological one, and perhaps even better at rendering itself invisible. It is rationally evasive, especially to its own keenest adherents, disappearing into a miasma of inevitability, rendering objection "naive." And yet, *we all know* that to suggest that things could not be better when most of the world lives in abject poverty, or that the market is always right when it buys comfort only for the few, is as blithe and Panglossian as saying that every single instance of pain and suffering is part of God's plan: more power to the righteous (now read rich).

To make that point is not simply to gesture towards the hidden costs of the current economy, though we should certainly do that. The United States is not really in "peacetime," for example, despite the ease with which that adjective trips off the tongue of the president and every self-satisfied commentator on the Sunday morning panel shows. At any moment, the United States is engaged in several small-scale foreign wars and has hugely expensive aircraft carriers and ground forces stationed all over the world. Its 1999 military budget was $271 billion, greater than the amount spent by the next six biggest military spenders combined. A single aircraft carrier, the great symbol of American sovereignty when dispatched to the Indian Ocean or the Persian Gulf, costs $444 million a year to operate.

More people may be working, furthermore, but many of them are working longer hours, for less money – and yet generating bigger profits for the people who employ them. In 1995 U.S. businesses earned an average of $1.85 for every $1.00 spent on employee salaries and benefits; that figure has now risen to $2.15 for every $1.00 spent. More than half of the American population now invests in the stock market, but 90 percent of controlled shares are still owned by less than 10 percent of the population, 65 percent by less than 2 percent of the population. Growth has not been spread evenly – the top 1 percent of the population saw their incomes double between 1977 and 1999, but the vast majority were still struggling. The disparity between the wealth of the United States as a whole and the rest of the world is equally stark. Even Canada, blessed with numerous natural advantages, is a poor nation by comparison, with an ailing currency and declining quality of life everywhere outside the five major cities of Toronto, Vancouver, Montreal, Calgary, and

Edmonton. One could multiply the examples endlessly, but we have all heard this story before. Noting gross disparities in wealth has become so commonplace, in fact, that the statistics take on an air of invisibility.

More absurdly still, even using GDP as a measure of economic success is a mug's game, since it counts as productive activity any transaction involving goods or services, regardless of what effect it might have on society. The O. J. Simpson trial, for example, contributed an estimated $200 million to America's GDP during the mid-1990s in the form of legal fees, television airtime, and newspaper commentary. Degraded environments are GDP bonanzas, from the value of products produced in the rape of a given biosystem, through to the costs of (say) site cleanup and medical care for citizens poisoned by incidental toxic waste. As some leading economists put it in an article in the *Atlantic Monthly* not long ago, "By the curious standard of the GDP, the nation's economic hero is a terminal cancer patient who is going through a costly divorce." Or, as the economist Herman Daly said even more succinctly, "The current national accounting system treats the earth as a business in liquidation." One thing we must always remember when we are told about successive quarters of economic growth is that growth, by all the current measures, is not just value-neutral but severely skewed. We would be in a growth economy even as we were bombing each other into oblivion, or using up the planet's natural resources in a single generation.

The bottom line is this: American-style growth and expansion, which is what people usually mean when they use the opaque signifier *globalization*, look terrific only because they are measured at a level of abstraction, and with a narrowness of vision, that conceals everything from the unjust distribution of that wealth to the imperial adventures and exploitation of those who make it possible. Infinite growth, the goal of the internal logic of capitalism, is ultimately (and necessarily) self-defeating, for it will eventually – and maybe much sooner than we usually imagine – destroy the very site of its success, the natural environment of this planet. Left to its own devices, the Market god is really nothing like the benevolent, omniscient, omnipotent perfect being of the Christian imagination. It is, instead, as wrathful, punishing, and unresponsive as the God of the Old Testament could be.

———

Even if the prosperity were spread more evenly, however, and even if that staggering military budget were taken out of GDP calculations – even if a desire for sustainable and reasonable economic growth were matched by keen environmental awareness – what would the *point* of all this be? That is an ethical question, not an economic one. In other words, it is a question that has a hard time getting asked these days. But sooner or later, as individuals, we come up against a version of it. Suppose you have been struggling to get a foothold in the professional sector of your choice, making sacrifices for education and entry-level opportunities, and finally begin succeeding quite nicely. You find yourself, perhaps for the first time ever, modestly wealthy. Now, do you leave it at that, content to explore the possibilities of your identity as householder and cultural being, the many joys and lessons of Roles One through Six? Or do you ask what this good fortune means in terms of political opportunities and obligations? Do you wonder whether there are corresponding political duties and virtues to pursue, public spaces to maintain, dreams to entertain?

Perhaps this second choice seems far-fetched or impossibly demanding. Perhaps you simply give it no attention at all. And yet I believe many thoughtful people are troubled by the unstable relationship between success and meaning in this world we are so busily creating, and often find today that their sense of self is corroding under the mindless imperatives of personal economic expansion and financial success. They want to know what it all means, what their personal prosperity is in aid of: fulfillment, virtue, happiness, something. They want a *telos* of some kind, in other words, an end in view that helps to make life worth living – even if it is ever the case that any such *telos* is provisional, indistinct, even enigmatic. They also want the social roles and tables of relevant virtues to go with that *telos,* to provide the materials of everyday action and character. If they find no answers at all to these often inarticulate longings, no sense of possible direction to life, they are justifiably unsettled.

That sense of discomfiture, so often fleeting and vague, is an intimation of what I have been trying to show, in my backwards fashion, in the course of this book. Without some form of rich political commitment, we are somehow *less than ourselves* – we stand unfulfilled. This is not the only form of fulfillment we seek but, importantly, it is the most social and visible kind. It may also be the most lasting in effect, touching not just the people around us but also the institutions, social relations, and material conditions of life. No wonder we feel uneasy when this form of human commitment is confused or unavailable. We usually hide from such unease, covering it over with projects and tasks and speedy consumption; or translate it into something else, like a picture of the world itself as *inevitably* unbalanced or *naturally* unjust. But even if we did not make the world, we are nevertheless the ones making these pictures of the world, and we cannot reach any genuine insight about ourselves or our social-cultural environment – those co-determining poles of the social order of things – until we see the burden and joy of that peculiar responsibility. How do we create the world we want, rather than a world that just happens to us?

Well, what sorts of teleological conceptions of the world have made sense in the past? Aristotle thought the polis, buoyed by sufficient material wealth, was a site of human self-realization, the place where we worked out the inner logic of our natures. Saint Augustine talked of working towards the greater glory of God.

Machiavelli believed the point of military and material success was something less teleological and more modern: the glory of man, not God. Montaigne wanted privilege to be tempered by gentleness, disagreement managed with tolerance. Benjamin had an even more expansive vision of emancipation and belonging, a vision rooted in the materials of everyday life. All of them addressed their disagreements to a larger agreement, namely, that material wealth and personal comfort mean little in themselves; they are only good for what they make possible. And that is true for polities as much as for individuals. We cannot possibly begin to clarify any new political values for ourselves, or even recover the valuable aspects of existing ones, without moving past this crudest imaginable notion of a guiding principle, simple acquisitiveness. A constant greed for more, as every student of the human soul knows, is always a sign of some deeper, usually bewildered, desire.

The classic liberal conception of politics says, Here is the problem: we have two people who want the same thing. What are we going to do about that? We're going to manage their conflicting desires with a social contract, a non-aggression pact. From the liberal point of view, all desires are good desires and the only issue is effective and efficient management of them – this is the GDP of the soul. But just as there are conflicting desires *between* people, there are, as Plato and Marx and Freud all well knew, conflicting desires *within* people. Politics is not just about the smooth management of existing desire; it must also be about probing the roots of desire itself. Market liberals think that any teleology is too much teleology, that this talk of internal conflict and the meaning of life puts us on the slippery slope to moral tyranny. But they need to rethink their own impoverished teleology, their own cramped conception of human nature – a conception used, as much as any naturalistic vocabulary of inevitability about the market itself, to wave off objections they find uncomfortable. We are humans. Whatever else is true of us, we are vastly more complicated in our motivations and needs than pure social-contract or rational-decision theory can account for. For us, the question is never simply *What do we want?* It is also, often more crucially, *Why do we want it?*

In North America today you will hear little talk of that kind, of course. In this new directionless world of wealth, consumption has become a national obsession, an irresistible drive. Observe the massive personal debts and free spending, which make care with money seem strange, eccentric, even a bit wimpy, like someone who inexplicably opts out of a game of touch football. Notice the gargantuan high-fat meals delivered in restaurants, usually at short-order speed, and consumed with every appearance of desperation, as if there were a concealed referee timing the results for a prize. ("Becoming obese," said the University of Colorado health researcher James O. Hill, "is a normal response to the American market." Twenty percent of Americans are currently obese, and the numbers grow yearly, especially among young people: if nothing changes, within a few generations almost all American will be overweight. Market growth in action.)

Where are we going after all those big fast meals? What is all that borrowing and spending in aid of? It's a sign of the times that such questions are all but unintelligible right now. We have all been told that success breeds success. Here, in addition, success has become its own, purely self-reflexive, standard of value. Social conformity, conspicuous consumption, and heedless gain are not new features of the human scene; Socrates worried about their caustic effects on the souls of his fellow citizens more than two millennia ago. What may be new is that in this new postmodern version of prosperity, lack of content is the only content. This is prosperity for prosperity's sake alone. Never before, I suspect, have so many people been so rich to so little purpose.

When my first-year philosophy students write their final examination each year they are asked, among other things, to comment on
this statement taken from the philosopher Alasdair MacIntyre: "The
good life is the life spent seeking the good life." *Discuss. True or false.
Agree or disagree.*

Don't worry. I always tell them this beforehand. There isn't much
point, after all, in springing something like that on a nineteen-year-
old who's sitting in a chilly gym at 9 a.m., probably wondering what
she's going to do for a summer job or, maybe more to the point, why
he signed up for philosophy in the first place. I try to give them all
the breaks I can. On the other hand, I also want to unsettle them as
much as possible. What is the good life? MacIntyre's deliberately
puzzling formulation is an attempt to rise above the shifting sands of
time and fashion. It neatly captures the paradoxical nature of critical
reflection on the possibilities of life, because its logic undermines
the blithe assurance of those whose knowingness gives them all the
answers to our problems, usually doled out during dinner-party
debates or in 750-word chunks on the op-ed pages of newspapers.
This odd-sounding answer to the basic ethical question constantly
reminds us of the disruptive elements in our attempts to make sense
of ourselves and our place in the world.

That is an important reminder, even if we are rightly suspicious of
philosophers (or anyone else, for that matter) who seem to think that
the answer to all our problems lies in further theorizing and more
explanation. *Reflection* as I have been defending it in the previous
pages is conceptually distinct from *theory*. It is much more modest in
its aims and aware of the intellect's shortcomings – but also much
more searching and powerful in its potential effects. Reflection
involves the always incomplete attempt to make sense of who we are
and what we are up to, trying all the while to do that most difficult of
things, to live better. Theory believes it provides answers. Reflection
knows that it merely pursues questions, and does that often enough
only tentatively or in the midst of perplexity and sadness.

Even reflection has limits when it must cut so much against the spirit of the age. What constitutes success in living seems always to be changing, and that variation can lead to a judgment of relativism: the ultimately self-defeating notion that there is no fact of the matter about the good life – so knock yourself out in your chosen quest, for power or money or sexual pleasure. You might as well live like a depraved moral lunatic! Why not? What is there to stop you? These days, such judgments even draw a measure of social sanction and become the nihilistic common sense of the age. In the process they send ethical debate to the bleakly humorous margins so effectively rendered in contemporary films, usually about Los Angeles. The bickering armed robbers of *Reservoir Dogs*, the morally decentred group of bachelor-party buddies in *Very Bad Things*, the nuance-disputing drug dealers of *Go*: they all enact a kind of twisted Platonic dialogue about how to go on. "Sure we'll kill him, but not *that* way. Of *course* I'm going to commit a hit-and-run, but not without leaving the body where it can be discovered." Nobody sane would draw their notions of the good life from such material, of course, but these visions do serve to mark the decline of our reasoning about what Socrates considered the foundational philosophical question, What is the life worth living?

That question has lately become more about things than wisdom, more about brand names than the common good. These days, indeed, it is difficult to keep any discussion of "the good life" from sliding, sometimes immediately and sometimes by imperceptible stages, into a seminar on material comforts and lifestyle aids. The phrase "living well" has almost entirely shed its ethical connotations. That is why looking at certain lifestyle magazines can make you feel faintly sick: their lack of shame about materialism is, at one remove, shaming. This is certainly not to say that material goods are irrelevant to happiness, or that the good life involves nothing of what those tasty, coated-paper magazines deliver to us in their backlit visions. Try telling someone without the means to buy a television, or to make a phone call, that they shouldn't long for these double-edged toys of modern life. And anyone who has had the luck to enjoy some luxury now and then must agree with Aristotle that a truly blessed life involves a measure of wealth and the chance to enjoy its fruits. But we seem to have lost our ability to think clearly about these matters, and for fairly precise historical and economic reasons.

Today we are not really materialists. We are, rather, fetishists of the material. If we were truly materialist, as the critic Raymond Williams once pointed out, we would be *satisfied* with the acquisition of material goods; they would make us happy in themselves. We are precisely the opposite of this, ever-conflicted victims of the vice the ancient Greek philosophers called *pleonexia*: wanting more, the more we have. We do not really desire the goods most of the time, only the complicated feelings of pleasure that acquiring the goods makes possible. Strummed by advertisers and marketers like plummy mandolins, surrendering to our own internalized desires, we are forever in search of the next consumer hit. Well, so what? This is hardly news. Lots of people will tell you that it was ever thus, or that we can't expect anything else. Actually, both claims are false – it was not, and we can. But it is worth wondering why such argument-ending claims have the cachet they do, given how weak they are.

Part of the motivation for thinking in that reductive way, maybe a large part, is defensive. Consider an example. There is nothing more common in disputes about the state of the world today than what we might agree to call the Evasive Elision. I mean the way important distinctions, say between art and advertising, or between argument and self-promotion, are these days eagerly rubbed out in a face-saving attempt to suggest that everything is for sale and therefore nothing is untainted. Ironically, the arguments about a lack of purity are most often made by those who would otherwise shrink from the idea that purity matters, and from the idea that engagement with the market signifies impurity. This is a clear sign of the cynicism of the position, which proceeds not from conviction but from self-protection. Levelling charges of hypocrisy is always the fastest, and cheapest, route to the moral high ground – something Montaigne knew very well when he condemned the move as a moral evasion in the course of the *Essays*. The trouble is, that move doesn't help anybody except the leveller, who now gets to dodge criticism but only at the cost of shutting down debate altogether.

Indeed, such erasures recall Oscar Wilde's definition of the cynic as the person who knows the price of everything but the value of nothing. And that kind of apparently sophisticated attitude, perversely, makes us more comfortable with our weaknesses, not less. If the nihilism of the fastidious professional killer or mildly scrupulous drug dealer is not for all of us, this more general piece of cynical self-protection certainly is. The good life? Nowadays it is the life spent fending off all those naive challenges to one's acquisitiveness, throwing out facile charges of bad faith at those who dare to suggest things might be better, and claiming to find it baffling that anyone really thinks the adventitious privilege of birth might entail positive duties to the less fortunate. In this weirdly protracted battle for the modern soul, the glossy consumer objects, so ubiquitous and fetching, are themselves an unanswerable challenge to political awareness, a carapace of brand-name armour. Benjamin again, circa 1928: "The luxury goods swaggering before us now parade such brazen solidity that all the mind's shafts break harmlessly on their surface."

The real trouble, of course, is that all this acquisition does not seem to make us any happier. In this sense, the Evasive Elision and its cousins are mere window-dressing, the distracting appearance of argument that does not touch the core problem. The renegade economist Robert Frank notes that there is no logical stopping point to acquisition, and yet beyond a certain level there is no correlation between wealth and happiness. "Behavioral scientists," he says, "have found persuasive evidence that once a threshold level of affluence is achieved, the average life-satisfaction level in any country is essentially independent of its per capita income." Which is one reason why the 39 percent rise in U.S. per capita income between 1972 and 1991, say, left a legacy of lower average happiness levels. At the heart of this apparently bizarre result is the confused nature of our conceptions of happiness. We are competitive and envious creatures, whether by nature or by some complex of natural and social factors, and so our sense of well-being is dangerously dependent on what is going on with others.

Thus studies consistently indicate results surprising only in their honesty about human desire. Beyond the levels of basic subsistence, we want to have things and wealth relative to what other people have, not for themselves. Most people, for example, would prefer earning $50,000 while others made $25,000 to earning $100,000 while others made $250,000. This kind of result holds even when it is true that a flatter income-distribution level would be advantageous to everyone. As long as individuals measure themselves against other individuals, we are caught in what Frank calls the "smart for one, dumb for all" trap. Instead of channelling money into cheap and reliable public transit, for example, we all strive to buy sporty convertibles or massive trucks – though they clog the highways, pollute the air, cut us off from one another, and regularly crash. Instead of reflecting on the possibility that need and want may be distinct concepts, we immerse ourselves in the nearly overwhelming pleasures of the unstable material world.

These are real pleasures, of course, and there is real joy to be found in the marketplace. That is why merely denunciatory critics of consumerism are doing nobody but themselves any good. If we want to engage this world of ours with real results, we have to accept and understand the fact that watching a thirty-second television ad can sometimes be an exhilarating experience, that shopping is indeed a form of release and pleasure for many people, that putting on an expensive suit can occasion a liberating and wonderful feeling of well-being. Only then should we even attempt to separate that kind of exhilaration or pleasure from the consumer impulse that seems to accompany it. Why attempt that separation at all, ever? Well, because once we take a first step on the road to luxury, there is little to prevent a kind of consumerist arms race, with small gaps or advantages in material goods closing as fast as they open. Ever in search of a competitive advantage or pocket of enviable happiness, we are now driven to newer and more inventive forms of acquisition. Standard luxury items like Rolexes and ChrisCraft speedboats sell on the basis of their exclusivity, a combination of outrageous cost and artificially limited supply, in order to make them markers of success in the envy stakes. *I have it — and you don't!*

By the same token, the contemporary branding and narrativizing of consumer products, which compresses desire and expectation into the slick miniature plot of a television commercial, makes all of us into de facto experts on names and logos and spokespeople. Our overwhelming exposure to these micro-tales of success and beauty transforms acquisition into a kind of hyper-competitive graduate school, with Phil Knight or Bill Gates or Michael Jordan our presumptive professors. All the buying and selling of cool naturally comes down to this: I know more than you do about the available brands, I am more *au courant* with the latest narrative, I discovered this logo sooner, and therefore I have an advantage over you. You may catch up, finally buying your Kangol golf cap or FUBU shirt – or whatever it now is, for time overtakes a writer's examples as relentlessly as a person's expectations – but I will already be gone. We all know this is true, because marketers and their critics (who are sometimes, in another elision, the very same people) have been telling us this for years. And yet we seem unwilling to act on that knowledge.

It is hard to know whether the sharply unequal distribution of wealth we now observe in the world is a direct result of these aspects of our current notions of the good life, or whether we construct visions to match our situation. I think the relationship is symbiotic, complex, and hard to analyze with anything like a clarity that would issue in a course of action. The competitive impulse of all this envy drives a system away from horizontal distributions, even as it sharpens the unhappiness felt by the majority that, of necessity, finds itself unable to scale the pinnacles of the resulting x-y curve. It is certainly the case, for example, as the economist Robert Samuelson has argued persuasively, that most North Americans are far better off in absolute material terms now than during the 1950s. Rare today is the home without running water, a television or two, even a car. North Americans eat out more than twice as often now as they did during the 1950s, and spend vastly more on toys, travel, and entertainment.

There are fewer servants in North America today, it's true, because local wage expectations make them too expensive. Appliances and home shopping alleviate the need for most people, while cheaper foreign labour is once more making the domestic servant a familiar sight, at least in the homes of the very wealthy. Some people still live in abject poverty, but a larger proportion of the population is provably more comfortable than their parents' generation – and yet they think of themselves as poor because, compared with what they see and expect, they are. Visions of luxurious living clearly contribute strongly to this impression, since in the contemporary mediascape it becomes nearly impossible to avoid images of a life more desirable than your own. From Martha Stewart's mad domestic perfectionism to the cool-to-rule kids of the fashion glossies, there's always somebody somewhere who has it better than you. This leads in turn to a sense that life is letting you down, that there is no good reason for relative differences in comfort, and therefore no good reason for the social structures that permit them.

Envy may be the basis of democracy, as Bertrand Russell once said, but it is also the most common source of unhappiness. By 1995, household debt in the United States had grown to 81 percent of disposable income, not least because going into debt is the only way most people can acquire the things they crave. Those of us in the most prosperous parts of the world now work longer hours, commute farther, and sleep less – all in the service of the good life. People will do anything, apparently even to their own detriment, to find some manner of what they think constitutes "better living." On the surface, then, we observe more luxury goods, more seductive visions of individual achievement and self-creation, and more subtle comparisons. But we also see more unhappiness, more resentment, and more imminent social unrest. Programs of voluntary simplicity or renewed spirituality, the countertenor of the era's loud chorus, keen and warble their dissent but don't really affect the dominant melody of getting and spending.

Is there a solution to this crazy merry-go-round? Some economists propose a luxury tax to counter our upward spiral of acquisition, a bold attempt to turn individual self-interest away from itself by sharply raising the opportunity costs of indulgence. Individuals would have to decide on and declare a single luxury pursuit, preserving a measure of choice thereby, but would then be bound in their spending by the redistributive constraints of steep marginal tax rates. (The argument is that such a directed tax is fairer than across-the-board progressive income tax, which is indiscriminate in its application of redistributive burdens.)

Others would have us return, as if that were possible, to a less rapacious, fifties-style version of North America. For those who would not actually endorse the social and tax policies of any allegedly simpler era, there is always the costless option of nostalgia. Wander through the high-end home stores of Chelsea or Yorkville or SoHo and you will be struck by the ubiquity of a watered-down modernist style, a generalized and somehow bleakly appealing version of the good life as distributed, in the main, by cinematic imagery: skyscrapers in cool black and white, silver frames, bullet-headed cocktail shakers. We all want to live on this film set, to inhabit this fantasy. But like all fantasies, it is structurally unstable, important for what it hides more than what it reveals. The more of these literally fantastic goods there are to purchase, the more they, and the well-being they promise, seem to slip through our fingers. Nostalgia cannot aid us here, because its wispy attractions are meretricious; it leaves everything as it is.

I have a different suggestion. Denunciations of materialism and consumerism so often fall on deaf ears because at a deep level they miss the point. Appearances sometimes to the contrary, we are all struggling, in our different ways, to bestow meaning on the world of our everyday experience. We are trying to forge identities from the play of cultural materials. And the basics of the good life have not really changed, though this became harder and harder to see as we reached the end of the expiring decadent century and sifted through our trunks of mechanically reproduced images, faux memories, and siren calls to comfort. The relentless acquisition of goods is just a symptom of a deeper ailment, a lack of secure placement in a world of shared understanding, a failure to be at home. Denouncing the symptom instead of the illness, we would miss the point – and fail in our duty as social critics.

The important thing to see here is the currents of desire beneath the pretty surfaces, the wishes and fantasies there facilitated. What do they point to? The sociological studies bear out something that philosophical inquiry can see without taking a survey. We are, finally, happier not with more stuff but with more meaning: more creative leisure time, stronger connections to groups of friends, deeper commitment to common social projects, and a greater opportunity to reflect. In short, the life of the well-rounded person, including crucially the orienting aspect of life associated with virtuous citizenship. Nor is this basic social commitment something we should pursue for ourselves alone, a project simply to promote our personal happiness. At its best, it is an expression of commonality that creates something greater than the sum of its – let us be honest – often self-interested and distracted members. It creates a community.

Even this measure of political optimism may strike some readers as utopian. And that is indeed the bugbear of choice in our current debates, not least because the twentieth century was so hard on the idea of utopias. We seem to have lost our taste for thinking big in politics, for reasons that are not hard to trace.

Born in revolutionary optimism, determined to pursue Pound's brave demand for *news* in art, the century soon collapsed into bouts of cynicism, war, and that ageless downside of ideological commitment, zealotry. Numerous endings have been confidently proclaimed just in the past few decades: the end of war, the end of poverty, the end of ideology, the end of work, even the end of history itself. Each declaration bravely heralds a new world, only to fall quickly into brutality or modishness. As early as 1922 Robert Musil, author of *The Man Without Qualities*, noted with disgust that "[e]very new 'ism' that arrives is hailed as the forerunner of a new humanity, and the end of every academic year rings in a new epoch!" Virginia Woolf's "change in human sensibility" barely survives the century's first decades. Pound himself eventually succumbs to the lure of creeping fascism, ending his days caged and mad. Making it new is always, it seems, a risky business.

But that is no longer really our problem, here in the twenty-first century. The most recently declared endings – "the end of the end of the end of ideology," as the historian Russell Jacoby recently put it in an ironic commentary on the discursive state of play – are different in kind from these earlier ones. Self-referential and mocking, stacked up like planes over wintertime Chicago, they signal that our problem now is not firebrand optimism but, instead, an enervating self-consciousness. We begin the new century and the new millennium skeptical of the very idea of political change. It was the German philosopher Jürgen Habermas who first noted the "exhaustion of utopian energies" that stole over many people in the wake of the startling events of 1989. In the resulting limbo time of quiet complacency, political optimism has stalled.

Over the last decade and a half we have witnessed a calm lack of dreams that is, in its way, almost as disturbing (if not as violent) as the once-utopian nightmares that dominated the mid-century. These days, *everything* has ended because everything is fine – certainly as fine as it's ever likely to be. Utopia has become another victim of capitalist triumphalism, killed off by the harbingers of the market theodicy who proudly proclaim that we will never have to risk crazy revolutionary ideas again. Their favourite image? That infrastructural consummation of post-war prosperity, *the highway*, where we are all going the same way, even if driving at different speeds. Just one route and just one destination: so-called democratic capitalism. The soft-noose consensus of production and consumption goes mostly unchallenged. Hope, insofar as it still exists, is now deflected into purely personal projects of self-renovation, the hollowed-out "you-topias" of the advertising universe, where everything is possible but nothing is political.

All this smooth certainty is founded on a misunderstanding. Utopias do not exist – that is precisely their function. They are not blueprints for political reality but expressions of unreal possibility, meant to arouse hope and focus action. Imaginative disruptions in the smooth functioning of political thinking, they are the rude intrusion of wishes or fantasies into the otherwise normal course of business as usual, the otherwise unbroken course of deciding who gets what within the existing rules. In this sense, utopian thinking finally takes seriously the deep meaning of that ordinarily cynical definition of politics as *the art of the possible*. Utopian ideas remind us that even if the superhighway of consensus is actually there, and most of us feel we're on it willy-nilly, there are still exits and off ramps. There are side roads and cul-de-sacs. There are routes going back the other way and ones splitting off in other directions.

The first utopias were frankly supernatural, the otherworldly perfections of Plato's *Republic* or Augustine's *City of God*. (Though, as

I have suggested, Plato had a much more complex task in hand.) Later, in an era of imperial expansion, they became *spatial*: Thomas More's eponymous republic was to be found in the uncharted New World. More lately still, they become *temporal*, pushing us not into other realms or other places but other times, visionary futures. And yet, because we are so impatient, we demand that future now; or else we simply give up on the idea of making a better one. That is why our visions of the future have recently fallen into such stylish emptiness. We don't believe we can do much about the shape the future will take, so we make a complex, slick joke of our own thwarted desires for a better world. Nowadays, our taste runs to pop-savvy dystopias and cognitive distortions like *Snow Crash* or *The Matrix* – science-fiction books and films that trade on the vertiginous conceit of perception not being what it seems. Or we amuse ourselves with Pynchonesque conspiracy theories and second-order, meta-ironic anti-corporate satires like David Foster Wallace's sprawling *Infinite Jest*.

There is of course a lot of pleasure to found here, not least the self-congratulation of being so damn clever; but by leaving us inside our own heads, these diversions end up leaving everything outside just as it is. The hazard today is no longer that the future we imagine is too ideal, and therefore likely to encourage heedless revolutionary zeal and violence. It is rather that we have become paralyzed determinists about what is coming. Like TV commercials and globalization and consumerism on the Web, the future is now annoying but inevitable, something that just happens, usually much faster than we'd like. We are in danger of losing the idea that a future is created, bit by bit, out of our political desires and choices. That's why we need positive visions to balance the fashionably cynical ones, need them now more than ever. Political dreams often go awry, sometimes spectacularly so; but without them we are unmoored, cut loose from ourselves. Not everything the human soul craves can be found in what is already the case. And we haven't yet traced the limits of human justice.

As a new era dawns, should we dare to be utopian again? Well, why not? After all, it's always too early to give up on the future of our dreams. The times could not be riper for a playful but serious utopianism, an open-minded but political consciousness, an imaginative but hard-headed idea of civic participation. How else can we hope to fashion the world we want? We don't know what the future will bring, but that's because we are ever in the process of creating it, not because it is an alien force to which we will have to submit. And certainly we do know this: just as with a first-year philosophy course, the question of *how best to live* is always on the exam. In this life, on our troubled and beautiful planet, that question *is* the exam.

The project of universal justice? Let us say something that is neither banal nor unrealistic: we're working on it. In the meantime, be a citizen of the world. Donate 10 percent of your income to international relief every year. Take back some public space every week. Listen to somebody as unlike you as possible, including machines and animals, every day. And argue with anyone who says that this is the best of all possible worlds – or even just a world beyond changing. It is neither.

BIBLIOGRAPHIC ESSAY

In order to keep the main text as readable as possible I have avoided footnotes and other forms of direct reference. The following essay indicates the main research sources, roughly in the order they appear in each chapter. Works not specifically cited but present as background are found in the sections on the first and last chapters.

1   *The World We Have*

There is a vast and growing scholarly literature on the topic of citizenship, and I have not seriously attempted to engage its details here, a task that would involve many volumes. Will Kymlicka and Wayne Norman offer a critical map of the field in "Return of the Citizen: A Survey of Recent Work on Citizenship Theory," *Ethics* 104 (1994), pp. 352–81. Among the most influential works in the field are Will Kymlicka, *Multicultural Citizenship: A Liberal Theory of Minority Rights* (Clarendon, 1995); James Tully, *Strange Multiplicity: Constitutionalism in an Age of Diversity* (Cambridge, 1995); Jeff Spinner, *The Boundaries of Citizenship: Race, Ethnicity and Nationality in the Liberal*

State (Johns Hopkins, 1994); and Yael Tamir, *Liberal Nationalism* (Princeton, 1993).

Among edited collections of articles, the most important are David Batstone and Eduardo Mendieta, eds., *The Good Citizen* (Routledge, 1999); Ronald Beiner, ed., *Theorizing Citizenship* (SUNY, 1995); Gisela Bock and Susan James, eds., *Citizenship, Feminist Politics and Female Subjectivity* (Routledge, 1992); and Will Kymlicka, ed., *The Rights of Minority Cultures* (Oxford, 1995). It is striking how many of the leading theorists of citizenship – Kymlicka, Tully, Beiner, Norman, also Joseph Carens, Leslie Green, Judith Baker, Denise Réaume – are Canadian: evidence of both an ongoing constitutional crisis in the country and (perhaps by the same token) a willingness to think beyond the limits of crude nationalism.

Robert Putnam's theory of social capital and its relation to civil society, an idea with a long and complicated pedigree in political theory, is detailed in his book *Bowling Alone: The Collapse and Revival of American Community* (Simon & Schuster, 2000), based on the famous article of the same title. Some criticisms of Putnam were summarized by Stanley Katz in a lecture called "Constitutionalism and Civil Society," delivered at the University of California, Berkeley (2000). The notion of the various roles of human life and the place of citizenship within them was first suggested to me by James Nickel in a paper he delivered to the University of Colorado Conference on Media and Democratic Discourse (1999). A comment from Shirley Tillotson, who heard an early version of my own use of the schema, prompted further revision.

My book on justice and the political virtue of civility is *A Civil Tongue: Justice, Dialogue, and the Politics of Pluralism* (Penn State, 1995). Stephen Carter's book *Civility* (Basic, 1998) is a part of a pair on citizens' virtues that also includes *Integrity* (HarperCollins, 1997). Carlo Rosselli's tart little essay, *Liberal Socialism*, is published in English translation by William McCuaig (Princeton, 1994), and his life and work assessed in Stanislao G. Pugliese's fine book, *Carlo*

Rosselli: Socialist Heretic and Antifascist Exile (Harvard, 1999).

There are too many thoughtless denunciations of civility to bother citing them, but a thoughtful one can be found in William Chaloupka, *Everybody Knows: Cynicism in America* (Minnesota, 1999). Chaloupka finds recent calls for civility self-serving and thus cynical in a pejorative sense; he advocates "activist cynicism," which is cynical in the positive sense of constantly resisting what I have discussed here under the labels of "knowingness" and "the already-thought." It should be clear that without wanting to surrender the notion of civility as Chaloupka does, I agree with the necessity of this positive kind of cynicism. Indeed, the present book might be seen as an attempt to reconcile these two seemingly opposed desiderata: being cynical while being civil.

If for some reason you don't agree with me that life is too short to look at more capitalist cheerleading about global domination, see two particularly egregious examples of the genre: Thomas Friedman, *The Lexus and the Olive Tree: Understanding Globalization* (Farrar, Straus & Giroux, 1999); and Lester Thurow, *Building WEALTH: The New Rules for Individuals, Companies, and Nations in a Knowledge-Based Economy* (HarperCollins, 1999). A more considered, and considerable, analysis is found in Walter LaFeber, *Michael Jordan and the New Global Capitalism* (Norton, 1999), which takes the world-famous former basketball star as a dominant image of the new global culture – at least circa 1999. The cultural evolutionist Robert Wright, taking up the mantle of Herbert Spencer in rather glib fashion, makes a potted case for historical determinism (not to mention the triumph of capitalism) in his book *Nonzero: The Logic of Human Destiny* (Pantheon, 2000).

The debate about plain language and the commodification of ideas, in which Adorno is such an uncompromising figure, is one of those things that, like death and taxes, are ever with us. Adorno is matched against the great advocate of plain writing, George Orwell, in a thoughtful essay – itself smoothly crafted – by James Miller: "Is

Bad Writing Necessary?" *Lingua Franca* (December/January 2000), pp. 33–44. But the debate is not just endless, it is misplaced. Critics of obfuscation in academic prose are not against complexity in ideas or strategies of social resistance. They simply want to be convinced that a given degree of opacity is strictly necessary to the ideas in question. If it is not, then there is nothing going on in complicated language other than (variously) laziness, arrogance, intimidation, or old-fashioned scholarly necromancy. Those things may be forgivable or fun, but they cannot be defended as intellectual integrity.

2   Rights and Duties

There are many English translations of the three Platonic dialogues discussed in this chapter: *Euthyphro*, *Apology* (or *Defence*), and *Crito*. I have used, variously, those of David Gallop (Oxford, 1997) and Hugh Tredennick (Bollingen, 1961). Like all students of Plato, I am deeply indebted to Gallop's lucid introduction and commentary in his one-volume translation of these three dialogues.

A note on the rather stringent conventions of Athenian legal proceedings, adapted from Gallop: Socrates was accused by three of his fellow citizens, indicted by a council of five hundred peers, and appeared at a one-day trial; he mentions several times the pressure of time on his argument. (In Sparta, by contrast, capital cases were allowed three days.) The proposed penalty, if he was convicted of the charges of praising false gods and corrupting youth, was death. Following arguments from prosecution and defence, the jury voted on the charges. A convicted citizen was allowed to suggest an alternative punishment, and then the jury selected between the two options; they were not permitted to introduce a third. Therefore in this case they could not exile the convicted Socrates after he proposed, as an alternative sentence, celebrating him as they would a sports hero. Nor was there any right of appeal on conviction: the five hundred was the highest judicial body in this system.

Plato's account of this trial is of course the most famous, and is probably a more accurate rendering of the historical Socrates than is to be found in later Platonic dialogues such as the *Republic*, where Socrates is often used as a mouthpiece for the metaphysical theory of Platonism. Xenophon, in his *Memorabilia* and *Defence of Socrates*, differs on a number of points from Plato's account. He says, for example, that Socrates never suggested a fine (as happens in Plato's *Apology*), and that Socrates was more preoccupied with the imminent pains of old age than with making a personal sacrifice of himself.

In general, Xenophon's picture of the trial is much less the portrait of a martyr to rational inquiry than we find in Plato's stylized, and perhaps somewhat self-serving version. Certainly Plato and the other close followers of Socrates had to flee Athens for Megara soon after the trial, the anti-Socratic feeling was so strong. For more on the trial and death of Socrates, including a provocative argument that the Athenians were justified in eliminating so disruptive a presence in their nascent democracy, see I. F. Stone, *The Trial of Socrates* (Anchor, 1989).

Jonathan Lear's illuminating Freudian interpretations of Plato and Aristotle are collected in his book *Open Minded* (Harvard, 1998). I have been influenced here particularly by the essays "Eros and Unknowing: The Psychoanalytic Significance of Plato's *Symposium*," pp. 148–66, and "Inside and Outside the *Republic*," pp. 219–46. Details of the formation of Athenian democracy and the importance of public spaces are discussed in Murray Bookchin, *The Rise of Urbanization and the Decline of Citizenship* (Sierra Club, 1987), especially chs. 3 and 4.

Charles Taylor's contribution to Amy Gutmann, ed., *Multiculturalism and the Politics of Recognition* (Princeton, 1992) is the best brief statement of his nuanced position. Linda McQuaig, in *The Cult of Impotence* (Viking, 1998), argues that technology's ability to track market transactions outweighs its tendencies to make them invisibly fast. But even if that is true, ability is not reality: there are few encouraging signs that this feature of technological prowess is actually working to control the blind speed of trading. Fredric Jameson discusses Mandel and the geography of late capitalism in *Postmodernism, or, the Cultural Logic of Late Capitalism* (Duke, 1991), quotations from p. 276 and pp. 384–86.

Hannah Arendt's *Eichmann in Jerusalem: A Report on the Banality of Evil* (Viking, 1964) is still the best examination of how evil functions when it takes on bureaucratic form, and a cultural discussion of the Holocaust's impact that holds up to continued scrutiny. The first inversion of Arendt's famous phrase – blandness as itself reprehensible – is the sense that John Ralston Saul gives to banality in his description of former Canadian prime minister Brian Mulroney in *The Doubter's Companion* (Viking, 1994), p. 40.

The classic statement of mass culture's deadening power is Theodor Adorno and Max Horkheimer's exquisitely pessimistic essay, "The Culture Industry: Enlightenment as Mass Deception" (orig. 1945), reprinted in Simon During, ed., *The Cultural Studies Reader* (Routledge, 1993), pp. 29–43. My discussion here of simulacral culture is a slightly modified version of the postmodernism of Jean Baudrillard, whose idea of the simulacral, or hyperreal, arises with the (alleged) death of the representational and real. A representation is always a representation *of* something, something real, whereas a simulacrum is merely one of many equivalent things without need (or possibility) of something they represent. Thus the disappearance of reality as a meaningful category in the flood of identical mass-produced tokens. See Baudrillard, *Simulations* (Semitotext(e), 1983), passim. A note to dedicated pop-culture watchers: a hollowed-out copy of Baudrillard's *Simulacrum and Simulation* is where Neo (Keanu Reeves) hides his secret software in the opening scenes of the Cartesian epistemo-action thriller *The Matrix* (1999).

For an illuminating discussion of the form of specifically cultural reification associated with the technological bonus, see Jameson, "Secondary Elaborations," ch. 10 of *Postmodernism*, pp. 314–18. By Jameson's reasoning, even emphatically modern cultural markers, which focus on the unique act of production by an artist, can be reified via consumption. The idea of hybrid identities is addressed, in quite different fashions, in Homi K. Bhabha, *The Location of Culture* (Routledge, 1997), and Michael Ignatieff, *Blood and Belonging* (Viking, 1993) and *The Warrior's Honour* (Viking, 1998).

Judith Shklar makes a compelling argument about humanity's mundane limits while discussing Montaigne in "Putting Cruelty First," ch. 1 of her superb book, so Montaignist in spirit, *Ordinary Vices* (Harvard, 1984). For Rorty's discussion of Shklar's insight see, among others, his collection *Contingency, Irony, Solidarity* (Cambridge, 1991), especially the essay "The Last Intellectual in Europe: Orwell on Cruelty," pp. 169–88. (I will leave aside for now the interesting question of whether this gloomy characterization of intellectuals was prompted by – or directed towards – Rorty's colleagues in academic philosophy.)

Compare, on the issue of everyday culture as it relates to politics, Rorty's denunciation of academic cultural studies in *Achieving Our Country: Leftist Thought in Twentieth-Century America* (Harvard, 1998). I cannot agree with Rorty's straightforward dichotomy between "activist" leftists and "spectatorial" ones: sometimes accurate cultural diagnosis is the necessary prologue to effective political action. I do agree that the former is no substitute for the latter.

Michel de Certeau is illuminating on the productive possibilities that, paradoxically, seem to reside in consumption: tactical manoeuvres of transformation, alteration, and subversion. Using the very systems of representation that stand over them, resistant consumer-producers can sometimes engage in a critique of consumption that "redistributes its space" and "creates at least a certain play in that order, a space for maneuvers of unequal forces and for utopian points." See de Certeau, *The Practice of Everyday Life*, Stephen Rendall, trans. (California, 1984), p. 18; also Henry Jenkins, *Textual Poachers: Television Fans and Participatory Culture* (Routledge, 1992), ch. 6.

3   Virtues and Vices

I have relied on the most widely available English text for all quotations from Montaigne, namely *Essays*, J.M. Cohen, trans. (Penguin, 1958). Quotations in the opening section are taken from the essays "On friendship," "On smells," and "On experience." Other quotations in this chapter are drawn from the essays "On liars," "On the power of the imagination," "On the education of children," "That it is folly to measure truth and error by our own capacity," "On cannibals," and "On cruelty."

La Boétie is known to most people today only through Montaigne's appreciation, and is little quoted; but Elizabeth David, in her *Mediterranean Cooking* (Penguin 1950), includes this appropriately philosophical epigraph from him in her opening section, on soups: "*Le plus entendu de touts n'eust pas quitté son écuelle de soupe pour recouvir la liberté de la respublique de Platon.*"

John Rawls's brief discussion of the political virtues is found in *Political Liberalism* (Columbia, 1993), pp. 193–95, in a significant revision of his basic theory as defended in the canonical work *A Theory of Justice* (Belknap, 1971). Leslie Green's claim is that civility is the distinctively political virtue for the sake of which citizens will tolerate imperfections in our public institutions; see his *The Authority of the State* (Clarendon, 1988), ch. 6. Stephen Carter defends the virtues of political life in *Civility*, cited above. William Galston ranks political virtues among other virtues (general, economic, public) of the liberal citizen; see his *Liberal Purposes: Goods, Virtues, and Duties in the Liberal State* (Cambridge, 1991), pp. 221–24.

The civic republican defence of civility as traditionalism is offered by Michael Oakeshott in "On the Civil Condition," essay two of his *On Human Conduct* (Oxford, 1975), pp. 108–84. Benjamin Barber also defends civility in his challenging republican manifesto, *Strong Democracy: Participatory Politics for a New Age* (California, 1984). But Barber's demands for a "publicly oriented" civic virtue are criticized by Shelley Burtt, "The Politics of Virtue Today: A Critique and a Proposal," *American Political Science Review* 87 (1993): 360–68. Burtt cites Stanley Elkin, *City and Regime in the American Republic* (Chicago, 1987) and Bruce Ackerman, *We the People* (Harvard, 1991) as examples of more persuasive – because politically more plausible – accounts of "privately oriented" civic virtue. I attempt a defence of civility as what Burtt would call a privately oriented civic virtue in *A Civil Tongue*, cited above, especially chs. 2, 6, and 7.

For an illuminating reading of the place of the virtues in recent citizenship theory, see Kymlicka and Norman, "Return of the Citizen," cited above, especially pp. 365–69, on liberal virtues. For further discussion of political virtue in general, see also J. Budziszewski, *The Resurrection of Nature: Political Theory and Human Character* (Cornell, 1986), which argues for an Aristotelian conception of public virtue; Stephen Macedo, *Liberal Virtues: Citizenship, Virtue, and Community in Liberal Constitutionalism* (Clarendon, 1990) and Rogers Smith, *Liberalism and American Constitutional Law* (Harvard, 1985), who both call for a liberal culture of participatory virtue; and Shelley Burtt, *Virtue Transformed: Political Argument in England 1688–1740* (Cambridge, 1992), which traces the history of civic virtue and limitations of publicly conceived virtue.

Alasdair MacIntyre's widely influential analysis of virtue is *After Virtue: A Study in Moral Theory* (Duckworth, 1982). See also J. Budziszewski, *The Nearest Coast of Darkness: A Vindication of the Politics of Virtues* (Cornell, 1988). Donald McCloskey, "Bourgeois Virtues,"

American Scholar 63 (1994), pp. 177–91, extends MacIntyre's discussion of Ben Franklin's table of virtues. David Frum's rather perverse discussion of bourgeois virtue is found in *Dead Right* (Basic, 1996), which argues that Ronald Reagan and George Bush were *not conservative enough*; Irving Kristol's essays and articles are collected in *Neo-Conservatism: The Autobiography of an Idea* (Free Press, 1997); and William Bennett's astonishing best-seller of conservative nostrums is *The Book of Virtues* (Simon & Schuster, 1993). I discuss some further implications of this conservative annexation of virtue in Kingwell, *Better Living: In Pursuit of Happiness from Plato to Prozac* (Viking, 1998), chs. 7 and 8.

The arguments about the relationship of democracy and wealth are made best by Amartya Sen, who suggests that individual freedom has an economic value that should be factored into assessments of development in emerging countries; see his *Development as Freedom* (Knopf, 1999). That this argument even needs to be advanced is proof of the wide influence of studies purporting to show that authoritarian "Asian tiger" economies of the middle 1990s were more "successful" than economies of emerging democracies like India. This deplorable situation indicates, if nothing else, how dominant purely growth-based definitions of success have become in contemporary debate. See Jeff Madrick, "Economic Scene: Democracy has the edge when it comes to advancing growth," *The New York Times* (13 April 2000), p. C2.

Contemporary defenders of Aristotelian civic virtue wish to defend and cultivate those traits that make for the *best* life, as opposed to liberal and republican defenders of virtue, who wish only to cultivate those traits that make for good citizens and a healthy public life. Compare, on this important point, Charles Larmore, *Patterns of Moral Complexity* (Cambridge, 1987), chs. 1 and 2. Larmore argues that Aristotle's monism – that is, the presumption that there is one and only one answer to the question, What is the good life? – makes his ethico-political conception largely inapplicable to our pluralistic world. The notion of politics *as conflict* is absent from the conception, and that is why the Aristotelian temptation regarding virtue must be resisted, even if we are (as I am) otherwise willing to agree with Aristotle's general emphasis on the virtues in ethics. On the idea that conflict is essential to political life, see also Chantal Mouffe, *The Return of the Political* (Verso, 1993), chs. 3 and 5; and Carl Schmitt, *The Concept of the Political*, George Schwab, trans. (Rutgers, 1976).

Stuart Hampshire poses his challenge to unworldly moral philosophers in *Innocence and Experience* (Harvard, 1989), and pursues it in *Justice as Conflict* (Harvard, 1999). Judith Shklar, as mentioned, discusses Montaigne and the issue of cruelty in *Ordinary Vices*. For quotations from Aristotle, I have relied here on Aristotle, *Nicomachean Ethics*, Terence E. Irwin, trans. (Hackett, 1985).

The most sustained discussion of Machiavelli's attempt to subvert the traditional princely virtues is found in Felix Gilbert's well-known, extremely lucid paper, "The Humanist Concept of the Prince and *The Prince* of Machiavelli," *Journal of Modern History* 11 (1939), pp. 449–83; reprinted in abridged form in the Norton edition of *The Prince*, Robert M. Adams, trans. (Norton, 1977). I have for the most part followed Gilbert's analysis in these paragraphs. The simpler (and nicely illustrated!) version of Machiavelli's advice is found in Claudia Hart, *A Child's Machiavelli: A Primer on Power* (Penguin Studio, 1998).

For more on the republican tensions in Machiavelli's thought, see Leo Strauss, *Thoughts on Machiavelli* (Chicago, 1958). For the record, I do not mean to suggest here that *The Prince* represents Machiavelli's considered views on political virtues, only that it presents one form of reductive temptation in discussing them: cynical political realism. Thus the view in question is probably "Machiavellian" rather than Machiavellian. But even in *The Discourses* the virtues of the leader are not always what we would approve today. The ruler is advised to be opportunistic (Book II, ch. 9), instrumentally deceptive (Book II, ch. 13), and to rely on fear rather than love. At the same time, Machiavelli emphasizes the need for a commitment to the common good (Book I, ch. 3), princely generosity (Book I, ch. 25), and the rule of law (Book I, ch. 43). For more on Machiavelli's republican virtues, see Quentin Skinner, *Machiavelli* (Oxford, 1981), ch. 3, "The Philosopher of Liberty."

Peregrine Worsthorne's admiration of Montaigne was part of a larger argument (with which, as usual, I do not agree) that utopianism is no longer of any interest in contemporary politics: "Dickens's responsibility for the disappearance of mighty conceptions and the rise of Gerrards Cross," *The Spectator* (27 November 1999), p. 42. For the full argument for Montaigne's role in altering conceptions of nobility, in effect creating a sixteenth-century version of *noblesse oblige* within the bloody context of the wars of religion, see David Quint, *Montaigne and the Quality of Mercy* (Princeton, 1999). Stephen Toulmin's *Cosmopolis: The Hidden Agenda of Modernity* (Chicago, 1992) argues that the Cartesian version of what it means to be modern should be corrected by a Montaignist one – an argument I also make, though far too briefly, in a new preface to the U.S. edition of my book *Better Living*, cited above, published as *In Pursuit of Happiness* (Crown, 2000); the new preface also appears in the paperback Canadian edition (Penguin, 1999).

The standard early texts of liberal citizenly virtue are, as mentioned, Locke's *Letter on Toleration* (Blackwell, 1956) and Spinoza's *Tractatus Theologico-Politicus* (Hackett, 1998); one might also add Hobbes's *De Cive* or *On the Citizen* (Cambridge, 1998), which is a more accessible and systematic exposition of the ideas presented in his famous but more sprawling text, *Leviathan*. I discuss further the role of civility in eighteenth-century moral philosophy in an essay called "Politics and the Polite Society in the Scottish Enlightenment," *Historical Reflections / Réflexions Historiques* 19:3 (Fall 1993), pp. 363–87. For more on politics and politeness in this period, see J.G.A. Pocock, "The Varieties of Whiggism from Exclusion to

Reform: A History of Ideology and Discourse," Part III of his *Virtue, Commerce and History: Essays on Political Thought and History, Chiefly in the 18th Century* (Cambridge, 1985). The quotation used here is from p. 236 of that work; emphasis added. Not surprisingly, Pocock labels this variety of Whiggism "polite Whiggism." I defend the distinction between manners and civility at greater length in *A Civil Tongue*, cited above, chs. 6 and 7.

Leah Bradshaw analyzes the Platonic idea of the tyrant in "Tyranny: Ancient and Modern," *Interpretation* 20 (1992), pp. 187–203. "[The timocrat] is compelled to think about the good, however limited, of those he rules," says Bradshaw. "The worst excesses of political life are not, as [Leo] Strauss suggests, occasioned by giving the quest for honor and recognition the highest place among human ends, but by discrediting the honor-seeker in politics. When the pursuit of honor is denigrated in politics, and the ambition to rule is thwarted by praise of the fulfillment of private desires, the great and insatiable desires of tyrannical types meet with little resistance. When the desire to rule is condemned as 'unethical,' the worst and most devious of men come easily to power" (p. 199).

As Bradshaw notes, this dangerous shift in how power functions, all too familiar in our own day, may not always occur in the well-guarded halls of public governance. It may also begin in the less obviously scrutinized realms of the corporate boardroom or the scientific laboratory. "We miss the mark when we stand guard over aspiring 'princes' and regard as harmless the eugenics researchers," says Bradshaw. "The tyrant is *not* an essentially political man. As a person of mad desire, he will satisfy that desire in any form that fosters it. Bureaucracies and science laboratories may be far more hospitable terrain for the tyrant than a publicly scrutinized political arena" (pp. 201–2).

The most influential statement of the "dualist" view of citizenship – that is, private most of the time, public when necessary – has been given by Bruce Ackerman in his *We the People*, vol. 1 of his projected

three-volume history of the U.S. Constitution, cited above. Ackerman argues for a society in which "intermittent and irregular periods of public virtue," pursued during "rare periods of heightened
public consciousness," mark a break from the routine interest-
brokering and factionalism of politics. For a brief overview of the
argument, see Ackerman, "The Storrs Lectures: Discovering the
Constitution," *Yale Law Journal* 93 (1984): 1013–72.

4   *Spaces and Dreams*

The letters between Benjamin and Adorno are published in English
as *The Complete Correspondence, 1928–1940*, Henri Lonitz, ed., and
Nicholas Walker, trans. (Harvard, 1999). I benefited from having
access to that material in page proofs, as I did with the monumental
new English translation of *The Arcades Project*, Howard Eiland and
Kevin McLaughlin, trans. (Harvard, 1999). This is the first complete
English translation of the *Project,* but some parts of Benjamin's mas-
terwork have been published in English before, most notably the
book-within-a-book, *Charles Baudelaire: A Lyric Poet in the Era of High
Capitalism*, Harry Zohn, trans. (Verso, 1997).

Important book-length interpretations of *The Arcades Project* can
be found in Susan Buck-Morss, *The Dialectics of Seeing* (MIT, 1991),
and Pierre Missac, *Walter Benjamin's Passages*, Shierry Weber
Nicholsen, trans. (MIT, 1995). My rather idiosyncratic comparison
volumes here are Roland Barthes, *Mythologies*, Annette Lavers,
trans. (Paladin, 1973), and Marshall McLuhan, *The Mechanical Bride:
Folklore of Industrial Man* (Vanguard, 1951; reissued by Beacon,
1967). Further English translations of Benjamin's own writings can
be found in various books and collections. The most accessible are
Illuminations, Harry Zohn, trans. (Harcourt, Brace, 1968); *One-Way*

Street and Other Writings, Edmund Jephcott and Kingsley Shorter, trans. (Verso, 1979); and *Reflections*, Edmund Jephcott, trans. (Harcourt, Brace, 1978). See also the collection *Prisms*, Samuel Weber and Shierry Weber, trans. (MIT, 1981).

Benjamin's often scattered work is only now being collected in definitive English translation. There are two volumes so far of Walter Benjamin, *Selected Writings*, Michael W. Jennings, Rodney Livingstone *et al.*, trans.; Michael Jennings, Howard Eiland, and Gary Smith, eds. (Harvard, 1999). There is an extensive secondary literature on Benjamin, especially in German, which I will not try to cite here; but see the very good apparatus included in the Harvard volumes. For the complete texts in German, see Walter Benjamin, *Gesammelte Schriften*, Rolf Tiedemann and Hermann Schweppenhäuser, eds. (7 volumes; Suhrkamp, 1972–89); also Theodor W. Adorno, *Gesammelte Schriften*, Rolf Tiedemann, ed. (20 volumes; Suhrkamp, 1970–86).

Important background argument to any understanding of *The Arcades Project* is Theodor Adorno and Max Horkheimer, *The Dialectic of Enlightenment*, Joseph Cummings, trans. (Continuum, 1982), a benchmark in their culturally pessimistic form of critical social theory, which remains an important position in debates about modern/postmodern reason. Also, for various analyses of a crucial Arcades figure, see Keith Fester, ed., *The Flâneur* (Routledge, 1994).

The quotations taken from Don DeLillo, *White Noise* (Random House, 1985), can be found on pp. 3–4 and p. 41. For more on the notion of "post-cultural identity," see Christopher Clausen, "Nostalgia, Freedom, and the End of Cultures," *Queen's Quarterly* 106:2 (Summer 1999), pp. 233–44; Clausen is also at work on a book that addresses the subject of post-culturalism. Naomi Klein, *No Logo: Taking Aim at the Brand Bullies* (Random House, 1999), and Kalle Lasn, *Culture Jam: The Uncooling of America* (Eagle Brook, 1999), explore the pathologies of branded culture from, respectively, an activist and a culture-jamming point of view.

Michael Walzer's views on political interpretation and the limits of theory are contained in, among others, *Thick and Thin: Moral Argument at Home and Abroad* (Toronto, 1994). John Rawls makes his version of the liberal argument for justice in, most recently, *Political Liberalism*, cited above, and *The Law of Peoples* (Harvard, 1999). A dissenting view on the possibility of civic virtue, from a feminist perspective, is Iris Marion Young, "Polity and Group Difference: A Critique of the Ideal of Universal Citizenship," *Ethics* 99 (1989), pp. 114–41; and "Impartiality and the Civic Public," in Seyla Benhabib and Drucilla Cornell, eds., *Feminism as Critique* (Polity, 1987), pp. 57–76. From a feminist perspective critical of Young and sympathetic to Michael Oakeshott, Chantal Mouffe has attempted to navigate a middle course between civic republican monism and liberal fragmentation. See Mouffe, "Democratic Citizenship and the Political Community," ch. 4 of her *The Return of the Political*, cited above.

Pierre Bourdieu's dissection of nostalgia and journalistic narratives is found in his little book, *On Television*, Priscilla Parkhurst Ferguson, trans. (New Press, 1999). I discuss Bourdieu's views on television and discourse at greater length in my essay "Fear and Self-Loathing in Couchland: Eight Myths about Television," *Queen's Quarterly* 107:1 (2000), pp. 3–24. The history of modernism in the twentieth century – in art, architecture, literature, music, and politics – is brilliantly told by Peter Conrad in *Modern Times, Modern Places* (Knopf, 1999), from which I have learned a great deal and borrowed some key details.

A good discussion of the absence of everyday things in the discourse of most political theory can be found in Bruno Latour, *Pandora's Hope: Essays in the Reality of Science Studies* (Harvard, 1999). Latour seeks to disrupt the distinction between political (discursive) reality and natural (fact-based) reality by, among other tactics, reminding us of the etymology of the word *thing*, which in many European languages originally meant (and in some still does) a political assembly. Thus the original meaning of the "republic" as *res publica*, the public thing, is bent back to inform our otherwise apolitical attachment to the thing as fact or as consumer object. For more on the relationship between the design of public spaces and the culture of consumerism, see the various contributions to Rem Koolhaas, ed., *The Harvard Guide to Shopping* (Monacelli, 2000). Koolhaas analyzes the subversive potential of cities in his classic book, *Delirious New York: A Retroactive Manifesto for Manhattan* (Oxford, 1978; reissued by Monacelli, 1994), a discussion recently pursued by (among others) Lars Lerup in *After the City* (MIT Press, 2000).

Gaston Bachelard's *The Poetics of Space*, Maria Jolas, trans. (Beacon, 1969), is the classic text on twentieth-century philosophy of dwelling and architecture. Marjorie Garber deftly analyzes the house as a complex cultural metaphor and commodity fetish in her witty book *Sex and Real Estate: Why We Love Houses* (Pantheon, 2000), including an illuminating treatment of the idea of "the dream house." Terence Riley's essay to accompany the exhibit on "The Un-Private House" was published in photocopy by the Museum of Modern Art (6 January 1999) and is included in the catalogue book of the exhibit. Donna Haraway's celebrated article, "A Cyborg Manifesto: Science, Technology, and Socialist-Feminism in the Late Twentieth Century," was originally published in *Socialist Review* 15: 2 (1985) and later included in her collection *Simians, Cyborgs, and Women: The Reinvention of Nature* (Routledge, 1991), pp. 149–81.

5   *The World We Want*

For more on the pathologies of wealth and its uneasy relation to happiness, see Robert H. Frank, *Luxury Fever: Why Money Fails to Satisfy in an Era of Success* (Free Press, 1999), and Robert J. Samuelson,

The Good Life and Its Discontents: The American Dream in the Age of Entitlement 1945–1995 (Vintage, 1995). See also Robert Frank and Philip Cook, *The Winner-Take-All Society* (Free Press, 1995).

I borrowed quotations and some details of argument about the absurdity of gross domestic product as a measure of economic success from Bill Bryson, "The Numbers Game," in his collection *Notes from a Big Country* (Doubleday, 2000), p. 68. Pico Iyer's very readable book *The Global Soul: Jet Lag, Shopping Malls, and the Search for Home* (Knopf, 2000) is an attempt to read the new global landscape from the ground up, including a brief discussion of the multicultural politics of Toronto.

Bertrand Russell discusses the role of envy in human happiness in his excellent little book, *The Conquest of Happiness* (Liveright, 1912), which I discuss throughout *Better Living*, cited above. The latter also includes more detailed arguments about twisted ideas of "better living" that abound in contemporary society, and the possibilities of virtue as a more stable foundation for happiness.

Finally, the most uncompromising argument I know for the duty to aid those in less developed countries is contained in Peter Unger, *Living High and Letting Die* (Oxford, 1996), which advocates a tough-minded, even extreme form of utilitarianism that denies any moral significance to the relative proximity of suffering. Read it.

COPYRIGHT ACKNOWLEDGEMENTS

Quotations reprinted by permission of the publisher from *The Arcades Project,* by Walter Benjamin, translated by Howard Eiland and Kevin McLaughlin, Cambridge, Mass.: The Belknap Press of Harvard University Press, copyright © 1999 by the President and Fellows of Harvard College.

Quotations from *The Complete Correspondence,* by Walter Benjamin and Theodor Adorno, Henri Lonitz ed., reprinted with the permisson of Polity Press.

Quotations from *Dead Right*, by David Frum, copyright © 1996, published by Basic, used with permission.

Quotations from *Essays*, by Michel de Montaigne, reprinted with permission.

Quotations reprinted by permission of the publisher from *Innocence and Experience,* by Stuart Hampshire, Cambridge, Mass.: Harvard University Press, copyright © 1989 by Stuart Hampshire.

Quotations from *Modern Times, Modern Places*, by Peter Conrad, reprinted with permission from Alfred A. Knopf, a division of Random House Inc.

Quotations from *Nicomachean Ethics*, by Aristotle, translated by Terence E. Irwin (Hackett, 1985), used with permission.

Quotations from *Political Liberalism*, by John Rawls, copyright © 1993, published by Columbia, used with permission.

Quotations from *Simians, Cyborgs & Women*, copyright © 1990. *From Simians, Cyborgs & Women* by Donna Haraway. Reproduced by permission of Taylor & Francis, Inc./Routledge, Inc., http:// www.routledge-ny.com.

INDEX